Life Writing

Autobiography, Biography, and Travel Writing in Contemporary Literature

Proceedings of a Symposium Held by the Department
of American Culture and Literature
Haliç University, Istanbul, 19-21 April 2006

Edited by
Koray Melikoğlu

Cover illustration:
Rembrandt: Self Portrait, 1629

Koray Melikoğlu (Ed.)

LIFE WRITING

Autobiography, Biography, and Travel Writing in Contemporary Literature

Proceedings of a Symposium Held by
the Department of American Culture and Literature
Haliç University, Istanbul, 19-21 April 2006

ibidem-Verlag
Stuttgart

Bibliografische Information Der Deutschen Bibliothek

Die Deutsche Bibliothek verzeichnet diese Publikation in der Deutschen Nationalbibliografie; detaillierte bibliografische Daten sind im Internet über <http://dnb.ddb.de> abrufbar.

A CIP catalogue record for this book is available from:
Die Deutsche Bibliothek
http://dnb.ddb.de

All rights reserved. No part of this publication may be reproduced, stored in or introduced into a retrieval system, or transmitted, in any form, or by any means (electronic, mechanical, photocopying, recording or otherwise) without the prior written permission of the publisher. Any person who does any unauthorized act in relation to this publication may be liable to criminal prosecution and civil claims for damages.

∞

Gedruckt auf alterungsbeständigem, säurefreien Papier
Printed on acid-free paper

ISBN-10: 3-89821-764-7

ISBN-13: 978-3-89821-764-4

© *ibidem*-Verlag
Stuttgart 2007
Alle Rechte vorbehalten

Das Werk einschließlich aller seiner Teile ist urheberrechtlich geschützt. Jede Verwertung außerhalb der engen Grenzen des Urheberrechtsgesetzes ist ohne Zustimmung des Verlages unzulässig und strafbar. Dies gilt insbesondere für Vervielfältigungen, Übersetzungen, Mikroverfilmungen und elektronische Speicherformen sowie die Einspeicherung und Verarbeitung in elektronischen Systemen.

Printed in Germany

CONTENTS

Contributors · xi

Acknowledgements · xiii

Welcome Address · xiv

Foreword · xv
Koray Melikoğlu

I COMPREHENSIVE STUDIES

**Travellers and Traces: The Quest for One's Self
in Eighteenth- to Twentieth-Century Travel Writing** · 1
Manfred Pfister

**Say It Isn't So: Autobiographical Hoaxes
and the Ethics of Life Narrative** · 15
Sidonie Smith and Julia Watson

**Telling Life Stories:
The Rhetorical Form of Biographical Narratives** · 35
Gerald P. Mulderig

**Too Far For Comfort?
A Discussion of Narrative Strategies in Biography** · 47
Rana Tekcan

**A Culture of Everyday Life:
Exploring Blogging as Cyber-Autobiography** · 67
Leman Giresunlu

A Historical Approach to Turkish
Women's Autobiographies   83
Nazan Aksoy

Reception and Audience in Life Writing and Healing   99
Wendy Ryden

II CASE STUDIES

Henry James' *Autobiography* (1913-1915):
Creating "The Master"   113
Laurence Raw

Samuel Beckett's Trilogy: The Picture
of the Artist Trying to Represent the Self   125
Oya Berk

Art and Artifice in Sylvia Plath's Self-Portrayals   141
Richard J. Larschan

Auto/biography, Knowledge, and Representation:
The Theory and Practice of Filial Narrative   159
G. Thomas Couser

Anglo-American Women Travellers
Writing on the Self and on Oriental Women   171
Tea Jansson

Istanbul: Edouard Roditi's Mirror of the Self?   187
Clifford Endres

The Empirical Journey to the Self:
Memory, Language and the Re-construction
of Identity in Moris Farhi's *Young Turk*   199
Bronwyn Mills

Quest for the Lost Mother:
Autobiographical Elements in Jean Genet's
Un captif amoureux (*Prisoner of Love*)   211
Clare Brandabur

The Brother, the Friend, the Stranger and I:
Uwe Timm's Biography of a Post-War
German Generation   231
Jutta Birmele

Being in Time: Reading the Written Self
in Alev Tekinay's *Nur der Hauch vom Paradies*
(Only the Breeze from Paradise)   241
Özlem Öğüt

Theorizing Life: Argentinean History Recovered   253
Claire Emilie Martin

Resisting Dis/closure:
Autobiography and Orhan Pamuk's *İstanbul*   263
Dilek Doltaş

Traces of the History of Turkish Modernization
in Orhan Pamuk's *Yeni Hayat* (*The New Life*)**:**
The Oscillation between Fascination with
and Resistance to the "West"   281
Ayse F. Ece

Home Away from Home:
Diaspora Experiences of Turks and Greeks in the 1920s   293
Banu Özel

The Dancer and the Dance:
A Study of Mrinalini Sarabhai's Autobiography   307
Leena Chandorkar

Wire Writing as Life Writing:
The Portraits of Alexander Calder 321
Barbara B. Zabel

Contributors

Aksoy, Nazan, Prof.—Bilgi University, Turkey.

Berk, Oya, Assist. Prof.—Haliç University, Turkey.

Birmele, Jutta, Prof.—California State University, Long Beach, USA.

Brandabur, A. Clare, Assist. Prof.—Doğuş University, Turkey.

Chandorkar, Leena, Dr.—Abasaheb Garware College, India.

Couser, G. Thomas, Prof.—Hofstra University, USA.

Doltaş, Dilek, Prof.—Boğaziçi University, Turkey.

Ece, Ayşe, Dr.—Marmara University, Turkey.

Endres, Clifford W., Prof.—Kadir Has University, Turkey.

Giresunlu, Leman, Assist. Prof.—Dokuz Eylül University, Turkey.

Jansson, Tea, MA.—University of Tampere, Finland.

Larschan, Richard J., Prof.—University of Massachusetts, USA.

Martin, Claire Emilie, Prof.—California State University, Long Beach, USA.

Melikoğlu, Koray, Re. Assist.—Istanbul University, Turkey.

Mills, Bronwyn, Assist. Prof.—Kadir Has University, Turkey.

Mulderig, Gerald P., Assoc. Prof.—DePaul University, USA.

Öğüt, Özlem, Assist. Prof.—Boğaziçi University, Turkey.

Özel, Banu, Instructor—Haliç University, Turkey.

Pfister, Manfred, Prof.—Freie Universität Berlin, Germany.

Raw, Laurence, Assist. Prof.—Başkent University, Turkey.

Ryden, Wendy, Assist. Prof.—Long Island University, USA.

Smith, Sidonie, Prof.—University of Michigan, USA.
Tekcan, Rana, Assist. Prof.—Bilgi University, Turkey.
Watson, Julia, Assoc. Prof.—Ohio State University, USA.
Zabel, Barbara B., Prof.—Connecticut College, USA.

Academic Committee

Berk, Oya, Assist. Prof.—Haliç University.
Ece, Ayşe, Dr.—Marmara University.
Erbora, Ayşe, Prof.—Istanbul University.
Gumpert, Sırma Soran, Assist. Prof.—Haliç University.
Öğüt, Özlem, Assist. Prof.—Boğaziçi University.
Özbayrak, Çiler, Assist. Prof.—Haliç University.
Özel, Banu, Instructor—Haliç University.

Organizing Committee

Berk, Oya, Assist. Prof.—Haliç University.
Demir, Defne Türker, Re. Assist.—Haliç University.
Gumpert, Sırma Soran, Assist. Prof.—Haliç University.
Özbayrak, Çiler, Assist. Prof.—Haliç University.
Özel, Banu, Instructor—Haliç University.
Sobutay, Meriç, Re. Assist.—Haliç University.

Acknowledgements

We wish to extend our warmest thanks to the participants of the symposium for their illuminating and thought-provoking presentations which led to stimulating discussions on the theory and practice of life writing during the symposium. We are also deeply grateful to the Academic Committee and the Organizing Committee for their invaluable work; without their contribution this event would not have been realized. We would also like to thank our colleague, Oya Berk, for her help with the proceedings as well as for her commitment and support during the organization of the symposium.

Our heartfelt thanks go to Professor Atilla Özalpan, Vice Rector and Dean of the Faculty of Arts and Sciences at Haliç University at the time of the event for his invaluable help and support throughout all stages of the organization of this symposium. We also want to express our sincere gratitude to the Rector, Professor Ahmet Çakır, and to Professor Gündüz Gedikoğlu, Chairman of the Board of Trustees of Haliç University, for their generous support and encouragement.

Çiler Özbayrak
Department of American Culture and Literature
Chair
Haliç University

Welcome Address

Dear Guests,

It is my great pleasure and honor as president of the board of trustees of Haliç University to welcome you all to the symposium on 'The Theory and Practice of Life Writing.'

I would like to extend my deep appreciation and many thanks to the organizing committee for realizing this symposium.

Events such as this one are very important bridges for scholarship and exchange of knowledge both nationally and internationally, and more lectures, symposia and congresses will contribute to world peace and the improvement of international scholarship.

As you attend our symposium, please take the opportunity to visit our lovely city. As you know Istanbul is a beautiful city bridging Asia and Europe. It is also a bridge between civilizations, cultures and historical eras. We count amongst our treasures the legacies of the Roman, Byzantine and Ottoman Empires. You can see these cultural crossroads in many of our prominent landmarks, such as the Topkapı Palace and its walls that date back to Byzantine times. And you can see it in the commingling of churches, mosques and synagogues which represent the peaceful co-existence of the three great religions of the world.

Our cuisine, whether it is our famous Turkish coffee or our world-renowned Turkish Delight, also represents a bridge between the East and the West.

I will finish by welcoming you again to Istanbul, to Halic University and to our interesting and stimulating symposium and by thanking you for your important contributions.

Prof. Dr. Gündüz Gedikoğlu
Chairman
Board of Trustees of Haliç University

Foreword

Showing one of the dozens of self-portraits by Rembrandt, the cover of this volume may lead the reader to reflect on possible parallels between the history of one of these in particular and life writing, the subject of these proceedings: At the beginning of the new millennium the portrait by one of Rembrandt's pupils of a fictitious Russian aristocrat was revealed to hide underneath its layers of paint a self-portrait by the master himself, who had apparently ordered the transformation in order to make an unsold painting profitable by adapting it to a marketable pattern of his time (see, e.g., Johnston; "'Lost' Rembrandt" [with illustrations]; Vogel). From the first suspicion in the 1930s to the final confirmation of the picture's palimpsestic nature it went through a number of stages in which the Russian nobleman gradually was robbed of his features, hat, some hair, parts of his moustache, and earrings to allow for his predecessor underneath to appear. This display of both a real and a fictitious person's features at the same time and the resulting tension between self- and other-portrait may lead one to consider the difficulties attendant on judging the accuracy of any biographic or autobiographic account, no matter which medium it utilises—a consideration which is aided, for example, by the fact that Gore Vidal called his first memoir *Palimpsest*.

Interestingly, it is not so much Rembrandt's self-portrait than its transformed version that may hold a lesson for students of autobiography, the latter picture making evident a possible trait to the real artist's character that the former with its many mates might conceal: What was taken as a sign of introspectiveness in Rembrandt, the proliferation of his self-portraits, may turn out to have been a commercial strategy designed to leave several sale options open (see Johnson).

Of course the reflections do not stop here. If at some future time the authenticity of the newly-discovered Rembrandt should be questioned, as happens with so many works attributed to the master, this would offer further interesting perspectives on the present volume.

Many of the studies in these proceedings deal with difficulties of this kind. They grew out of the international symposium 'The Theory and Practice of Life Writing: Auto/biography, Memoir and Travel Writing in Post/modern Literature,' held at Haliç University, Istanbul, on 19-21 April 2006. The majority of contributions to this event, some of them heavily revised for publication, is collected in this volume.[1] The symposium was the fourth in a series organised by the Department of American Culture and Literature at Haliç University.

A first group of the papers included here, treatments of more comprehensive and/or theoretical aspects of life and travel writing, discusses genre history (Nazan Aksoy; Manfred Pfister), typology (Manfred Pfister; Sidonie Smith and Julia Watson), issues of narration (Gerald P. Mulderig; Rana Tekcan), the recent phenomenon of blogging (Leman Giresunlu), and therapeutic narrative (Wendy Ryden).

A second group—whose concern often heavily overlaps with that of the first in that it also pursues theoretical goals—concentrates on individual authors and artists: Sabâ Altınsay and Dido Sotiriou (Banu Özel), Samuel Beckett (Oya Berk), the sculptor Alexander Calder (Barbara B. Zabel), G. Thomas Couser and his filial memoir, Moris Farhi (Bronwyn Mills), Jean Genet (Clare Brandabur), Henry James (Laurence Raw), Orhan Pamuk (Dilek Doltaş; Ayşe F. Ece), Sylvia Plath (Richard J. Larschan), the British and American Oriental travellers Caroline Paine, Sophia Poole, and Mary Eliza Rogers (Tea Jansson), Edouard Roditi (Clifford Endres), Sara Rosenberg (Claire Emilie Martin), the dancer Mrinalini Sarabhai (Leena Chandorkar), Alev Tekinay (Özlem Öğüt), and Uwe Timm (Jutta Birmele).

Questions relating the history of the Rembrandt portrait to many of these discussions come to mind immediately: Can the traces of the

---

[1] Of the participants, Hülya Adak, Sema Bulutsuz, John Eakin, Trevor Hope, Meltem Kıran Raw, Margaret Russett, and Daniel Roux did not submit their papers for inclusion in this volume.

original painting visible in the transformed version be accommodated in Pfister's typology of traces? Was the reworked picture a hoax of the kind discussed by Smith and Weston or was it rather the contrary, because it understated the significance of its subject? Is the interplay between artistic and commercial considerations in Rembrandt similar to that which Larschan claims for Sylvia Plath's works? Is our route to Rembrandt via the Russian aristocrat a complexly mediated process of the kind described by Couser which brings us closer to the real Rembrandt than an unmediated study of his works would have done, just as Couser feels his posthumous reading of his father's papers gave him a better knowledge of the deceased than his parent's actual presence did?

The reader is invited to extend this list of questions. Among them may be the question whether the confidence emanating from Rembrandt's features on the cover of this book stems from his youth or from his knowledge that a portrait that cannot be sold can always be painted over.

Koray Melikoğlu

Works Cited

Johnston, James. "Rembrandt Self-Portrait That Was Covered up for 300 Years Expected to Fetch £5m." *Scotsman* 28 Apr 2003. 2 Dec. 2006 <http://thescotsman.scotsman.com/index.cfm?id=4832 92003>.

"'Lost' Rembrandt Fetches Nearly £7m." *BBC News*. 10 July 2003. 2 Dec. 2006 <http://news.bbc.co.uk/2/hi/entertainment/3052491.stm>.

Vidal, Gore. *Palimpsest: A Memoir*. 1995. London: Abacus, 1997.

Vogel, Carol. "Inside Art." *New York Times* 14 Mar. 2003, late ed., East Coast: E.2:38.

I COMPREHENSIVE STUDIES

Travellers and Traces: The Quest for One's Self in Eighteenth- to Twentieth-Century Travel Writing

Manfred Pfister
Freie Universität Berlin

Abstract: Travelling is always a travelling in traces—looking for traces of past cultures or following the traces of previous travellers. These traces can be material or textual, visual, performative or mnemonic. In some of the best of twentieth-century travel-writing such quests for traces do, however, take an inward and self-reflective turn in which travel writing becomes a form of self-writing and self-staging.

In my presentation, I will survey this development from the eighteenth century to the present, beginning with Grand Tour accounts of journeys to Italy, to then focus on modernist and postmodernist travel writing. This will take us not only to *Etruscan Places* with D. H. Lawrence or Patagonia with Bruce Chatwin, to Asia Minor on *Alexander's Path* with Freya Stark or to the Caribbean with Amryl Johnson but back into these writer's lives, their deepest memories and desires. What should emerge in my readings is how writing the Other can become a way of writing the Self.

I

Travellers search for and follow traces—and they leave their own traces in turn. Both, the traces followed and those left, are inscribed in the cultural memory relating to a particular place and can become powerful *topoi* in the mnemonic archive that makes up culture—*topoi* revisited, re-cited and re-enacted. 'Places' and 'traces' do not only rhyme, they also converge semantically as powerful inscriptions in our cultural memory: without traces there are no places and vice versa, and together they construct both cultural difference and identity.

Travel writing plays an important role here. Even if there have always been travellers who have insisted on not following traces and on relying for their accounts on autopsy alone, only on what they have seen with their own eyes, at a closer look it becomes evident—be it only in their forceful gestures of negating intertextuality and erasing traces—that they, as all travellers, have always tapped the archives of the cultural memory of both their own and the other culture (cf. Pfister, "Intertextuelles Reisen"). And this is, of course, particularly true of a place like Istanbul, which is itself so rich in multi-layered cultural traces and which has been so densely overwritten with the traces of generations of travellers that the impossibility of saying anything new about it has become an often evoked exordial *topos*.

II

It is at this point, however, that I should, perhaps, explain what I mean by 'traces' in this context.

Let me, as a first step, distinguish between material and textual traces. **Material traces** must be considered as the semantic prototype of what we call 'traces': footprints in the sand or the field, which previous travellers have left and which continuous traffic can gradually turn into trails and beaten tracks; the sedimentations, relics and landmarks they or previous inhabitants of the lands have left and which the traveller follows and will try to decipher in his text. The Grand Tourists of the seventeenth and eighteenth centuries followed such material traces, which had turned into beaten tracks (cf. Buzard), a network of connections made up of roads and passes, of coaching and guides, of ancient ruins, splendid buildings of the past, important collections and other *videnda*, other sights one had to have seen to qualify as a true traveller. Such material traces are part of the archives of cultural memory—both of the traveller's and the travellee's culture.

Material traces are often under- or overwritten by **textual traces**, i.e. the accounts of previous travellers distilled into maps, guidebooks or travelogues, but also texts originating in the other culture. This is what entangles travelling and travel writing in a web of intertextual references and allusions. Shakespeare's contemporary Thomas Coryate on his way to Venice already saw himself as a "tombstone traveller" (1611) and traced with great enthusiasm the birth and burial places of classical authors, and with the Romantic period the abodes of English poets in Italy—Keats, Byron, Shelley, the Brownings— have became the destination of literary pilgrimages for British tourists in Italy, not to mention Giulietta's or Julia's balcony in Verona! Before them, in the eighteenth century, a Grand Tourist like Joseph Addison travelled through Italy in the tracks of the classical Greek and Roman poets—whom he considered much more a part of his own, than of Italian culture—with the express intention "to compare the natural face of the country with the landscapes that the poets have given us" (*Remarks on Several Parts of Italy*, 1705; qtd. in Pfister, *Fatal Gift* 467)). As Horace Walpole put it cuttingly: "Mr Addison travelled through the poets, not through Italy" and he "might have composed [his travels] without stirring out of England" (letters to Richard West, 2 Oct. 1740, and to Henry Zouch, 20 Mar. 1762; qtd. in Pfister, *Fatal Gift* 467). In one particular case, a few lines of verse sufficed to launch generations of English travellers on a poetic quest: Milton's epic simile comparing the hosts of fallen angels in *Paradise Lost* with

> [. . .] autumnal Leaves that strew the brooks
> In Vallombrosa, where the Etrurian shades
> High overarched imbower [. . .] (page 480, I, 302-304)

sent hosts of Grand Tourists on a "Milton trail" to the monastery hidden in dense forests a day's ride away from Florence[1]—a classic case of a poetic trace turning into a trail and that trail turning into a beaten track and overwriting the Italian landscape with the travellers' own "pretexts" and cultural memories!

When D. H. Lawrence in 1927, on his last journey, turned towards reading the traces of *Etruscan Places*, he sought to liberate himself as much as possible from the intertextual burden of previous writings and follow alone the **mnemonic traces** of a life-affirming and death-

---

[1] Cf. Pfister, *Fatal Gift* 321-322 and 451-452.

accepting mode of existence in the depth of his own unconscious. Such mnemonic traces are the third category of traces I wish to identify. They may, to a certain extent, be part of an intertextual web of associations and be conditioned by the formations of a cultural memory, yet the textual inscriptions lie so deep here that they cannot be adequately described in terms of specific verbal pretexts. They are, therefore, less immediately related to textual traces than to **iconic** and **performative traces**—to traces of images going back to one's earliest memories or dreams, which, consciously, half-consciously or unconsciously, give orientation to the traveller's desires; traces of earlier, kinaesthetically remembered performances, which can give to travelling the sensation of a re-enactment.

III

The quest for traces of buried memories merits a separate category, if only because much of modernist and postmodernist travel writing is programmatically dedicated to it. Bruce Chatwin's memories of a prehistoric piece of brontosaurus skin in the glass-fronted cabinet of his grandparents' living room, which had stimulated his childhood fantasies and which sends the adult on a quest to its place of origin, is the postmodern *locus classicus* for this phenomenon. His search for traces of the lost material relic does not only take him to the "Lost Hope Sound" at the end of the world, in Patagonia, and back to a lost palaeontological past and its traces in the European cultural memory, the archives of images and texts about Patagonia, but also back to his childhood. As the great searcher for traces, W. G. Sebald, commented in an essay on Chatwin: his "wanderings to the end of the world are search expeditions for the lost boy in him" (140; qtd in Pfister, Nachwort 359; my tanslation).[2] Chatwin's *In Patagonia* is just one instance of a general tendency in modernist and postmodernist travel writing to

---

[2] "Auch für Chatwin waren die Wege an das Ende der Welt Suchexpeditionen nach einem verloren gegangenen Knaben [. . .]."

stage self-consciously what previous travel writers have tended to play down: the fact that travelling is always a travelling in traces, is always the pursuit of traces to be followed and read, and that the reading of these traces is more of an adventure or challenge than the travelling itself. Rather than erasing traces modernist and postmodernist travellers tend to foreground the material, textual and mnemonic traces which motivate and orientate the journey in complex and often aporetic narrative structures. For what is at stake in the reading of traces is both the traveller's and the travellee's cultural memory, and the private memories of the individual traveller. In an attempt to substantiate this claim, I shall highlight four variants of such travelling in pursuit of traces, which self-consciously turns the quest for traces into the main concern of travel narrations and which seem to me of particular significance in recent travel writing.

My first variant is the **archaeological quest**. Let me take as an example for this a travelogue that bears the notion of a trace already in its title: Freya Stark's *Alexander's Path* of 1958. In contrast to her best-know book, *The Valleys of the Assassins* of 1934, where this archetypal British women traveller still staged herself in a typically female pose as travelling without a purpose, for travelling's sake—"I travelled single-mindedly for fun" (*Valleys* 9; cf. Bode)—here she is engaged from the beginning in a geographical, archaeological und ethnological project. What she intends to do is to reconstruct the Persian campaign of Alexander the Great in Cilicia, Pamphylia und Lycia. For that she has studied beforehand the sparse classical sources, Arrianos' *Anabasis* in particular, and read all the available accounts of modern travellers before her, and now checks their frequently contradictory information *in situ* by carefully reading the material traces and literally counting her footsteps to get things right at last. Exploring the inland regions of the Turkish Mediterranean coast on often impenetrable or abandoned paths, she constantly looks up from her old maps and texts to the landscapes surrounding her and back from the landscape to the text to work out some kind of congruence between the material and textual traces, yet still finds time to compare Alexander's path with the marks of modernisation and progress which Kemal Pasha's new Turkish national state has imprinted upon the landscape. Negotiating between the contradictory writings and maps of ancient and modern historians and explorers, she puts all her trust in what she sees with her own eyes and experiences with her own body and not in her throughout male authorities, whom she puts in place with sportive condescension: "They were splendid young men, however erratic their time-table may have been up the hill" (*Alexander's Path* 183).

But why all this physical and intellectual effort to trace Alexander's path more precisely than before? Was it learned pedantry or know-it-all arrogance, or did she need a scholarly pretext to give the dignity of a serious purpose to mere adventuring. The answer she herself proffers—"The pure wish to understand, the most disinterested of human desires was my spur" (168)—cannot really satisfy as it withholds her own fascination with him whose traces she follows, and with what the traces lead her to: her fascination with Alexander the Great, "the most dynamic being that the world has perhaps ever known" (230), and with his vision of an *oikumene* of Occident and Orient, which found its first expression in the Persian campaign und was to culminate—and fail tragically—in his march towards India. It is for this that Freya Stark's quest for the traces of Alexander ends elegiacally in an identification of her own failure with the failure of Alexander's dream:

> So the young dream died, of the brotherhood of men. [. . .] That, I thought suddenly, is why I am so unhappy. I have failed this brotherhood. I should have stayed. [. . .] Alexander's vision ended and was lost for over two thousand years; and we, who are dreaming it again, look extremely like failure at the moment [. . .]. (225)

And this dream of a *West-östliche Divan* takes her far back in her life, back to her childhood, where it began with a book: "An imaginative aunt who, for my ninth birthday, sent me a copy of the *Arabian Nights*, was, I suppose, the original cause of the trouble" (*Valleys* 9).

In my second variant the search for traces is focussed on one particular previous author and his work. Intertextuality is, therefore, paramount here, though material and performative traces can also play an important role. I am speaking about biographies cast in the mould of travelling in the traces of the biographee, of following his footsteps across the trajectory of his life. Let me call this type **biography as travelogue**. Of course, researching a biography has always involved a certain amount of fact-gathering travelling in the footsteps of the author, but in the writing of the biography the traces of these journeys have then been usually erased. After all, who wants to know how the biographer got hold of the facts? It's the facts that count. More recently, however, we increasingly find texts which position themselves between travelogue and biography and make the biographer's search for the traces of his author, and not the author's life itself, the dominant principle of narrative organisation. To my knowledge, the first to do so was James Albert Symons in his *Quest for Corvo* (1934), drawing attention to the novelty of his method in the subtitle *Experiment in Biography*. This is not the life-story of the mysterious and scandalous *fin de siècle* writer Frederick William Rolfe, who called himself Baron Corvo, but the story of the quest for Corvo, the search for traces of his life, which takes Symons to strange and dark places in Venice or Rome. Accordingly, Corvo's life is not narrated in a linear and conclusive fashion, but emerges in a series of journeys by a literary sleuth dedicated to identifying and reading the traces of the various phases of Corvo's life and of the various places his texts project in order to unravel its mysteries. What is particularly modern about this "Experiment in Biography" is, of course, that it does not only drop the conventional claims of biographers to be able to offer the truth, the whole truth, about an author and his works, but exposes such claims as mere pretence. Since then, many have followed Symons' model in factual or fictional travelogues, among them Julian Barnes in his novel *Flaubert's Parrot* (1984), which takes an English dentist and hobby Flaubert specialist to Normandy to establish once and for all the actual model for the parrot in "Un coeur simple," only to end up in an aporia of proliferating parrots. Or, to give another example closer to our immediate concerns here, the travel writer, critic and biographer Richard Holmes has given to his book about English Romantic poets in Italy the significant title *Footsteps* (1986) and has defined his biographical project as "a kind of pursuit, a tracking of the physical trail of someone's path, a following of footsteps," as "acts of self-identification" or "self-projection" sought and performed in the encounter with "landscapes, buildings, photographs, and above all the actual trace of handwriting on original letters and journals" (Holmes 27 and 67).

"Travelling in pursuit of traces" always involves tapping into the archives of cultural memory. There is, however, a specifically postmodern version of engaging with the resources of cultural memory in travel writing which I would like to call, in Bakhtinian terms, the **carnivalisation of traces**. Pitt-Kethley and her engagement with the Sibyls of Italy have already provided us with an example of this mode. It highlights traces by playing games with them, in particular with traces of great cultural status, with traces that represent great cultural capital. This can begin already with the narrative form: Travelling in pursuit of traces, as we have already seen, often invokes the time-honoured myth of a quest, a quest for some sacred site, object or experience as in the Arthurian romances of the Middle Ages. Postmodern travelling in pursuit of traces, however, where it evokes this narrative archetype, tends to subvert and exploit its cultural pretensions and sacred aura to comic effect. Thus, for instance, William Dalrymple alludes quite explicitly both in the title and the subtitle of his *In Xanadu: A Quest* (1989) to the pregnant shape cultural memory has given to journeys to make them significant and memorable. The title quotes, of course, the first line of Coleridge's opium and Chinese dream, "In Xanadu did

Kubla Khan," which in turn evokes a host of European travelogues about China, and at the same time it commemorates the great modernist classic of literary sleuthing, John Livingston Lowes' *The Road to Xanadu* (1927), which unravels the textual traces underlying Coleridge's romantic poem. One of these traces is Marco Polo's *Milione* and it is Marco Polo's quest for the *meraviglia* of the East that Dalrymple's "Quest" re-enacts. But he does no longer undertake it with the scholarly high seriousness with which, say, Freya Stark followed *Alexander's Path* or Richard Holmes the *Footsteps* of his poets. Indeed, Dalrymple follows Marco Polo from Venice to Xanadu without bothering much about reconstructing his exact traces or reading his readings of cultural traces. What he focuses upon instead are the often absurd adventures on his way, which highlight the performative differences between his own modern mode of travelling and that of his legendary forerunner and stage them with comic narrative zest. Marco Polo's *meraviglia* do not, of course, survive unimpaired such carnival conjunctions of high and low, of myth and modern banality. The disenchantment they work begins already with the phial of Holy Oil, which Dalrymple, like his medieval precursor, carries from Christ's burial chapel in Jerusalem to China: his modern oil does not burn miraculously for ever, but has to be renewed and refilled from a mundane can of sunflower oil and is transported in an equally banal plastic bottle from Body Shop. And, of course, reaching the destination is not the moment of ecstasy a quest would suggest; it is a let-down rather, neither Marco Polo's nor Coleridge's China: "Our vision of Xanadu was nearer the heath scene in *Lear* than the exotic pleasure garden described by Polo" (Dalrymple 298).

All the travels in pursuit of traces and the quests for traces I have discussed so far have been, in terms of colonial voyages, "voyages out," not "voyages in," journeys away from one's origins and not towards them. It is, however, mainly "voyages in" that we find among my fourth variety, which I will give a rather Proustian name: **journeys of remembrance of one's origins**. Though they do occasionally occur in male travel writing, they are more typically the form that female travelling tends to take.[3] I have chosen an example from a postcolonial context, Amryl Johnson's *Sequins for a Ragged Hem* (1988). This is the account of a *nostos*, a homecoming by a Black British writer in search of the traces of her origins in the Caribbean. Such a journey cuts across the colonial divide of "voyage in" and "voyage out," for it is at one and the same time a quest for Johnson's homelands and thus a "voyage in" and, as a journey away from the long-time home of the naturalised Briton, a "voyage out." Accordingly, the perspective of the traveller is an instable one, oscillating between that of a British tourist sightseeing in former colonies and that of a migrant without a fixed centre to her life far away from her island of birth.

The journey Amryl Johnson narrates is already her second journey home. During the first, the previous year, she was traumatised by an initial shock: the experience that her house of birth had just been destroyed, together with all material traces of what had always been present in her memories. Her nostalgic desire to tread again in the footsteps of her childhood, to literally to re-live her childhood once again and re-enact it in a commemorative performance—"Heel to toe within every footprint, matching the outlines until I was back on that one road. The same I had travelled" (Johnson 12)—had ended in a void. The traces she now follows on her second journey are mnemonic traces that go beyond the individual, private memories of her childhood, embedding them in deeper, half-lost sediments of a cultural memory of the Middle Passage and of slave labour on the sugar plantations. Fittingly, it is a monument that shows her the way into these depths of cultural memory—a huge iron wheel on Tobago, both material trace and symbolic reminder of the lost world of her origins. "The visit to the wheel becomes the postcolonial turning point of her entire passage, the point from where the scars of history inscribed on Caribbean landscapes can be retraced so that her tour turns from touristic

---

[3] Cf. for this gender aspect of travelling K. R. Lawrence.

travelling into a *rite de passage* of personal redefinition" (Döring 47). Only after this act of commemoration and remembrance does a personal homecoming become possible for her, the encounter with her mother, with which the book ends—and not with her return to England.

Having finished this paper, I bought and read Orhan Pamuk's *Istanbul: Memories of a City* (2005) to tune myself into the history and life of a city I had not visited before. Too late I realised that I might have—perhaps even should have—based my entire paper on this wonderful book. Pamuk, travelling peripatetically in his own city, is a searcher for, and a reader of, traces if ever there was one: the cultural traces left by its Greek, Byzantine, Jewish, Armenian, Anatolian, Ottoman and modern Turkish populations, the traces inscribed upon the city by the travellers from the West such as Nerval, Gautier or Flaubert, and, last but not least, the traces of his own childhood in Istanbul. The "Memories of a City" Pamuk evokes are both his own memories of Istanbul and Istanbul's memories of its own past. His book is therefore a double, interconnected quest for Istanbul and for his own identity. By tracing the one he traces the other, as he realises late in his book: "I have described Istanbul when describing myself, and described myself when describing Istanbul" (265). And in the end his quest for origins for the identity of his city and himself "come[s] full circle, for anything we say about the city's essence, says more about our lives and our own states of mind. The city has no centre other than ourselves" (316).

Nor has the world. This is, indeed, where all the traces travellers follow end.

Works Cited

Barnes, Julian. *Flaubert's Parrot*. 1984. London: Picador, 1985.
Bode, Christoph. "*The Valleys of the Assassins and Other Persian Travels* (1934) oder 'Ich bin ein *hillman*.'" *West Meets East: Klassiker der britischen Orient-Reiséliteratur*. Ed. Christoph

Bode. Anglistische Forschungen 246. Heidelberg: Winter, 1997. 117-134.

Buzard, James. *The Beaten Track: European Tourism, Literature, and the Ways to Culture, 1800-1918*. Oxford: Clarendon, 1993.

Chatwin, Bruce. *In Patagonia*. Ed. Manfred Pfister. Universalbibliothek Fremdsprachentexte. Stuttgart: Reclam, 2003.

Coryate, Thomas. *Coryat's crudities*. London: William Stansby, 1611; facs. ed. 1978.

Dalrymple, William. *In Xanadu: A Quest*. London: Collins, 1989.

Döring, Tobias. *Caribbean-English Passages: Intertextuality in a Postcolonial Tradition*. London: Routledge, 2002.

Holmes, Richard. *Footsteps: Adventures of a Romantic Biographer*. Harmondsworth: Penguin, 1986.

Johnson, Amryl. *Sequins for a Ragged Helm*. London: Virago, 1988.

Lawrence, D. H. *Etruscan Places*. New York: Viking, 1957.

Lawrence, Karen R. *Penelope Voyages. Women and Travel in the British Literary Tradition*. Ithaca, N.Y.: Cornell University Press, 1994.

Lowes, John Livingston. *The Road to Xanadu: A Study in the Ways of the Imagination*. Boston; New York: Houghton Mifflin, 1927.

Milton, John. *The Poems*. Ed. John Carey and Alastaire Fowler. London: Longmans, 1968.

Pamuk, Orhan. *Istanbul: Memories of a City*. Trans. Maureen Freely. London: Faber and Faber, 2005. Trans. of *İstanbul: Hatıralar ve Şehir*. İstanbul: Yapı Kredi, 2003.

Pfister, Manfred, ed. *The Fatal Gift of Beauty: The Italies of British Travellers: An Annotated Anthology*. Amsterdam: Rodopi, 1996.

Pfister, Manfred. "Intertextuelles Reisen, oder: Der Reisebericht als Intertext." *Tales and "their telling difference." Festschrift für Franz K. Stanzel*. Ed. Herbert Foltinek et al. Heidelberg: Winter, 1993. 109-132.

Pfister, Manfred. Nachwort. *In Patagonia*. By Bruce Chatwin. Ed. Manfred Pfister. Universalbibliothek Fremdsprachentexte. Stuttgart: Reclam, 2003. 353-377.

Pitt-Kethley, Fiona. *Journeys to the Underworld*. London: Chatto & Windus, 1988.
Sebald, W. G. "Das Geheimnis des rotbraunen Fells." *Chatwins Rucksack: Portraits, Gespräche, Skizzen*. Ed. Hans Jürgen Balmes. Frankfurt am Main: Fischer, 2002. 133-142.
Stark, Freya. *Alexander's Path: A Travel Memoir*. 1958. Woodstock, New York: Overlook, 1988.
___. *The Valleys of the Assassins and Other Persian Travels*. 1934. Harmondsworth: Penguin, 1952.
Symons, Alphonse James Albert. *The Quest for Corvo: An Experiment in Biography*. London: Cassell, 1934.

Say It Isn't So: Autobiographical Hoaxes and the Ethics of Life Narrative

Sidonie Smith
University of Michigan

Julia Watson
Ohio State University

Abstract: Although autobiographical hoaxes are not a recent phenomenon, the last few decades have seen both an increase in the kinds of autobiographical fakery and intensified cultural attention to their exposure. This essay examines such cultural disturbances by offering a taxonomy of hoaxes that sets out critical distinctions, generic scripts, and ethical implications of the problematic of hoaxes. Our typology surveys several kinds of hoaxing: scam lives; prosthetic enhancements; ethnic impersonation; fantasized lives; plagiarized lives; fabricated lives; and false witnessing. Probing these different manifestations of autobiographical hoaxes suggests questions about the cultural anxieties provoked through the scandal of the hoax: anxiety about the terms of the autobiographical pact; ethical investments in the "truth" of increasingly fragmented lives; the media production of celebrity self-narrators; the heterogeneous desires of readers seeking alternative identities; the impetus to self-reimagining through narratives posing possibilities for ersatz authenticity; and the global commodification of narratives of suffering and survival. Finally, we call for rethinking both the conceptualization of the hoax and its implications for theorizing life narrative in the media and moment of globalization.

Autobiographical hoaxes are not a recent phenomenon. The persona of Silence Dogood, a virtuous middle-aged Puritan widow, was adopted by sixteen-year-old Benjamin Franklin, in fourteen "letters" that comprise the earliest essay series in America, for his brother's *New England Courant* in 1722 (15, n. 2). More generally, the eighteenth and nineteenth centuries, in the United States and elsewhere, saw the proliferation of narratives of Indian captivity, Barbary Coast adventures, and other genres, whose "authenticity" in some cases was debunked as impersonation or outright invention. Men posed as women; journalists posed as pirates. But writers could make a living and, sometimes, large profits, from a gullible and sensation-seeking public eager for stories of other worlds.

In the last few decades, autobiographical fakery has taken a postmodern turn. In 1972, Clifford Irving attempted to publish a bogus autobiography of Howard Hughes based on in-person interviews that he invented. Unlike Franklin's, Irving's caper netted him a sixteen-month prison sentence. Since that attempt, however, Irving has not only established himself as a novelist. His book about it, entitled *The Hoax*, was a publishing success; and the escapade became the subject of a Lasse Hallström film, *The Hoax* (2006). Ironically, Irving tried to sue Hallström, alleging that he was incorrectly represented in the film, which the *New York Times* called "a hoax about a hoax" (Broeske 13).

On the surface a hoax seems a transparent thing, especially a hoax autobiography. It is a narrative claimed to be autobiographical that is actually inauthentic, fabricated, untruthful. But how do we know this is the case? What evidence is cited when the charge of fraud or "hoaxiness" is attached to a published life narrative?

We will briefly summarize the aspects of narratives that elicit the charge of hoax, adapting historican Thérèse Taylor's schema for analyzing one such case (see "Truth"). **External** evidence may include the following: the degree of specificity in the story's geography and its correlation with a "real" world; the version of history it circulates or advocates; the extent to which it includes documentation that verifies both personal life and historical events; evidence about a counter life and/or counter identity; expert testimony on social issues the story raises, such as the status of repressed or recovered memory; and conspicuous attention in the media or what we might call a text's celebrity effect.

Internal evidence may involve the hoax's peritextual apparatus—for example, the use of authoritative endorsements that, by shoring up the story's "authenticity," incite readers' suspicion that the life is in fact invented; and the presence or absence of documentation, particularly the use of claims or allegations without evidence. Several narrative issues may also raise suspicion: multiple improbabilities in the story; contradictions or discrepancies from one part of the text to another; the use of a sensationalistic script such as the melodrama of beset victimhood; repeated vagueness about details; and a narrative voice that has a formulaic or generic quality.

In other words, readers inclined to suspect the veracity or authenticity of what a writer claims is his or her life story might read for multiple indices of inconsistency that signal "hoaxiness." Indeed, while some readers and audiences might allege all autobiographical work is fakery—"lies, damn lies, and statistics," to paraphrase Mark Twain—the pressures of this historical moment, the heterogeneous desires of partisan audiences, and the commodification of life narrative in the "age of memoir" argue that we need to distinguish among kinds of hoaxes and adopt a more suggestive continuum of terms. We offer the following taxonomy of autobiographical hoaxes to complicate critical thinking about the cultural work that the hoax does and, conversely, the work that its unmasking performs.

A. Scam Lives

Perhaps the easiest hoaxes to expose and the most egregious are what we might call **scam lives**. These are exemplified by the email messages sent by what the website *Scamorama* calls "the lads from Lagos." Such writers fabricate a pedigree and dire circumstances in making urgent appeals for financial help. Theirs might be relabeled **spam lives,** since appeals from around the globe can arrive in our in-boxes at a staggering rate. Scam lives are financial lives, invented as compelling dramas of fortunes in ruins and calculated for quick profit. Literally asking for an investment in the life story, scammers position email readers as gullible investors. Most readers would concur that scam lives blatantly misrepresent and intend to deceive, that the life is a con and the goal a quick buck, and that readers best beware. Other kinds of suspect life narratives, however, are less transparent in their appeals.

B. Prosthetic Enhancements of Life

Of course, autobiographical narratives, as most theorists influenced by postmodernism would argue, are informed by and incorporate fictive elements. For instance, culturally intelligible and valued fictions of selfhood, such as the *Bildungsroman* or narrative of social development, offer genres of emplotment. Narratives using detailed dialogue certainly invite our suspicion, especially if the scene of narration would have taken place many years before the time of writing. Moreover, autobiographical narratives participate in regimes of truthtelling, as Leigh Gilmore has convincingly argued. But there are limits, however difficult to specify, to the degree of fictionality that is credible, and to the centrality of a fictional scene or plot. In the US this debate about the limits of acceptable fictionalizing recently played out in national media, hinting at the investment readers have in the murky relationship of the referential and the fictive.

In early January 2006 the publishing world was rocked by an exposé that appeared on the scandal-mongering website *Smoking Gun*. It searingly denounced James Frey's best-selling memoir, *A Million Little Pieces*, as a hoax, "a million little lies" ("Million"). Frey's narrative recounted his struggle during his college years with drug addiction, his arrest and conviction on several felonies, his time in prison and his subsequent struggle out of degradation. His life, like his body, he asserted, had been shattered into pieces and had to be rebuilt step by step. Telling his narrative was part of a process of self-reconstruction. Frey followed the format for confession that writers since Augustine have used in describing their wayward lives: early wanton transgression; an awakening through shock to the error of one's ways; and conversion to more enlightened selfhood enabled by readers' absolution of the teller's waywardness (while readers vicariously participate in order to confirm the error of such excess). Frey's story of addiction to drugs and alcohol conformed closely to the Alcoholics Anonymous version of recovery narrative, as Helena Michie and Robyn Warhol describe it. The life he told was ready-made for sale to sensation-seeking readers.

But *Smoking Gun*'s exposé claimed Frey's narrative was something quite different, a highly fictionalized account. Drawing on several authoritative sources, it alleged that Frey had spent almost no time in jail and had not been charged with the serious crimes he claimed to have committed.[1] In other words, Frey had exaggerated his criminality, suturing his story to the narrative of severe addiction as a kind of prosthetic to enhance his life. In what television "fake news" commentator Stephen Colbert calls the age of "truthiness," what counts is what is said to be true—think, "weapons of mass destruction in Iraq." Similarly, *New York Times* op-ed critic Frank Rich saw Frey's memoir as symptomatic of an American hunger for sensationalism and tolerance of what "can be sold as truth," though he dismissed the memoir itself as "harmless diversion [for] suckers" (16).

Indeed, television played a key role in adjudicating the Frey affair. Oprah Winfrey, the queen of talk shows who had made the fortune of *A Million Little Pieces* by naming it a Book Club choice in 2005, initially issued a statement of support for Frey. But, a month later, when she had him return to her talk show "Oprah" for a frank discussion of *A Million Little Pieces*, Oprah challenged Frey's version of events item by item and, in a phrase used by almost every commentator, "took him to the woodshed." She demanded that Frey make a public apology to her, to the television public, and to his readers, for having willfully misled and deceived them. Subsequently, not despite, but *be-*

---

[1] *Smoking Gun* drew on several sources—police reports and public documents, interviews with people who had known Frey in 1997 during the period of his rehab and alleged criminal activity. This challenge to the veracity of Frey's narrative was the tabloid-style exposé that wouldn't go away. *Smoking Gun* allegations were quickly followed by reports in prominent national sources.

cause of, this public humiliation, sales of the book increased steadily; a sequel has been rushed into print.

The Frey hoax is an instance of the celebrity effect that attaches to the writer whose life story feeds readers' hungers for stories of debasement and redemption, linking seediness and neediness. With a little prosthetic manipulation, the author turned a small-town story of youthful waywardness into one of spectacular excess and self-abasement. A life made for sale, the prosthetic life story exposes how the paradoxical relationship of exposure and profit fans readers' desire for the story. As the context of fraud becomes part of the text, readers are increasingly titillated and the writer laughs all the way to the bank.

C. Ethnic Impersonation

A different kind of calculated opportunism is evident in narratives of ethnic crossing or passing. In Australia the narrative *My Own Sweet Time*, alleged to be by "Wanda Koolmatrie," involved cross-cultural impersonation. Published in 1997, it told the story of an indigenous woman's wandering from her hometown of Adelaide to the urban world of Melbourne. Critics hailed *My Own Sweet Time* as representative of the voices of a hip new generation of indigenous Australian writers, a mixed-blood generation cut off from traditional community but at ease in urban Australia's multicultural maze. When the book won a literary award a year later and the publisher requested a meeting with Koolmatrie, the impersonation was revealed: Wanda Koolmatrie was the fictional persona of a young white man named Leon Carmen. Annoyed because he felt white men could no longer find publishers for their work, he cashed in on the popularity of personal narratives told by indigenous Australians.

In *My Own Sweet Time* Leon Carmen deliberately exploited the contemporary commodification of aboriginal life narratives. During the 1990s publishers in Australia sought stories by indigenous Australians for several reasons: partly because of increasing national engagement with the stories of the "stolen generation"; partly because the UN Decade of Indigenous Peoples called attention to indigenous rights movements around the world; and partly because the marketing of "victim" stories played to a desire among the more privileged for the stories of "authentic" sufferers, with whom they could feel empathy. Carmen's impersonation traded on cultural receptivity to "real" stories of indigenous life.

Readers' desire for the verifiably real might be said to stimulate a range of autobiographical practices that involve impersonation and the exploitation through stereotypic simplification of ethnically-marked lives. Like Australia, the United States, as Laura Browder argues in *Slippery Characters*, has been a hotbed of autobiographical impersonation for at least two centuries. An example of such impersonation occurred in *The Education of Little Tree*, published in 1976 under the name of Forrest Carter. Carter presented his story as an autobiographical account and himself as a "half-breed" Cherokee child of the mountains who was raised by his grandparents, sent at age five to an orphanage, then rescued by a Cherokee adult to grow up as an "unlettered" cowboy. His criticism that the US government's historical policy of assimilating Indians was cruel and incompetent received acclaim in the wake of the American Indian Movement's (AIM) confrontation with federal marshals at Wounded Knee, South Dakota in 1973, and the book enjoyed widespread sales (Lang). It has, however, been unmasked as an act of sheer impersonation by Asa Earl Carter, a white man raised in Oxford, Alabama, in a family of four children. After attending the University of Colorado, Boulder, Carter became a political speechwriter for then-white supremacist governor George Wallace and assumed the leadership of a Ku Klux Klan branch, a group noted for its virulent anti-African American and anti-Semitic views. According to informants, Carter knew very little about Cherokee culture.

In the aftermath of the exposure of the Carter hoax, critics have weighed in with differing assessments of both the narrative and its effects. Henry Louis Gates initially defended the quality of his narrative as a novel (though it was classified as an autobiography at that time, 1991). But Eileen Elizabeth O'Connor Antelek critiqued its white supremacist bias in portraying Little Tree as a stereotypic native American "mystically attuned to his environment"; she suggests that Carter's "mythologizing of the Cherokee people" treats their heritage as "just another stereotype" (Antalek 45; qtd. in Bollmann). Laura Browder regards Carter as a "slippery character," seeing the narrative as "a fantasy about Native American primal spirituality [. . .] attuned to [. . .] the recovery movement" and portraying "the inner child Indian, a figure that represents lost innocence and a sense of wonder" (134). Carter, defending his shrewd use of Noble Savage and generic Indian stereotypes, told one informant that he would give the Cherokee nation part of the profits from his book, and its fame would help them get on television talk shows. No Native group receiving profits has, however, been located to date. Carter died in 1979 and the 25th anniversary edition of the narrative has been reissued as "fiction."

Multi-cultural nations in which diverse ethnic communities coexist, such as the US, are especially open to practices of voluntarily-passing from one cultural identity to another, as a means of shifting cultural positionality. The foundational American national myth of the assimilable citizen implies that ethnic differences are fixed, often through racist stereotypes. Impersonating another's ethnic identity, however, offers imaginary escape from everyday life for profit and celebrity. As Browder suggests, "in a multiethnic society, Americans have always shifted identities" (6), at once evading the pressure to conform to stipulated, hierarchical identities and intensifying cultural anxiety about the stability of national identity. Browder argues that ethnic impersonation is a particularly American phenomenon through which we see the "logic of class" (understood as fluid) applied "to a construct of race and ethnicity" (understood as fixed) (7). Ethnic impersonators expose the logic of "passing," and work to escape or "free themselves from the historical trap of an unwanted identity by passing into a new one" (10).

D. Fantasized Lives

A complex example of the hoax is the **fantasized life**, a by-product of world-historical events and projects of collective remembering. Since the memoir boom of the 1990s, testimonial writing has become a favored site of such narratives. One widely publicized autobiographical hoax was *Fragments: Memories of a Wartime Childhood*, translated into English in 1996 and alleged to be by "Binjamin Wilkomirski," known as Bruno Dösseker.[2] G. Thomas Couser summarized the history of counter-evidence to the narrative's asserted evidence, including "Wilkomirski's" refusal of DNA testing, that led to his publisher's subsequent withdrawal of the book and his literary agency's investigation of its narrative assertions (173-174). Stefan Mächler's 2001 biography exposed *Fragments* as a fictional collage weaving together memories of survivors from various literary and historical sources. The question of whether this misrepresentational collage was intentional is, however, more complex, in that "Wilkomirski's" painful fragmented memories of a Swiss foster home may have contributed to a sense of persecution. He continues to insist that his identity is that of a Jew and a survivor of the Holocaust (Couser 174-175), although his book has been withdrawn from bookstores, condemned as either delusion or opportunistic identity theft, and now republished as a novel.

The debate around *Fragments* underscores how an historical event may be particularized and re-presented as a fantasy of cultural belonging. For someone like "Wilkomirski," close to the traumatic event but not a survivor of it, the desire to claim a shared past of victimage of-

---

[2] Following G. Thomas Couser, we place the name "Binjamin Wilkomirski" in quotation marks because the Swiss citizen using this "signature," who alleged he had a Latvian-Jewish father and was imprisoned in Nazi concentration camps before adoption, has the birth name of Bruno Grosjean and the adoptive name of Bruno Dösseker.

fered a personal way to understand the past and situate himself inside world memory. What this apparent delusion illustrates, as Ross Chambers argues, is that certain traumatic stories become so much a part of world memory shared across cultures that an individual can imagine himself "truly" in them. The categorizing of a text as autobiography lifted its narrator out of obscurity and conferred celebrity and cultural value on a life lived in, and as, suffering. Had it been released as "fiction," *Fragments* would not have garnered the attention, awards, or eventual notoriety that it did. In this instance the hoax exposes the mechanism through which particular life stories gain cultural purchase, becoming the stuff of fantasy about heroic avatars.

E. Plagiarized Lives

Bizarrely, some writers may get a life by borrowing incidents, struggles, plots, character, dialogue, and/or drama from someone else's story for insertion into their own narratives. Such lives come ready-made, fashioned by someone else, without even the need of invention. Scenes can be slotted in, voices adapted, dialogue assigned from other historical actors. With a plagiarized life the suspicious reader has to become a sleuth of copyright infringement, reading not just between the lines but beyond the covers. Intriguingly, plagiarizing another's story for autobiographical incorporation implies that releasing lives, through publication, into the public sphere, renders them material for remixing and rematching, surfing and inserting. Certainly, the pastiche lives presented in eighteenth-century broadsheets (see Ann Fabian) and in some Barbary Coast captivity narratives are patchwork creations from many sources. And the practice continues.

Native American writer Sherman Alexie recently claimed that the author of *The Blood Runs like a River Through My Dreams*, one "Nasdijj," stole parts of his short story entitled "This is What It Means to Say Phoenix, Arizona" for his memoir. Another recent example from the realm of autobiographical fiction is Harvard student Kaavya

Viswanathan's heralded "chick-lit" first novel, *How Opal Mehta Got Kissed, Got Wild, and Got a Life*. Viswanathan was outed by the *Harvard Crimson* (see Zhou) for stealing large portions of her story of adolescent angst from two novels by young-adult author Megan McCafferty (*Second Helpings* and *Sloppy Firsts*).[3] While a paucity of life experience might explain a teenager's cribbing of another's story, the promise of fame, profit, and acceptance to Harvard suggests the cynical calculation that may underlie the wholesale borrowing of others' stories. Identifying texts as identity theft relies not on internal discrepancies but on readers' acts of detection. It calls for critical detection attentive to plagiarism, theft, and appropriation of copyright material enabled as never before by ever-more sophisticated technologies of circulation, manipulation, and reproduction.

F. Fabricated Lives

It seems to us that something different and interesting is happening in what we call "found lives," life narratives constructed through various effects of the real, and validated with a documentary apparatus, as in W. G. Sebald's *Austerlitz*. This manifestly fabricated life of the character Austerlitz—a name conflating references to the Napoleonic battle site in Czechoslovakia, a Parisian train station, the Theresienstadt concentration camp site—is embedded in a text rich with documents and historical references that seem to verify its status as autobiographical. Performing a composite life, Sebald inserts photographs, purportedly of Austerlitz, that are in fact of himself, the apparently disinterested narrator. Here, the life fabricated as autobiographical narrative is not a hoax in historical fact, but a conflation that signals a sense of complicity in the Holocaust (despite Sebald's infancy at the time). There is an ethics to constructing a collaborative biographical

---

[3] See e.g, the *International Herald Tribune* 26 Apr. 2006, page 9, for a detailed story, and followup on 29 Apr. about Little, Brown and Co.'s pulling of unsold copies of the book from stores.

life in this way that an historical biography arguably could not perform. We might read this fabricated life as an oblique personal narrative: the author engages imagination and memory with the materials of remembrance in a post-memorial act of reading the archive of the past. A fabricated life narrative such as *Austerlitz*, linking disparate times, places, and identities, suggests both the complicity of historical actors in histories of violence that pre-date them and the trans-historical connections that acts suturing memory and imagination enable. It functions as a metanarrative of the politics, aesthetics, and ethics of autobiographical narrative at the psychic and imaginative center of its time.

G. False Witnessing

Hoaxes may, or may not, be cynical. But they profit from, cater to, and capture certain cultural formations of this historical moment. These include: a history of violence, injury, and harm; the rise of transnational activism; the often-marginalized social location of the witness; the spectacle of lives erased from history that can be revived as somehow "exotic," instructive, and/or representative; the commodification of particular kinds of life stories; and historical apparatuses and rhetorics of authentication. Autobiographical hoaxes, thus, are yoked to the commodity cultures of late capitalism and to the cultural responses to oppression and violence. With the advent of heterogeneous and multiple rights movements in the last three decades and the capacity for narratives to travel globally in the wake of new technologies, a relay has occurred between the global forces of commodification and the public's desire for narratives of suffering. The effect of this relay is to intensify the stakes of exposing an autobiographical hoax, or shifting a narrative into the category of hoax. Hoaxes can become political events that link genres of the autobiographical to the transnational politics of truth-telling and the commodification of victim stories.

Especially in western countries, readers seek first-person narratives about the rest of the world that expose the "gritty details" (in Paul Farmer's phrase [31]) of violence, suffering, and survival and put a human face on suffering. These stories activate a sense of intimacy by promising access to "authentic" experience and attaching reader affects to stories of injury and harm. Readers can feel educated about issues around the world, identify and empathize with those they consider less fortunate, and gain agency in recognizing the suffering of the other while imagining themselves part of a rescuing culture. But in their desire for sentimentalized tales of suffering and survival they can also find themselves manipulated by acts of false witnessing.

An example is Norma Khouri's post-September 11, 2001, narrative entitled, in the UK and Australasia, *Forbidden Love: A Harrowing True Story of Love and Revenge in Jordan* (in the US called *Honor Lost: Love and Death in Modern-Day Jordan*). As narrator, "Norma Khouri" observes her friend Dalia's fate in a melodramatic plot involving Dalia's star-crossed love for Michael, a Catholic in the Royal Army. An old tradition calling for the killing of women considered to have dishonored their families results in her death at her father's hand. In narrating the story of Dalia's death, Khouri acts as witness to an intimate's fate, a recognizable form of authentication. As a witness/narrator—a participant observer who must escape in order to survive—she creates herself as a center of danger. This tactic gives the narrative its gripping, you-are-there quality, its affective charge, and affords the reader the opportunity to observe a clandestine affair. By playing to the Western fantasy of violent patriarchs and beset womanhood under Islamic law and tradition, the narrative draws readers into a melodrama of Islamic victimhood that reifies both the victim and the perpetrator of violence.[4]

---

[4] Norma Khouri's *Forbidden Love* was enthusiastically received in Australia, until the *Sydney Morning Herald* exposed her fraud in summer 2004 (see Knox) and her publisher (Random House Australia) withdrew the book.

A similar example is the narrative *Burned Alive*, first published under the pseudonym "Souad" in France in 2003 (*Brûlée Vive*), in collaboration with Jacqueline Thibault (and in English with the subtitle *A Survivor of an "Honor Killing" Speaks Out*). It chronicles the struggle of a young rural Palestinian woman, pregnant after a liaison with a neighbor, to survive a so-called honor killing in which her father and brother attempted to immolate her. The narrative details her suffering in a West Bank hospital where social workers and doctors allegedly refused to intervene because of the Islamic honor code; her rescue by a Swiss social worker who helps her and her baby escape to Lausanne; and her survival in France, under an assumed name, with a family. This new sense of self ultimately enables her to speak out against patriarchal violence and raise funds for the aid organization Fondation Surgir, which has supported right-wing groups in Israel.

Historian Thérèse Taylor cites both internal and external evidence pointing to the falsity of the witnessing. It is sensational, "a drama of endless death." No factual evidence is presented for its serious allegations about treatment in the Palestinian hospital. The family home, said to be in an isolated village, has a telephone at a time in the 1970s when that would have been impossible. There are multiple errors about West Bank geography. The story inaccurately describes rituals of Arab women's private lives and makes a sweeping condemnation of Islamic patriarchy. The narrator could not have survived burns as severe as she describes. And Fondation Surgir has a link to Terre des Hommes, which has been used by conservative Israeli groups. In other words, Taylor marshals multiple kinds of evidence, internal and external, to suggest how *Burned Alive* discloses to the skeptical reader its status as false witnessing.

In such narratives, the use of human rights discourse, institutions, and mechanisms structures a victim story of injury and harm in ways that many readers immediately credit. In turn the global commodification of such stories of debasement, violation, and survival produces advocates for them, editors anxious to find them, activist groups mobilizing to use them, and readers willing to accord the narratives uncritical acclaim and the writers celebrity status. But in such geopolitical contexts, false witnessing can harm communities and individuals. For example, women activists in Jordan expressed concern about the damage Khouri's hoax had done to their work on behalf of Jordanian women threatened by honor killing. Harm can also be done to a collectivity of people, as in the serious charge in *Burned Alive* that Palestinian social workers and medical staff let women who were victims of honor killing die in hospitals.

For other readers and for various groups and officials, however, the charge of hoax can be used to strategic and instrumental political ends. Suspicious readers may seize on a few lapses in a text's verifiability as synecdochic evidence that undermines the claims of the entire life narrative, as occurred with David Stoll's attack on *I, Rigoberta Menchú*. To similar effect, the Ugandan government charged that China Keitetsi misrepresented her age at the time of her abduction into the army in her narrative of exploitation entitled *Child Soldier*, and thereby challenged Keitetsi's identification as a "child" soldier. In other instances, entire narratives can be dismissed as fabrications in the global politics of rights claims and counterclaims. Conservative Japanese apologists, responding to national and international outrage about the "comfort station system" (a system of organized brothels for military personnel during World War II in which women were in effect sex prisoners) condemned the personal witnessing of the former World War II sex prisoners as revisionist narration that opportunistically deployed the victimization script. Given the marginal social location of the witnesses to sex slavery, those defending the honor of Japan could dismiss the stories of victimization as lies by former prostitutes seeking reparations (see Schaffer and Smith 147).

Conclusion—Readers and the Aftereffects of Hoaxes

Are the kinds of hoaxing we have surveyed anything more than an amusing or bizarre sideshow in the main event of contemporary memoir, interesting certainly, but inconsequential for an understanding of cultural formations and anxieties? Or are such suspicious acts something far more important to our time and to the genres of the autobiographical? We think the latter is the case.

The taxonomy we have proposed intends to set out critical distinctions, generic scripts, and ethical implications central to the problematic of hoaxes. Other issues also deserve exploration. What is the appropriate terminology for such events—fakes, frauds, hoaxes, or fabrications? How are the conditions of belief that constitute the autobiographical pact undermined, threatened, or enhanced when a life narrative is revealed to be a fabrication? How does the writer's manipulation of the pact reconfigure readers' desires? How do we disentangle the imperative to verify representations in and through the referential world from cultural deployments of the rhetoric of authenticity to produce truth effects? How does the compression of time and space in new digital environments impact the contemporary globalization of life narratives and their surveillance? And what kinds of anxieties are refracted and generated through the production, circulation, and reception of hoaxes?

At this moment conflicting points of view and debates abound on the significance of hoaxes for the interplay of self-presentation and referentiality that has driven studies in autobiography for three decades. From one point of view, the heated conversation generated around the exposure of hoaxes could be understood as affirming that reader-consumers, the marketplace, and the media monitor the arena of autobiographical confession, at once legitimizing confessional practices and discrediting them (see McGill). But from another angle, the scandalous revelation of a hoax and its afterlife in the media suggest that it may not matter to some readers whether a life story is plagiarism, impersonation, or fabrication, if the experience of reading the story has been beneficial, educational, illuminating, pleasurable. To reprise Frank Rich's wry comment on the Frey affair, hoaxes expose what can be "sold" as truth at a particular historical moment, in a specific cultural context.

Alternatively, we might read the scandals surrounding hoaxes as creative, producing conditions for more informed and skeptical, less naïve kinds of reading practices. A different kind of reader might resist unmediated identification with the life narrator and engage the text intersubjectively, contributing to new ways of conceptualizing personhood. However we approach the significance of hoaxes at this time, we discover something about the persistence and intransigence of our desires for truth effects, the unpredictability and fluidity of the narratives that embody, transform, and resist those desires, and the mechanisms and motives of the institutions and vehicles that carry those desires toward us.

Works Cited

Alexie, Sherman. "When the Story Stolen Is Your Own." *Time* 6 Feb. 2006: 72.

Antalek, Eileen Elizabeth O'Connor. "Deforrestation Begins with a Little Tree: Uncovering the Polemic of Asa Carter in his Novels as Forrest Carter." Thesis Clark University, 1994.

Bollman, Amy Kallio. "*The Education of Little Tree* and Forrest Carter: What Is Known? What Is Knowable?" *NativeWeb*. 3 Sept. 2006 <http://www.nativeweb.org/pages/legal/carter.html>.

Broeske, Pat H. "Based on an Untrue Story." *New York Times* 27 Nov. 2005, sec. 2: 13.

Browder, Laura, *Slippery Characters: Ethnic Impersonators and American Identities*. Chapel Hill, NC: University of North Carolina Press, 2000.

Carter, Forrest [Asa Earl Carter]. *The Education of Little Tree*. Albuquerque: University of New Mexico Press, 1976.

Chambers, Ross. "Orphaned Memories, Foster Writing, Phantom Pain: The *Fragments* Affair." *Extremities: Trauma, Testimony, and Community*. Ed. Nancy K. Miller and Jason Tougaw. Urbana: University of Illinois Press, 2002. 92-111.

Colbert, Stephen. *The Colbert Report*. Comedy Central. 17 Oct. 2005.

Couser, G. Thomas. *Vulnerable Subjects: Ethics and Life Writing*. Ithaca: Cornell University Press, 2004.

Fabian, Ann. *The Unvarnished Truth: Personal Narratives in Nineteenth-Century America*. Berkeley: University of California Press, 2000.

Farmer, Paul. *Pathologies of Power: Health, Human Rights, and the New War on the Poor*. California Series in Public Anthropology 4. Berkeley: University of California Press, 2003.

Franklin, Benjamin. *Benjamin Franklin's Autobiography*. Ed. J. A. Leo LeMay and P. M. Zall. New York: W. W. Norton, 1986.

Frey, James. *A Million Little Pieces*. New York: N. A. Talese/Doubleday, 2003.

Gates, Henry Louis. "'Authenticity,' or the Lesson of Little Tree." Rev. of *The Education of Little Tree*, by Forrest Carter. *New York Times Book Review* 24 Nov. 1991: 1, 26-30.

Gilmore, Leigh. "Jurisdictions: *I, Rigoberta Menchú*, *The Kiss*, and Scandalous Self-representation in the Age of Memoir and Trauma." *Signs: Journal of Women in Culture and Society* 28.2 (Winter 2003): 695-718.

Hallström, Lasse, dir. *The Hoax*. Miramax, 2006.

Irving, Clifford. *The Hoax*. Sagaponack, NY: Permanent, 1981.

Keitetsi, China. *Child Soldier: Fighting for My Life*. Bellevue, South Africa: Jacana, 2002.

Khouri, Norma. [UK and Australasia:] *Forbidden Love: A Harrowing True Story of Love and Revenge in Jordan*. Australia Scoresby, VIC: Random House, 2003. [US:] *Honor Lost: Love and Death in Modern-Day Jordan*. New York: Atria, 2003.

Knox, Malcolm. "Bestseller's Lies Exposed: Literary Editor Malcolm Knox Uncovers Australia's Latest Hoax Author." *Sydney Morn-*

ing Herald 24 July 2004. 2 Apr. 2006 <http://www.smh.com.au/articles/2004/07/23/1090464854793.html?oneclick=true>.

Koolmatrie, Wanda [Leon Carmen]. *My Own Sweet Time*. Broome, Aus.: Magabala, 1994.

Lang, Debbie. "The Battle of Wounded Knee 1973: Resistance Stories of Lakota People." *Revolutionary Worker Online* 1038, 16 Jan. 2000. 3 Sept. 2006 <http://www.rwor.org/a/v21/1030-039/1038/wknee.htm>.

McCafferty, Megan. *Second Helpings: A Novel*. New York: Three Rivers, 2003.

___. *Sloppy Firsts: A Novel*. New York: Crown, 2001.

Mächler, Stefan. *The Wilkomirski Affair: A Study in Biographical Truth*. New York: Schocken, 2001.

McGill, Robert. "The Unfaithful Muse: Intimacy and Ethics in Autobiographical Fiction." Diss. University of Toronto, 2006.

Menchú, Rigoberta. *I, Rigoberta Menchú: An Indian Woman in Guatemala*. Trans. Ann Wright. Ed. and introd. Elisabeth Burgos-Debray, London: Verso, 1983.

Michie, Helena, and Robyn R. Warhol. "Twelve-Step Teleology: Narratives of Recovery/Recovery as Narrative." *Getting A Life: Everyday Uses of Autobiography*. Ed. Sidonie Smith and Julia Watson. Minneapolis: University of Minnesota Press, 1996. 327-350.

"A Million Little Lies: Exposing James Frey's Fiction Addiction." *Smoking Gun*. 12 May 2006 <http://www.thesmokinggun.com/archive/0104061jamesfrey1.html>.

Nasdijj. *The Blood Runs like a River Through My Dreams*. New York: Houghton Mifflin, 2000.

Rich, Frank. "Truthiness 101: From Frey to Alito." *New York Times* 22 Jan. 2006, sec. 4: 16.

Scamorama. 12 May 2006 <http://www.scamorama.com/>.

Schaffer, Kay, and Sidonie Smith. *Human Rights and Narrated Lives: The Ethics of Recognition*. New York: Palgrave, 2004.

Sebald, W. G. *Austerlitz*. Trans. Anthea Bell. New York: Modern Library, 2002. München: C. Hanser, 2001.

Stoll, David. *Rigoberta Menchú and the Story of All Poor Guatemalans*. Boulder, Colorado: Westview, 1999.
Souad, with Marie-Thérèse Cuny. *Burned Alive: A Survivor of an "Honor Killing" Speaks Out*. New York: Warner, 2005. *Burned alive: A Victim of the Law of Men*. New York: Warner, 2004. Trans. of *Brûlée vive*. Paris: Oh, 2003.
Taylor, Thérèse. "Truth, History, and Honor Killing: A Review of *Burned Alive*." *Antiwar.com*. 2 May 2005. 2 Sept. 2006 <http://www.antiwar.com/orig/ttaylor.php?articleid=5801>.
Viswanathan, Kaavya. *How Opal Mehta Got Kissed, Got Wild, and Got a Life*. New York: Little, Brown, 2006.
Whitlock, Gillian. "The Skin of the Burqa: Recent Life Narratives from Afghanistan." *Biography* 28.1 (Winter 2005): 54-76.
___. *The Skin of the Burqa*. Forthcoming University of Chicago Press, 2006.
Wilkomirski, Binjamin [Bruno Dösseker]. *Fragments: Memories of a Wartime Childhood*. Trans. Carol Brown Janeway. New York: Schocken, 1996.
Winfrey, Oprah. "James Frey and the *Million Little Pieces* Controversy." The Oprah Winfrey Show. ABC. WXYZ, Detroit, MI. 26 Jan. 2006.
Zhou, David. "Sophomore's New Book Contains Passages Strikingly Similar to 2001 Novel." *The Harvard Crimson Online Edition* 23 Apr. 2006. 12 Sept. 2006 <http://www.thecrimson.com/article.aspx?ref=512968>.

Telling Life Stories:
The Rhetorical Form of Biographical Narratives

Gerald P. Mulderig
DePaul University

Abstract: Contemporary discussions of biography have given significant attention to the genre's uneasy fusion of factual intent and fictional technique, a conjoining of opposites that writers, readers, and teachers of biography have found both provocative and vexing. Here I offer an alternative to theories of biography that have pitted the truth of fact against the truth of art. Indeed, I argue that truth in biography is less important to a proper understanding of the genre than is *apparent* truth. When we concentrate on the elements in a biography that make it *seem* true, I argue, we bring into focus the reader's participation in the text, and we foreground biography's rhetorical design.

In A. S. Byatt's novel *The Biographer's Tale*, a graduate student named Phineas Nanson decides, quite spontaneously, that he can no longer tolerate the study of postmodern literary theory and must find something more substantial to devote himself to. "I need a life full of *things*," he says in explaining his decision to one of his professors, "[f]ull of facts" (7). The professor suggests that Phineas consider biography because, unlike other literary genres, it is "an art of things, of facts, of arranged facts" (7)—precisely what Phineas feels is lacking in his life as a literary theorist in training. And so, within weeks, Phineas decides to write a biography of one Scholes Destry-Scholes, who himself was the biographer of a colorful Victorian scholar and traveler named Sir Elmer Bole.

But the facts of the life of Destry-Scholes that Phineas is able to discover turn out to be disappointingly insubstantial after all. He stands in front of the Yorkshire house in which Destry-Scholes was born and feels merely the ordinariness of the small brick building, whose current owner eyes him suspiciously from its upstairs windows.

The house is a very solid thing, and Destry-Scholes' life in it is a verifiable fact, but this thing and this fact seem to contain little meaning. Later Phineas acquires 37 manuscript pages apparently typed by Destry-Scholes, which after he has arranged them appear to be pieces of drafts of biographies of Henrik Ibsen, of the naturalist Carl Linnaeus, and of the geneticist Francis Galton. These manuscripts are also concrete things, but as Phineas reluctantly concludes, they offer little more substance than he had found in postmodern theory. Are they parts of one work in which Destry-Scholes planned to compare these three men, or are they notes compiled for three different books that Destry-Scholes planned to write? Moreover, Phineas learns, much of what Destry-Scholes wrote about Linnaeus in this manuscript was untrue. Was Destry-Scholes unaware of these falsifications, or was he perhaps compiling notes for a fictionalized life of Linnaeus? In short, what—and where—are the facts?

Finally, a niece of Destry-Scholes gives Phineas two boxes full of note cards written by her uncle, and Phineas sets about trying to make sense of them. But the fragmentary entries on these note cards and the wide range of subjects they address present him only with further incoherence and meaninglessness. As Phineas attempts to arrange the note cards into logical groups, he realizes that biographical research does not offer him the world of things and facts that he sought. Rather, it presents an endless succession of interpretive challenges as the biographer attempts to discover significance in facts and artifacts that are frustratingly mute. And in this interpretive task, each biographer is dominated by his or her own inescapable subjectivity, by the irresistible tendency "to translate everything, everyone, all reasoning, all irrational hope and fear, into our own Procrustean grid of priorities" (194-195).

The juxtaposition of fact and interpretation that Phineas discovered in his brief career as a biographer has been recognized since the nineteenth century, but it has been only rarely addressed, because biography remains a curiously undertheorized genre. When biography is theorized at all, writers, including biographers themselves, tend to focus on the relationship that exists between the biographer and the biographical subject—or more precisely, between the biographer and the materials about the subject that he or she collects and uses. Concepts such as "truth" or "accuracy" are always in the background of such discussions. Even as they acknowledge the artistic component of their work, biographers have for the most part continued to see themselves as writers constrained by a body of objective fact that must be accurately represented in narrative form. Leon Edel, for example, argued eloquently for the importance of incorporating techniques of fiction in biographical narratives but found little difficulty in separating the artistic form of biography from the "proveable and palpable fact" (185) on which it rests. "The fancy of the biographer [. . .] resides in the art of narration," he wrote in 1984, "not in the substance of the story. The substance exists before the narration begins" (15). Victoria Glendinning similarly privileges biographical "fact" when she describes the ultimate biographical challenge as

> writ[ing] a biography that [has] the tension and entertainment value of a novel, using all and any narrative techniques, but including nothing that could not be backed up by documents or other evidence, and suppressing nothing of significance, however inconvenient it might be structurally or artistically.
> (54-55)

For a twenty-first-century formulation of the same sentiment, consider P. N. Furbank's argument that neither the historian nor the biographer can claim to be an "artist" because such a writer "is not a free agent, able to mold his or her material just as he or she would wish" but must instead "respect the contingent and the accidental, the randomness of the archive and the obstinate arbitrariness of 'what happened'" (19). Gail Levin, similarly, has written that biography must be true to the life it depicts "while casting the truth in narrative form that is accessible, instructive, and entertaining" (121).

What such discussions of the relationship between truth and art, or fact and interpretation, in biography have in common is their focus on this issue as an authorial problem: given the biographer's need to find pattern and coherence in the subject's life, to make artistic sense of factual data, what are the proper limits of speculation and invention? How much interpreting can a biographer engage in without violating what Richard Ellman has called biography's essentially "archival" character (18)? I think this tension between fact and interpretation must indeed be a central concern in a theory of biography, but I want to frame this issue not in terms of the author's relation to the subject but instead in terms of the author's relation to the reader. In doing so, I wish to suggest that we should think of biographies not, primarily, as factual texts but rather as rhetorical texts.

Let me say first, though, that I don't believe that we as readers can simply ignore the factual intent of biography. Some critics, it is true, have attempted to do so: thus William C. Dowling argued that Boswell's *Life of Johnson* should be read with what he terms "a controlling awareness of its self-contained nature as a work of art" rather than as a text intended to depict actual people and events (79). Similarly, Judith Anderson, in her study of Tudor-Stuart biography, has claimed the essence of biography is a type of insight and judgment more characteristic of the novelist than the researcher, so that "to a greater or lesser extent, biography is inseparable from fiction" (13). Such an approach to biography is flawed because it overlooks a critical fact: biography offers us as readers pleasure different from that of fiction, pleasure inherent in its form and dependent in part on our acceptance of its factual truth. As Ralph Rader has, I think, correctly explained, a "true" narrative such as a biography

> makes sense only if we do think of it as referring beyond itself to what its author did not create; it presents itself as true—[as] reality referring—and our assumption that it is true governs our entire imaginative participation in its meaning

and value, so that if we do discover, for instance, that a fascinating true story is false, we do not think that we have been entertained with a good fiction; we think we have been told a lie. ("Defoe, Richardson" 41)

But on the other hand, the argument that the truth of biography consists, or should consist, of historical fact unaltered by any subjective decisions on the part of the writer is clearly untenable, neglecting as it does the inevitability of selection and emphasis—conscious or unconscious—as the biographer evolves his or her narrative. As readers we expect—we even enjoy—such subjective shadings. Indeed, our unarticulated skepticism about the absolute factual accuracy of any biography is revealed by our interest in other biographies of the same person by writers who select, configure, or interpret their data in different ways—a phenomenon that Gordon Bowker has aptly labeled "the infinitely revisable nature of biography" (269).

An effective theory of biography, I want to suggest, must accommodate both the particular pleasure that we as readers find in biographies as factual texts and our opposing awareness that biographical narratives at best only approximate objective reality. My approach to such a theory of biography is through what I call the authenticity, rather than the accuracy, of biographical narratives, a distinction explained by Paul Murray Kendall:

> We demand that a novel [. . .] be in some way true to life; we demand of biography that it be *true to a life*. There is a difference in meaning between the phrases; they join, however, in signifying not "factual" but "authentic"—and authenticity lies not only in what we are given but in what we are persuaded to accept. (8)

To talk about authenticity in biography is to shift our attention away from the data out of which biographers construct their narratives and instead to the readers for whom they write, from questions of accuracy to questions of believability.

What draws us to biography, I propose, is not the certainty that it is factually accurate but the possibility that it may be, and biographies succeed as putative factual texts, despite their inescapably interpretive character, to the extent that they affirm that possibility of truth. The success of a biography, in other words, is primarily a rhetorical achievement: it rests not on the authority of the biographer's accumulated "facts" but on the *reader's* belief that the biographer's artistic representation of those facts may correspond to historical reality. Whether biographers see themselves as reporting facts or as making subjective interpretations is ultimately irrelevant; consciously or unconsciously, through countless choices of detail and language, every biographer seeks above all to win the reader's assent to the validity of the image of the subject that the biography presents.

An authentic biography, in the sense that I wish to use that term, overrides the inevitable opposition between fact and interpretation by inspiring a reader's belief in the truth of the text even though its factual accuracy remains unverifiable—indeed, even if its accuracy is in dispute. To put it yet another way, truth in biography is less important to a proper understanding of the genre than is *apparent* truth. When we concentrate on the elements in a biography that make it *seem* true, I would argue, we shift the focus of critical attention from the data out of which biographers construct their narratives to the readers for whom they write, from questions of accuracy to questions of believability. In short, we foreground biography's essentially rhetorical character.

Perhaps the best case for understanding my argument that biographies succeed or fail according to their rhetorical effectiveness is provided by the biographies of nineteenth-century England. For nowhere is the tension between fact and interpretation in biographical writing greater. Victorian biography took shape just as the gap between interpretation and fact in modern historical writing was being defined.

Suspended between the old tradition of "literary" history, with its emphasis on the writer's insight and imagination, and the new school of professional historians dedicated to objective and verifiable knowledge, Victorian biography is an amalgamation, in constantly shifting proportions, of both modes of thought. For biographers in the nineteenth century, truth was a fluid concept—sometimes confirmed by mounds of documentary evidence, sometimes determined by the biographer's frankly intuitive understanding of his or her subject. What is so striking—and often so unsettling—to the modern reader is not just the notorious freedom with which Victorian biographers altered documents and details, but their concomitant, and apparently genuine, asseverations of their absolute fidelity to truth. Thus John Gibson Lockhart could write to William Adam that his objective in his *Life of Walter Scott* was "*telling the truth* in all things" (qtd. in Hart 10)—while at the same time he was discouraging his publisher from issuing a supplementary edition of Scott's correspondence that might reveal the silent textual alterations that he had made in the letters quoted in the biography (Grierson xxvii). And Elizabeth Gaskell, besieged by complaints from readers who felt that they had been misrepresented in her *Life of Charlotte Brontë*, could write in apparently genuine anguish to Brontë's friend Ellen Nussey, "I *did so try* to *tell the truth*, & I believe *now* I hit as near the truth as any one *could* do" (Gaskell 454)—even though Gaskell's decision to suppress completely any mention of Brontë's unrequited love for Constantin Heger had made it necessary for the biographer to antedate the crisis in Branwell Brontë's life by eighteen months in her narrative so as to create a plausible reason for Charlotte's sudden departure from Brussels in 1844 and her depression upon returning home (Gérin 171).

But the need to reconcile fact and interpretation in biography is just as important for our understanding of the genre today as it was for the Victorians. Consider the following three types of rhetorical strategies by which successful biographers foster their readers' belief in the authenticity of the text and thereby avert the collision of the truth of fact and the truth of art.

First is the relationship established in the text between the biographer and the reader. We do not come to know the person whose life is narrated in a biography without also forming an association with the biographer in his or her role as narrator—a bond shaped by the biographer's overt contributions to the narration in passages of commentary, explanation, clarification, or analysis but also by his or her indirect presence in the text through the presentation of background and setting, the choice of anecdotes and details, the selection and editing of documentary evidence, and the structuring of events for dramatic effect. As Diane Wood Middlebrook correctly observes, "No matter how subtly the biographer inserts herself into the text, she will have to be there behind the scenes, managing the chronology, not just documenting it" (159). Our apprehension of the dynamic relationship between biographer and subject that is played out before us as the narrative unfolds plays a major role in shaping our judgment about the validity of the text.

Second, what dominant ideas about the character and personality of the subject is the reader urged to accept? In his analysis of literary form in Boswell's *Johnson*, Ralph Rader suggests a further source of authenticity in biography: the coherence of the biographer's depiction of his or her subject. The unifying center of Boswell's text, Rader argues, is Johnson's character, which validates the biography by simultaneously evolving from and corroborating the evidence that Boswell presents. "The image [of Johnson] constructs the facts," he explains, "and the facts in turn construct the image; the process, circular and progressive, constitutes the linear coherence and material unity of the *Life*" ("Literary Form" 17). James Clifford explains that such unity has been considered essential in biography because of the cultural myth of "personal coherence" that readers of biography share. "And if the life does not take shape," he writes, "if we do not in reading [a biography] encounter a distinct person whose voice, gestures, and moods grow familiar to us, then we judge the biography a failure" (44). The believability that a biography achieves by conveying a unified image of its subject results, of course, from the biographer's selection and arrangement of his or her materials rather than from the data themselves. As Claude Lévi-Strauss has pointed out, individual pieces of information do not alone validate a historical text; they gain credibility only because they are consistent with a larger pattern of details established by the writer (57).

Finally, how is the story of the subject's life structured for the reader? Not only the coherent depiction of the subject, but the coherence of the narrative itself may contribute to the reader's belief in the biography's validity. "Biographers," as Isobel Grundy has written, "have to find the story in the muddle" (111). From the randomness and disorder that make up every human life, the biographer culls aspirations, setbacks, and accomplishments that, linked together, give the life a thematic or teleological dimension. The use of literary techniques to create meaning in historical narratives has received far more critical attention from historians than from biographers. Hayden White's term for this pattern-making power is "emplotment." Historical events, White explains,

> are *made* into a story by the suppression or subordination of certain of them and the highlighting of others, by characterization, motific repetition, variation of tone and point of view, alternative descriptive strategies, and the like—in short, all of the techniques that we would normally expect to find in the emplotment of a novel or a play. [. . .] *How* a given historical situation is to be configured depends on the historian's subtlety in matching up a specific plot structure with the set of historical events that he wishes to endow with a meaning of a particular kind. (85)

Martine Watson Brownley, similarly, has used the term "imaginative referent" to describe the vision of the historian that imbues historical evidence with "thematic structure and aesthetic coherence." The result, she writes, is the reader's perception of reality in the text, "the sense that what he is encountering is the historical truth" (14).

I titled this essay "Telling Life Stories," and the pun in that title was deliberate. For my interest is not only how a biographer tells the story of another person's life, but how he or she shapes that narrative into a telling story—an effective and convincing one. My argument has been that a biography can succeed only if the biographer makes the reader believe in its possible truth. Walter Ong has noted that "[a] reader has to play the role in which the author has cast him [. . .]" (12). The ways in which readers of a biography may be induced to assent to the validity of the text as they play out the roles the biographer defines for them constitute what I call biography's rhetoric of authenticity. In the intersection of biographer, subject, and reader, I believe, lies an approach to biography that not only reconciles biography's factual and fictional dimensions, but also enlarges our conception of the biographical enterprise.

Works Cited

Anderson, Judith H. *Biographical Truth: The Representation of Historical Persons in Tudor-Stuart Writing*. New Haven: Yale University Press, 1984.

Bowker, Gordon. "Constructing the Biographical Subject: The Case of Malcolm Lowry." *Writing the Lives of Writers*. Ed. Warwick Gould and Thomas F. Staley. Houndmills: Macmillan, 1998. 266-276.

Brownley, Martine Watson. *Clarendon and the Rhetoric of Historical Form*. Philadelphia: University of Pennsylvania Press, 1985.

Byatt, A. S. *The Biographer's Tale*. New York: Vintage-Random House, 2001.

Clifford, James. L. "'Hanging Up Looking Glasses at Odd Corners': Ethnobiographical Prospects." *Studies in Biography*. Ed. Daniel

Aaron. Harvard English Studies 8. Cambridge: Harvard University Press, 1978. 41-56.

Dowling, William C. "Boswell and the Problem of Biography." *Studies in Biography*. Ed. Daniel Aaron. Harvard English Studies 8. Cambridge: Harvard University Press, 1978. 73-93.

Edel, Leon. *Writing Lives: Principia Biographica*. New York: Norton, 1984.

Ellman, Richard. *Literary Biography: An Inaugural Lecture Delivered before the University of Oxford*. Oxford: Clarendon, 1971.

Furbank, P. N. "The Craftlike Nature of Biography." *Biographical Passages: Essays in Victorian and Modernist Biography Honoring Mary M. Lago*. Ed. Joe Law and Linda K. Hughes. Columbia: University of Missouri Press, 2000. 18-27.

Gaskell, Elizabeth. *The Letters of Mrs. Gaskell*. Ed. J. A. V. Chapple and Arthur Pollard. Cambridge: Harvard University Press, 1967.

Gérin, Winifred. *Elizabeth Gaskell: A Biography*. Oxford: Clarendon, 1976.

Glendinning, Victoria. "Lies and Silences." *The Troubled Face of Biography*. Ed. Eric Homberger and John Charmley. New York: St. Martin's, 1988. 49-62.

Grierson, H. J. C. "Sir Walter Scott in His Letters." Introduction. *The Letters of Sir Walter Scott*. Centenary Edition. Ed. H. J. C. Grierson. Vol. 1. London: Constable, 1932. xxvii-lxxix.

Grundy, Isobel. "'Acquainted with all the Modes of Life': The Difficulty of Biography." *Writing the Lives of Writers*. Ed. Warwick Gould and Thomas F. Staley. Houndmills: Macmillan, 1998. 107-124.

Hart, Francis R. "Proofreading Lockhart's *Scott*: The Dynamics of Biographical Reticence." *Studies in Bibliography* 14 (1961): 3-22.

Kendall, Paul Murray. *The Art of Biography*. New York: Norton, 1965.

Levin, Gail. "Biography and the Visual Arts: The Problematic Interface of Images and Life." *Biography and Source Studies*. Ed. Frederick R. Karl. Vol 8. New York: AMS, 2004. 121-137.

Lévi-Strauss, Claude. "Overture to *le Cru et le cuit.*" *Yale French Studies* 36-37 (1966): 41-65.

Middlebrook, Diana Wood. "Postmodernism and the Biographer." *Revealing Lives: Autobiography, Biography, and Gender.* Ed. Susan Groag Bell and Marilyn Yalom. Albany: State University of New York Press, 1990. 155-165.

Ong, Walter J., S.J. "The Writer's Audience Is Always a Fiction." *PMLA* 90 (1975): 9-12.

Rader, Ralph W. "Defoe, Richardson, Joyce, and the Concept of Form in the Novel." *Autobiography, Biography, and the Novel.* Papers Read at a Clark Library Seminar, May 13, 1972. Ed. William Matthews and Ralph W. Rader. Los Angeles: William Andrews Clark Memorial Library, University of California, 1973.

———. "Literary Form in Factual Narrative: The Example of Boswell's *Johnson.*" *Essays in Eighteenth-Century Biography* Ed. Philip B. Daghlian. Bloomington: Indiana University Press, 1968. 3-42.

White, Hayden. *Tropics of Discourse: Essays in Cultural Criticism.* Baltimore: Johns Hopkins University Press, 1978.

Too Far For Comfort?
A Discussion of Narrative Strategies in Biography

Rana Tekcan
Istanbul Bilgi University

Abstract: This essay is an attempt to look at the various ways in which a biographer re-creates the life of his/her subject in narrative. The different narrative strategies involved in this writing process are examined through the "distance" between the biographer and the subject in terms of time and space. Distance enables us to divide the genre into three categories: where the biographer and the subject personally know one another; where the biographer is a near contemporary of the subject; and where biographer and subject are separated by, in some cases, hundreds of years.

In all the narrative strategies used in the integration of primary material, narrative voice, tone, event selection and emphasis, biographers have to use selectivity in order to reach a sense of completeness. This seems to be the basic paradox of the genre. Furthermore, what creates the sense of vividness and lived-life, which is the aim of all biographies, is best achieved when the biographer imposes his own idiosyncrasies upon the text. This is what makes a biography a life-narrative that belongs both to the subject and to the biographer. Several biographies are used to illustrate how the approach to the subject and the employment of narrative strategies may vary: Johnson's *Life of Savage*; Boswell's *Life of Johnson*; Strachey's *Eminent Victorians*; Holroyd's *Lytton Strachey*; Honan's *Jane Austen* and Motion's *Keats*.

The main interest of this essay lies in the various ways of recreating a "self" in narrative by "another," in other words, the intricate relationship of the biographer and the subject. What exactly does a biographer *do* when he or she re-creates a subject in a biography? This is a question widely ignored both by readers and reviewers. Most reviews of biographies in newspapers and literary magazines—and there are many, since biography is a highly popular genre—see through the narrative strategies and styles as if they are not there and directly look at the content. They often consist of a summary of the life that is depicted in the work. That particular life's important events are highlighted and commented on. Rarely, if at all, a biography is reviewed as a product of choice and organization. As opposed to the narrative voice in an autobiography, which is always listened to with particular attention, the voice that tells someone else's life story is often ignored; it is rendered transparent, invisible.

But what is content without form? It is biographical form that gives shape to the biographical subject. Without it no "illusion" of a living and breathing person can be created on paper. Biography, after all, *is* a well-staged illusion. The recreation of the biographical subject is a complex endeavour and requires a complex narrative. In contrast to purely fictional forms, biography writing does not allow total freedom to the biographer in the creative act. Ideally, a biography's structure or backbone is formed by accurate historical fact—in that sense, it claims a kinship with history. But its soul lies elsewhere. Since the concern is "life," something more is needed. This "something more" is desired both by writers and readers of biography: It is the vivid sense of a "lived life"; nothing dry, cold or dead, but a well-rounded, vibrant impression of a life that is left in the air after one turns over the last page of a biography of any value.

Each biographer uses a different strategy to create this impression. However, he or she is, once again, unable to exercise total freedom. The use of narrative strategies cannot be arbitrary. It is, in my opinion, largely dictated by what could be called the "distance" between the biographer and the subject in terms of time and space (Alpers 12). Distance serves as a centre around which the issues of biographer and subject relationship can be discussed. Looking at biography in terms of distance also enables us to divide this diverse genre into three main categories: first, where the biographer and the subject personally know one another; second, where the biographer is a near contemporary of the subject; and third, where biographer and subject are distinctly separated, in some cases, by hundreds of years. Let us look at these in some detail.

The biographers in the first category are historically placed at such a privileged moment that they are able to see their subjects with their own eyes. Does it follow, then, that the strongest asset of any biographer is his/her personal knowledge of the subject—as Anthony Alpers says, "the author once saw Shelley plain, and there is no substitute for that" (12)? Is it true as Dr. Johnson said that "[n]obody can write the life of a man, but those who have eat and drunk and lived in social intercourse with him"?

Whether this unique situation is an advantage or a disadvantage in disguise has been a topic for debate. There are cases where the personal relation between the biographer and the subject produces disaster. The biographers in such cases are mostly relatives or close friends who may be just too close to write a reliable narrative. The primary commemorative instinct reigns above all other likely and often imperative considerations such as adherence to facts or attempt at objectivity. The outcome is a panegyric full of tiresome praise, distortions of fact and covering of faults.

Despite the possible abuses of this biographer-subject relationship, some of the genre's most famous examples are included in this category. For example *Life of Richard Savage* by Dr. Samuel Johnson and *Life of Dr. Johnson* by James Boswell. What significantly marks these two works is the biographers' personal acquaintance with their respective subjects. However, Johnson and Boswell differ in how they use this acquaintance.

For a while Dr. Johnson was writing anonymously for the *Gentleman's Magazine*. By 1742 he had published a short series of lives of scholars, physicians, scientists, priests and others. A year later his friend, the poet Richard Savage, died, and in 1744 Johnson wrote his friend's biography through which he established himself as a figure of major literary force and fame, alongside poems like "London" and "The Vanity of Human Wishes."

Why pick Richard Savage, who was little more than a frustrated genius even for his contemporaries, as a subject? For the answer we need to look in two different directions. One is personal: Savage was a friend of Johnson's youth. Together they suffered poverty. Johnson made it but Savage never did. After a life of misfortune, misunderstanding, waste and self-destruction Savage died in prison, penniless and virtually friendless. Johnson used this biography to justify Savage's ways to the public, to clear his name for posterity. Ironically he made his friend immortal through literature, something which Savage himself was unable to achieve with his own claim to genius and his literary output.

The second direction is Johnson's moralistic approach to biography which he later formulated in the two essays he wrote for the *Rambler* and the *Idler*. In *Rambler No:60* he writes:

> I have often thought that there has rarely passed a life of which a judicious and faithful narrative would not be useful. For, not only every man has, in mighty mass of the world, great numbers in the same condition with himself, to whom his mistakes and miscarriages, escapes and expedients, would be of immediate and apparent use; but there is such a uniformity in the state of man, considered apart from adventitious and separable decorations and disguises, that there is scarce any possibility of good or ill but is common to human kind. (95)

If so, what better material for a biography can there be than Savage's life? Within this relatively short work—especially if we think of the traditional biography of hundreds of pages—Johnson is in constant control of his material. He chooses to be apparently invisible, occasionally using the first-person pronoun in phrases like "whose name I am now unable to recollect" (511), implying the strong ties between the biographer's memory and his subject in this first category of life-writing. Since, for Johnson, the only kind of decent biography is written by people who have "eat and drunk and lived in social intercourse with their subjects," Johnson's references to his memory show that the record of a man's or woman's life is in the memory of the people who knew him, and that such knowledge can easily evaporate.

His invisibility is even more significant in the episode which became "a legend, almost an eighteenth century archetype, of the Outcast Poet, moving through an infernal cityscape" (Holmes 45). Here is what Johnson writes:

> He lodged as much by accident as he dined, and passed the night sometimes in mean houses, which are set open at night to any casual wanderers, sometimes in cellars, among the riot and filth of the meanest and most profligate; and sometimes, when he had not money to support even the expenses of these receptacles, walked about the streets till he was weary, and lay down in the summer upon a bulk, or in winter with his associates in poverty, among the ashes of a glass-house. (556-557)

From other accounts of these night-walks we know that Savage was not alone. "His associates in poverty" was nobody else but Johnson and Johnson alone. A careful look will show that Johnson did away with the "together" which he uses in other accounts. He detaches himself from Savage. He chooses to be a narrator only. This narrative detachment is also a reflection of his personal choice in life. He had chosen a different path. He had used his energy not as a force for self-destruction like his friend but as a force of self-creation, one outcome of which was writing Savage's life—as if he were looking at himself from behind the shadows and deciding to be otherwise.

The voice of the one who remembers—in this case Johnson—overlooks the whole text in a God-like manner. This omniscient voice blends itself masterfully with the background. It invites the reader to take Savage as Johnson believed him to be. In the narrative voice there is *an apparently* perfect balance of judgement and compassion. In this sense, the biography exudes a strange feeling of comfort—a sense of Savage being defended by a strong advocate at the final judgement.

The biography gains its primary strength from the narrative voice's understanding of human frailty and motivation. The text gives the impression of duplicating the effect Savage must have had on his finds. It charms just like Savage must have done, for his charm was legendary. Reading about the harsh justice that catches up with Savage in prison, one is made to feel not a sense of satisfied closure but rather a sadness and a strong sense of wasted life, misdirected energy and anger at the uncontrollable forces that inevitably direct one's life—even though one is plainly aware of Savage's faults which play a major role in his downfall. Johnson's voice always finds a way to bestow kindness on the subject. In a sense, the text becomes the revenge that Savage was unable to take for all the suffering life had to offer him.

Personal acquaintance between biographer and subject is not always expressed in such a "brief [and] ordered" (Shelston 43) manner as in *Life of Savage*. There is another way. At this far reach of the pendulum's swing we find Johnson again; but this time as the subject of the most famous biography in the English language: James Boswell's *The Life of Samuel Johnson, LL.D.*

Boswell writes, "So we drove on that stage in the dark, and were long pensive and silent" (705). Few biographies can boast of a sentence such as this. The "we" are Samuel Johnson and his friend and biographer James Boswell. Boswell's biography abounds in sentences like the one above, for as a biographer he chose to be fully present in his narrative both as a guiding, interpreting narrator and also as a character. Boswell personally knew Johnson in the last 21 years of Johnson's life. Only 276 days of these 21 years were spent in Johnson's company (Nicolson 102). But it feels as if Boswell was always there, watching Johnson from birth to death.

This biography also contains arguably the most extreme case of biographical manipulation. It shows us how personal acquaintance can be used in service of the biographer's art. As we know, Boswell specially concentrates on Johnson's conversations. He tries to write down every conversation he witnesses. He encourages Johnson to talk when there is really no occasion: "Desirous of calling Johnson forth to talk, and exercise his wit, though I should myself be the object to it, I resolutely ventured to undertake the defense of convivial indulgence in wine, though he was not to-night in the most genial humour" (490). This seems negligible; but, not so from the point of view of biography as a genre. Just the opposite. Boswell quits being just a biographer who *witnesses* what happens and records it for his work, and starts becoming an agent who actually generates conversation to write down. At first, he suggests certain topics that may interest his subject; but later he makes statements that he knows would make Johnson react strongly.

This might be considered somewhat innocent, but Boswell does not stop there. He tells Johnson what he hears about him from his friends or his enemies and records Johnson's amusement or anger. He then starts to contrive meetings between Johnson and certain people Boswell thinks would induce interesting conversation for the biography. One of these is Johnson's "arranged" meeting with General Paoli (409). Boswell hears Johnson talk against Corsicans and thinks it would be a good idea to bring these two men together and write down their potentially interesting conversation.

Another arranged meeting is Boswell's carefully executed plan to bring Johnson together with John Wilkes. This is an instance when one feels how strange a creature is Boswell the man and Boswell the biographer. "My desire," he writes, "of being acquainted with celebrated men of every description, had made me, much about the same time, obtain an introduction to Dr. Samuel Johnson and to John Wilkes, Esq. Two men more different could perhaps not be selected out of all mankind" (764). He sounds like a collector of exotic animals. Boswell may be, at this moment, at his most interesting: an "ordinary" man living vicariously through eminent personages. He enjoys meddling with lives. Actually, here, he sees his subject almost as a research animal, creates an artificial situation in which he tests his reactions:

> But I conceived an irresistible wish, if possible, to bring Dr. Johnson and Mr. Wilkes together. How to manage it, was a nice and difficult matter. [. . .] Notwithstanding the high veneration which I entertained for Dr. Johnson, I was sensible that he was sometimes a little actuated by the spirit of contradiction, and by means of that I hoped I should gain my point. I was persuaded that if I had come upon him with a direct proposal, [. . .] he would have flown into passion. (765)

So, instead of a direct proposal, he traps Johnson into going to a dinner where Wilkes is also going to be present. He writes with excitement, "When I had him fairly seated in a hackney-coach with me, I exulted as much as a fortune-hunter who has got an heiress into a post-chaise with him to set out for Gretna-Green" (767). Johnson gets very uncomfortable when he arrives at the house but he acts very civil. Then we come to a long section where the conversation is recorded in detail: the experimenter jotting down the actions and reactions of the subject of his experiment. The evening is treated in its entirety rather than in short impressions, as Boswell savours the delights of his trap. He uses his talents for storytelling to the full and he *is* talented. The dinner ends without any confrontation, the two men get on well. All that is left for Boswell to do now is to remind us of how ingenious it was of him to get these two men together. This is an astounding and twisted case of biography producing its own material, i.e. producing life. Can the biographer be any more "distanceless" from the subject?

Now to the second category: When it is historically impossible for a biographer to meet his/her subject, the main emphasis of the biography inevitably shifts onto a different axis. Neither Lytton Strachey (1880-1932) nor Michael Holroyd (b. 1932) had a chance to meet their subjects and the two different directions in which they moved from that point illustrates the possibilities of the second category of biographies.

Lytton Strachey's *Eminent Victorians* consists of four short biographies of Henry Cardinal Manning, Florence Nightingale, Dr. Thomas Arnold and General Charles Gordon. They are a carefully selected group each of whom represents a certain aspect of Victorianism: religion, humanitarianism, education and imperialism respectively. The title is ironic. However, it is a well-disguised sort of irony, parodying the titles of contemporary popular biographies. Biographies written around the time of *Eminent Victorians* quite often had similar titles given in all sincerity. Titles emphasized the respectability of the subjects as well as the manner the biographies chose to represent them. When *Eminent Victorians* was published on 9 May 1918, many readers picked the book up in stores totally oblivious to the irony its title entailed.

Strachey also reserves the traditional motive of the biographer, i.e. to document admiration for a subject. He wants to expose the "heroes" of an era for a new generation disappointed and frustrated by the false ideals symbolized in certain individuals. So, he picks his subjects as targets for attack. His aversion towards Victorianism at a social level and towards strong ambition at a personal level seem to be the twin triggers in his attack.

Strachey wrote the four biographies at a time when people who knew the subjects were still alive. However, he did not attempt to contact them and use their first-hand knowledge and impressions as source. His sources for each biography are given in a short bibliography at the end of each section. These lists consist of published biographies and, if possible, letters of the subjects as well as memoirs, autobiographies or correspondence of people that surround each subject. Strachey did not act as an investigative researcher-biographer, but chose to create what may be called a "second-hand" impression through already-printed material.

His staying away from primary research—a point of pride among biographers—is consistent with his overall attitude towards the genre. After all, what did piling of details contribute to those tiresome volumes of Victorian biographies? It was not the facts themselves but how one presented them that was important. The interpretive force behind the facts was art:

> When Livy said that he would have made Pompey win the battle of Pharsalia, if the turn of the sentence had required it, he was not talking utter nonsense, but simply expressing an important truth in a highly paradoxical way,—that the first duty of a great historian is to be an artist. The function of art in history is something much more profound than mere decoration [. . .] Uninterpreted truth is useless as burned gold; and art is the great interpreter. (Strachey, *Spectatorial Essays* 13)

In fact, the quotation above carries Strachey's de-emphasizing of fact further. The quotation from Livy is a fake, one of what Strachey calls his "well-known pseudo-quotations" (qtd. in Holroyd, 420).

He also includes imaginary scenes from the life of his subjects. Here is such an imaginary scene from the life of Florence Nightingale where he once again uses the image of an eagle to symbolize ambition:

> At times, indeed, among her intimates, Mrs. Nightingale [that is Florence Nightingale's mother] almost wept. 'We are ducks,' she said with tears in her eyes, 'who have hatched a wild swan.' But the poor lady was wrong; it was not a swan that they hatched, it was an eagle. (115)

The formal and contextual revisions Strachey made can be regarded as a demythologizing process. If biography is a form of modern myth-making (especially since Romanticism) Strachey reverses the mechanism.

What makes *Eminent Victorians* the biting, anti-heroic narrative that it is, is also laughter. This laughter turns the all-too-respectable, stuffy, gloomy and finally hollow Victorianism into a grim joke. Strachey's aim is to subvert Victorianism through its four paragons and he uses laughter as his tool. Bertrand Russell was to record the following about the time he was reading *Eminent Victorians* in his prison cell: "It caused me to laugh so loud that the officer came to my cell, saying I must remember that prison is a place of punishment" (qtd. in Holroyd, 69). In *Eminent Victorians*, the biographer's narrative voice "take[s] over, appropriate[s], and silence[s] the subject" (Backscheider 19), inducing the same laughter in the reader. And that is Strachey's strength.

Biographer Michael Holroyd, on the other hand, who stands at a similar historical distance from his subject as Strachey, refuses "to take over, appropriate, and silence the subject"; on the contrary, his famous biography of Lytton Strachey turns the narrative over to multiple voices as often as possible. Holroyd was born three years after Strachey's death. Many people who had known Strachey in different capacities were still alive when the young biographer embarked on the adventure of researching for his biography in 1962. He describes his first meeting with James Strachey, Lytton Strachey's brother, who looked very much like him. The old man who meets Holroyd at the door is a replica, a shadow of Holroyd's subject:

> In a more subdued and somewhat less astringent form, he shared many of Lytton's qualities—his humour, his depth and ambiguity of silence, his rational turn of mind, his shy emotionalism and something of his predisposition to vertigo. As he opened the front door to me, swaying slightly, murmuring something I failed to overhear, I wondered for a moment whether he might be ill. I extended a hand, a gesture which might be interpreted either as a formality or an offer of assistance. But he retreated, and I followed him in. (xii)

The scene has immediacy, vividness, and in one stroke we get to see the outlines of James Strachey and—at a distance—of Lytton Strachey himself. This is also retrospective writing. The young biographer will learn about the shared characteristics of the brothers much later, after reading the letters. However, in this scene Holroyd brings future knowledge and insight into the present moment at the first flicker of an opportunity to get that insight. He brings the now and the future together—something he will continue to do in Strachey's life narrative.

In *Eminent Victorians* Lytton Strachey does not give a complete picture of his subjects through the presentation of their diversity in all aspects of life, but a complete picture of one strong human trait that has put its stamp on almost all their actions. In this distorted completeness, subjects show the same traits of ambition even in their childhood. The completeness in the case of Holroyd's work, on the other hand, comes from the detailed treatment of Strachey's entire life in all its aspects and the thorough use of personal material given to the biographer by the subject's brother and close friends. Holroyd makes use of the advantage of being a near contemporary of his subject by making personal contact with people who knew Strachey. This is the most remarkable aspect of the book. The reader first encounters figures like James Strachey, Frances Partridge or Harold Nicolson in this preface, sitting face to face with the living, breathing biographer. Because of this first encounter, the reader feels an enhanced sense of connectedness when the younger selves of those people appear in the narrative. Holroyd successfully projects the sense that although he does not know his subject personally, he has the advantage of the next best thing.

Given the material at Holroyd's disposal, it was perhaps inevitable that he would write a biography which involved interesting biographical information about people other than the subject. Strachey's correspondence with his friends from Cambridge and fellow Bloomsbury members forms a significant and colourful backdrop to Strachey's life story. In this sense, Holroyd's biography presents a panorama of an era and consequently a group picture of some of the most talented and prolific intellectuals of that era. This brings Holroyd's biography close to Strachey's *Eminent Victorians*. On the one hand, the life of an individual is narrated, and on the other, a way of life and a state of mind are brought before the reader. Just as *Eminent Victorians* played a role in the comprehension and decoding of Victorianism, *Lytton Strachey* played a role in the late 1960s in the public advocacy of personal liberties, especially sexual ones. It also triggered an interest in the Bloomsbury group, both negative and positive. Since both biographies were written at times historically close to the eras they depicted, they had social and intellectual repercussions (although some would undoubtedly argue them to be quite minor).

This brings us to the last category: What about those biographers who do not have a chance "to eat, drink and live in social intercourse" with their subjects or those who are unable to meet close relatives or friends who actually had that privilege? Many biographers writing today are in this category. Being historically distanced from one's subject, in some cases by hundreds of years, carries with it the lack of all the advantages discussed in the previous chapters. However, it has one substantial advantage: freedom. A biographer writing a life lived many generations ago is almost never burdened by family authorization. There is no one who might be directly offended or seriously hurt by anything that may be written in the biography. There might be great-granddaughters or nephews or a large group of fanatic admirers; but they cannot be compared to an angry husband threatening to sue or a son preventing the publication of the product of years and years of arduous work. The available material can be freely used; the field of interpretation is open.

As examples we can look at Park Honan's 1987 biography of Jane Austen and Andrew Motion's 1997 biography of John Keats.

In *Jane Austen, Her Life*, Honan's primary interest is in the reconstruction of a picture in which the subject holds the centre-stage. In

Jane Austen's case, there is more biographical material available about people surrounding her, than material that immediately pertains to her. Honan uses this handicap very much to his advantage in his biography. He provides a social context around his subject made of all the available personal, familial and historical material. He shows us Austen's world through the eyes of everyone around her so that one, more or less, sees how the subject herself is informed. In doing this, he gets help from fiction, and being someone who lives and writes for an age dominated by visual images, from cinema. Such a reconstruction is essential for both the biographer and the reader. The age in which the subject lives should be presented thoroughly for a better understanding and evaluation of character, mood, emotion, reaction and action. The readers cannot be expected to do these without the help of the biographer since they are neither contemporaries or near contemporaries of the subject nor scholars of the period in question.

The biography opens with "Prelude: Frank Austen's Ride Home." Other chapters have similar titles reminding one of titles from novels: "Lady From France," "I Could Have Died of Laughter," "After Midnight," "Dancing in Kent," "Nelson Relaxes." "Prelude," the first of these, is written in the third person but follows Frank Austen's (Jane Austen's youngest brother but one) gaze upon the world around him. The actual biographical facts conveyed in this chapter are the following:

1. Frank Austen was Jane Austen's 20 months older brother.
2. He went to be trained as a midshipman at the Royal Academy of the Navy in Portsmouth.
3. He was ten years old at the time.
4. He left a detailed account of his years there.
5. He was allowed to go home for the holidays.
6. He travelled by coach most of the way, then briefly walked the rest.

Instead of stating these facts and quoting from Frank's account, Honan starts a third-person narrative directly informed by Frank's writings: "Let us begin at Portsmouth and follow Frank on a ride home" (1): a statement promising participation and visual detail, and drawing the reader into a cinematographic narrative. The "camera" first looks at a group of young trainees rowing out to an anchored ship, then singles Frank out. Colours abound: "the black, gold, orange, yellow and silver beakheads of the warships" (1), "black greasy ropes," "bright red bulkheads," "rose-coloured building" (2). Next to these visually stimulating images are put striking and gory details: The bulkheads are painted red because "red paint conceals blood" or a wounded boy "bite[s] into a leather gag as his leg [is] cut off" (2). These are very conscious choices on Honan's part. This harsher side of life does not appear in Austen's novels, which led many to believe that she was oblivious to it. On the contrary, Honan and other contemporary biographers of Austen want to show how war, revolution, social imbalance and injustice were quite within her domain. She was not the secluded, uninformed genius that people love to depict her as. Therefore, it is essential in Honan's biography that people surrounding Austen are shown as participating in different walks of life, communicating their knowledge either directly to her or to other members of the same household.

Honan wants the reader to participate in the creation of Austen's world through the use of association. This method is exemplified in the "Prelude"; in this sense the "Prelude" is a presentation of Honan's aims and provides a guideline as to how the reader should utilize the information in the biography. For instance, Frank "keeps a very neat 'Plan' of his training notes" (2). This should be associated with his sister's habit of neatness. The sailors on board ship drink a "fiery white wine called 'mistella,'" more popularly known as 'Miss Taylor' among the soldiers (3). This should later reverberate in our minds as the Miss Taylor of *Emma*. On his way home, Frank passes through from Wickham and there "Frank was not far from an arrogant James

D'Arcy whose name became a scandal" (5); of course the place and person names should echo in our minds. These names, places, events, mostly excavated through reading of peripheral material, may or may not have anything to do with Austen's later choices in her novels. However, Honan does something which I find to be unique among biography writers: He seems to want to create a subconscious area of associations, connotations, and reverberations similar to Austen's own. And this difficult yet quite rewarding endeavour works for this particular biography.

Little Frank Austen comes home. And as the opening sentence promises, we do follow him with our eyes and other senses as far as the text allows. Besides the social setting, the depiction of the physical look and feel of late eighteenth-century Hampshire is also important for Honan as a part of his recreation of Austen's milieu. "Bronze and white flecked" fields (7) elm and beech trees, the swallows, swifts and martins all have their place in this picture. "The sounds of horses' hooves clattering by on the flint" (7) brings us back to the coach Frank travels in.

> Frank left his coach at the inn where his sisters often collected the post, and then passed the white cottages. The lane here was overhung with greenery and so narrow that a coachman might complain of having varnish scratched off. In the Navy Frank tried to control his feelings, though his sister Jane never found him dull-hearted: now he might sense those feelings welling up uncontrollably. He would see his father's steepleless church, and beyond a curtain of elms the Digweeds' rented Tudor manor. Then he would come to downhill pasture and he might be running so hard he could barely see. An observer might find him rather absurd, as a small boy in an elaborate uniform running down a flinty land with fists in the air. But Frank had a sense of purpose: he was coming

home. He could talk with his father before returning to the red gundecks of King George's Navy, and with the affectionate greeting of a brother he might press his sisters to his heart.

(7)

Honan does several things in this paragraph. He brings the environs of the Austen house alive with sensory detail. He then adds to those the details that spring up from his informed imagination like the coachman complaining about having the varnish scratched off or the small running boy "with his fists in the air." He sprinkles this imaginative account with factual detail: The inn where Jane and Cassandra often collected their mail, bringing to mind their well-known correspondence, the steepleless church of Reverend George Austen, Jane's father, or the name of their neighbours the Digweeds. We see the countryside on a spring day through Frank's eyes or what Honan researched and imagined Frank to have seen, together with details of Frank's own account. All this merges to recreate an atmosphere. This is a method used often in the dramatized documentaries of our day. Honan works like a director who is in control of the information he wants to present and knows exactly the sense he wants to convey. He creates the scene in his imagination blending fact and fiction, even referring to an "observer" who watches the scene. The "observer" is both himself, the biographer, and us, the readers—allowed to "be there" as Frank Austen runs home. Honan puts the social, political, cultural, familial and physical together as if he were putting together the pieces of a jigsaw, which would incidentally be quite an appropriate description of his narrative strategy.

Andrew Motion, the second biographer in this last category, states his dissatisfaction with the present sentimental, "Romantic" image of Keats created both by his contemporaries and his subsequent biographers. He claims that his biography will unearth Keats' energetic, politicized, "robust" character and put the poet in the right perspective. This new look at Keats interests the reader as long as it informs him/her on Keats' poetry at a deeper level than before, because *Keats* is primarily the biography of a poet written by a poet. The dialogue between Keats' poetry and the life narrative is the driving force of this work. Although discussion of poetry can very easily fall into the trap of sentimentality, Motion avoids this not only in his discussion of the poems but also at every other point in the text. The narrative voice is knowledgeable and objective, and affords illuminating insights into the poetry of Keats. The use of the narrator's voice and the subject's voice is well balanced.

This last biography forms an interesting contrast with the other five and throws light on what might constitute a good biography. Motion's work gathers all the "ideal" qualities of biography as stated above. However, it does not have any "quirkiness" or idiosyncrasy which makes it memorable. Dr. Johnson's poorly disguised partiality; Boswell's delightful and sometimes infuriating ego; Strachey's irritated prejudice and ready-to-burst anger; Holroyd's freezing gaze and silent patience; Honan's insatiable need to integrate, integrate, integrate are what make their biographies some of the most remarkable examples of the genre. Motion's biography has everything but "the Motion touch," so his Keats does not come alive. After all, a dazzling illusion calls for a masterful magician.

Works Cited

Alpers, Antony. "Biography—The Scarlet Experiment." *The Literary Biography: Problems and Solutions*. Ed. Dale Salwak. London: Macmillan, 1996.

Backscheider, Paula R. *Reflections on Biography*. New York: Oxford University Press, 1999.

Boswell, James. *Life of Johnson*. Oxford: Oxford University Press, 1980.

Holmes, Richard. *Dr. Johnson and Mr. Savage*. New York: Vintage, 1994.

Holroyd, Michael. *Lytton Strachey: The New Biography*. New York: Farrar, Straus and Giroux, 1995.
Honan, Park. *Jane Austen, Her Life*. New York: St. Martin's, 1989.
___. *Shakepeare: A Life*. Oxford: Oxford University Press, 1998.
Johnson, Samuel. *Samuel Johnson: Rasselas, Poems and Selected Prose*. Ed. Bertrand H. Bronson. New York: Holt, Reinhart and Winston, 1971.
___. *The Idler and The Adventurer*. Ed. W. J. Bates, J. M. Bullitt, and L. F. Powell. *The Yale Edition of the Works of Samuel Johnson*. Vol. 2. New Haven and London: Yale University Press, 1963.
Motion, Andrew. *Keats*. Chicago: University of Chicago Press, 1999.
Nadel, Ira Bruce. *Fiction, Fact and Form*. New York: St. Martin's, 1984.
Nicolson, Harold George. *The Development of English Biography*. New York: Harcourt, Brace, 1928.
Shelston, Alan. *Biography*. London: Methuen, 1977.
Strachey, Lytton. *Eminent Victorians*. London: Penguin, 1986.
___.*Portraits in Miniature and Other Essays*. New York: Harcourt, Brace & World, 1931.
___. *Spectatorial Essays*. "A New History of Rome." New York: Harcourt, Brace, 1965.

A Culture of Everyday Life: Exploring Blogging as Cyber-Autobiography

Leman Giresunlu
Dokuz Eylül University

Abstract: Blogging, is a current popular medium of performative life writing on the cyberspace with inherent autobiographic qualities. In this respect blogging is a means of meaning making and transformation in a global setting. In popular media blogging strives for transparence in interpersonal relationships; it is an unrelenting media for sharing, collaboration, information exchange, and entertainment. In this context, conventional tools of everyday life such as the diary, memoir, and autobiographical narratives appear to have become multidimensional, and therefore inviting towards an accelerated evolution in the conceptualization of the self, other, and the communities built accordingly on the cyberspace. Barış Erkol's blog page on design and advertising exemplifies multidimensional traces left in the cyberspace as another venue for material culture studies. Thus L. Krasniewicz and M. Blitz, A. Kroker and M. A. Weinstein, N. Katherine Hayles, Brenda Laurel, George Landow, Gordon Graham, and Avital Ronell set the ground to conceptualize traces left by blogging. The mythical recognition of technology as both a "cure" and a "disease" along its cultural implications marks the boundaries of blogging as an ever-developing communications media.

This project aims to catch up with a most recent trend in cybercultures: blogging. Situating the popular concept of blogging as a medium of life writing and as a potential cyber-autobiography genre in a multi-layered hypertext format on the information superhighway allows focusing on its implications as a constantly transforming technological medium also enabling self-transformation and meaning making in a global setting. In this regard especially mythical codifications accompanying new technology help situate blogging in a philosophical context. Therefore the classical debate between the Luddites and technophiles opens venue to discuss the meaning of blogging along existent cyberculture criticism. Despite its promised healing aspect, technology is also codified with disease and eventually as a check to the risks of radical individualism.

Furthermore, blogging functions as an alternative communications and news media to the established press. In spite of arguments which express a fear of the "virtual class" appropriating the democratic potential of the internet (Kroker and Weinstein 147), blog pages make use of templates of the information superhighway. With the intermediary of blog pages, various companies and organizations disseminate information to their global clientele. Also "the "multiplicity of hypertext, which appears in multiple links to individual blocks of text, calls for an active reader" (Landow 102). This non-linear hypertext mindset, opens venue for the generation of new images and meaning in constant negotiation and exchange with the authors and the readers. The constant negotiation between authors and readers by means of blogging on a transient and hybrid setting allows for new types of selves to evolve.

In everyday human interactions the information superhighway offers its users anonymity as well as visibility. In this respect it is a space of freedom as well as commitment. For some it is an opportunity to explore one's self without social constraints, while to others it is a way of maintaining existing as well as building new communities. Barış Erkol's blog page on design and advertising displays design projects by himself as well as others (işitsel görsel dokunsal sanatsal dijital inovatif provokatif blog [audio-visual tactile artistic digital innovative provocative blog]). Since last accessed on April 14, 2006 the main logo of the site has changed from a syringe to a milk bottle. The blogger Barış Erkol states that he prefers the word 'sign' (*tabela* in Turkish) to 'logo' (personal e-mail correspondence, 6 Nov. 2006). These constant renovations of blog pages also show the ever-changing nature of meaning on these sites. To the visitor a page may at one time convey "cure" and "disease" simultaneously with the *syringe* used as a sign. However next, it may very well display a milk bottle for a freshness effect, whiteness and purity, and as a balanced emphasis on its multicolor content (same e-mail correspondence). This is an example of performative self-expression on a blog page: constantly shifting its form while staying loyal to its own content. It is just a pure display of utter playfulness enabled by blog page technology. The same syringe is now located on the *Buzdolap* blogspot, a project which is linked from Erkol's blog page and deals mainly with refrigerator door art: a typical material culture venue. This page is also an invitation to *Blog Kardeşliği* (fellowship of the blog). The archive of the site (a feature available in most blog pages) provides various displays of refrigerator door art. Similarly, the "fikir" (idea) link connected to Erkol's main blog page is used to host a presentation on blogging. This presentation is currently removed from the site. However, it is still available at its previous URL. Such shifts in the specific location of information present some difficulty for citation. However, it is possible to track any previously available site since there are archives made available on the blog page by the blogger. Other web engines too help track sites which were earlier available on their designated location. Technocrati.inc is one such search engine.

Even such an ever-changing media has to be defined. The *Webopedia* definition of 'blog' is as follows ("Blog"):

> **n.)** Short for *Web log*, a blog is a Web page that serves as a publicly accessible personal journal for an individual. Typically updated daily, blogs often reflect the personality of the author.
>
> **(v.)** To author a Web log.
>
> Other forms: Blogger (a person who blogs).

According to *Ask Yahoo* the term 'weblog' was coined in December 1997 by Jorn Barger in his *Robot Wisdom Weblog* ("What Are Blogs"). *Ask Yahoo* also offers the information that "[o]nline diaries have become absurdly popular over the past few years—witness the length of our <u>Online Journals and Diaries</u> category. From Serbian filmmakers to Singaporean teenagers to London accountants, thousands of people are baring their souls on the Internet on a daily basis" ("Are there Web Sites").

In a *Wikipedia* definition, blogs are indicated to show variety: they range from political, personal, cultural, topical, business, science, moblog (mobile blog), collaborative, eclectic, educational, directory, forum, to spam blogs. Although *Wikipedia* is itself a constantly renewed source of information and therefore problematic for academic use, here is an earlier entry from *Wikipedia* defining 'Online Diary' at a personal level as follows:

> Online Diaries, or Personal Blogs, are the most common implementation of the blog webpage format. The weblog format of an online diary makes it possible for users without much experience to create, format, and post entries with ease. People write their day-to-day experiences, complaints, poems, prose, illicit thoughts and more, often allowing others to contribute, fulfilling to a certain extent Tim Berners-Lee's original view of the World Wide Web as a collaborative medium. In 2001, mainstream awareness of online diaries began to increase dramatically.
>
> Online diaries are integrated into the daily lives of many teenagers and college students, with communications between friends playing out over their blogs. Even fights may be posted in the diaries, with not-so-veiled insults of each other easily readable by all their friends, enemies, and complete strangers.
>
> Personal opinions on experiences and hobbies are very common in the blog world. Blogs have given the opportunity for people to express their views to a mass audience. What may have been created to be used among a few friends may be viewed by the internet-using public. ("Online Diary")

In popular media blogging appears to strive for transparence in interpersonal relationships; to be a media for sharing, collaboration, information exchange, and entertainment. In this regard the conventional tools of everyday life such as the diary, memoir, and autobiographical narratives appear to have become multidimensional, and therefore inviting an accelerated evolution in the conceptualization of the self, the other and the communities we all live in.

The information superhighway is an interactive media of the everyday. It is an immediate opening to presence as well as absence simultaneously. The information superhighway in its evolved format known as hypermedia and hypertext is ready for access once necessary codes are typed in, identifications submitted and all rituals of inclusion accomplished. The aftermath is a mere play enacted in a virtual world simulating the real one and even unlike it with the impetus to blend in a variety of differences via the innovative urge of the imagination. According to Arthur Kroker and Michael A. Weinstein access to the "information highway" is an exchange of information for information to become information (149).

Contrary to Kroker and Weinstein, N. Katherine Hayles, another theoretician of the cyberspace, professes the seductive aspects of the information highway. On the other hand, Brenda Laurel envisions the metaphor of theater and performance as a move along the imagination "to create imaginary worlds that have a special relationship to reality—worlds in which we can extend, amplify, and enrich our own capacities to think, feel and act" (113). Alan Kay argues that the computer, more than a tool, can be defined as a "metamedium" since it

> can dynamically simulate the details of any other medium, including media that cannot exist physically. It is not a tool, although it can act like many tools [. . .] it has degrees of freedom for representation and expression never before encountered and as yet barely investigated. (113)

As a "metamedium" the development of the "hypermedia or hypertext," terms used interchangeably by George Landow, eventually gave way to "multilinear," "multisequential" web sites with the practical use of providing information (100). However, our main interest in this study is hypermedia formations defined as blogs which function rather on a performative level. Blogs beyond ideological constraints are geared mostly towards the fulfillment of a human striving to generate new meanings through a "multilinear," "multisequential" fountain fluxing into imagination and creativity. Although Kroker and Weinstein's unease in their definition of the "expert program [. . .] as the new center for pastoral power [. . .] still enacted under capitalism," requiring payments in return for the information provided, proves to be valid, it also invites the opposite where the free sharing and egalitarian spirit of the net are still alive and enable new ideas and compositions to flourish (149). This humane attitude of volunteerism, while allowing each and everyone to make use of intellectual property as such, also welcomes the gentlemen's agreement concerning proper referencing whenever needed. In such an environment where strict as well as yet emerging rules apply, the "expert program as the new center for pastoral power" (Kroker and Weinstein, 149) is just one of many frames and providers.

To Kroker and Weinstein "[t]he great agent of possibility becomes the master tool of normalization now a micro-normalization with high specificity [. . .] perhaps uniqueness! [. . .] The information highway is the way by which bodies are drawn into cyberspace through the seduction of empowerment" (149). In regard of the interaction experienced in and out of the blogs and as an example expanding further on the aspect of normalization that Kroker and Weinstein address, *New York Times* columnist Katie Hafner writes the following:

> Blogging is a pastime for many, even a livelihood for a few. For some, it becomes an obsession. Such bloggers often feel compelled to write several times daily and feel anxious if

they don't keep up. As they spend more time hunkered over their computers, they neglect family, friends and jobs. They blog at home, at work and on the road. They blog openly or sometimes [. . .] quietly so as not to call attention to their habit. [. . .]

The number of bloggers has grown quickly, thanks to sites like blogger.com, which makes it easy to set up a blog. Technorati, a blog-tracking service, has counted some 2.5 million blogs.

Of course, most of those millions are abandoned or, at best, maintained infrequently. For many bloggers, the novelty soon wears off and their persistence fades. [. . .]

Sometimes, too, the realization that no one is reading sets in. A few blogs have thousands of readers, but never have so many people written so much to be read by so few. [. . .] Indeed, if a blog is likened to a conversation between a writer and readers, [some] bloggers [. . .] are having conversations largely with themselves.

According to Katie Hafner, for some of the bloggers blogging is akin to an addiction, where one gets instant gratification and cherishes the hope that one has accomplished something. The blog pages invite commentaries from the readers on the blog page. Some positive effects of blogging that emerge from Hafner's text are feeling productive, a sense of community, connectivity, the illusion of immortality.

Katie Hafner also makes a political statement:

> Blogging for a cause can take on a special urgency. Richard Khoe, a political consultant in Washington who in his spare time helps run a pro-John Kerry group called Run Against Bush, posts constantly to the blog embedded in the group's Web site (www.runagainstbush.org). He blogs late into the night, although he knows that the site still attracts relatively few visitors.

Apparently, while laying out the positive aspects of blogging as a new fad, Hafner's article also seems to reiterate a "neo-luddite" tendency which Gordon Graham (1999) in the context of the internet identifies as a current form of vilification of new technology. Katie Hafner, by speaking of blogging as addiction, obsession, compulsion, pathology, anti-social behavior pattern, contributes to the Luddite argument of blogging as disease.

Hafner's selection of positive and negative comments on blogging suggests that the addictive aspect of blogging is healed once regular jobs come to the rescue. It is as if blogging amounts to a subversion of norms. Such behavior has to be evaded, since it does not provide any prospect for economic gain. In addition, the article, published in a newspaper with a Democrat orientation, critically suggests that even in blog format an anti-Bush campaign does not attract much attention. Thus the *New York Times* columnist scores against three parties at the same time: Bush, Kerry and the blog.

The use of the disease metaphor for the ethical questioning of new technology, especially computer technology, is also a feature of an article by Avital Ronell titled "A Disappearance of Community." To Ronell "[v]irtual reality, artificial reality, dataspace, or cyberspace are inscriptions of a desire whose principal symptom can be seen as the absence of community" (287). At this point the excesses of radical individualism seem to interfere with a more moderate lifestyle on a metaphorical level as disease and physical disturbances. Ronell, while enthusiastically employing, but also negatively contributing to the mythology built around Virtual Reality (VR), mentions the uses of VR during the Gulf War and the meaning load it has accumulated. According to Ronell, the generation of a rather virtual war was to the detriment of healing prospects to be offered to AIDS patients in the form of research, since the "costs of war" had "drained the resources for AIDS research" (289). The "aggressive" and especially the "clean" and "uncontaminated" aspect of the technology employed during the Gulf War and the mentality of the war itself were due to its "nanominimalist" contact with the "negated other." This position, while speaking for the unfortunate in both ends of the war—the HIV-positive body of the American, left devoid of prospects of healing, and the othered body of the enemy—also seems to keep a tight rein of the technophiles inviting a middle way, which Gordon Graham defines thus:

> Steering a reasoned middle course between Luddism and technophilia requires the following: that we are not swayed by technological innovation for no better reason than that it is innovatory, and that at the same time we remain open to its actual character and possible advantages. In short, we must be alive both to the possibility that computerized information technology may be a truly new way of doing things with real increases in value for those individuals and societies who adopt it, and to the possibility that its novelty and its advantages have been exaggerated. (15)

Before the publication of the Ronell article in 1996 a rather celebratory text by N. Katherine Hayles of 1993 defining computer technologies had addressed the following:

> To the extent they are reinforced, the patterns are more difficult to break; to the extent they are exposed, they become subject to analysis and therefore to change. Moreover, the technologies themselves can be—already are—agents of change. This is the double edge of virtual reality's revolutionary potential: to expose the presuppositions underlying the social formations of late capitalism and to open new fields of play where the dynamics have not yet rigidified and new kinds of moves are possible. Understanding these moves and their significances is crucial to realizing the technology's constructive potential. (307)

Although computer-related technology is fast progressing, it turns out that the positions taken towards it do not change much: the debate between technophiles and Neo-Luddites is always present, as Katie Hafner's article indicates. The following samples show Kroker and Weinstein's stance and style:

> Marx understood this first: every technology releases opposing possibilities towards emancipation and domination. Like its early bourgeois predecessors at the birth of capitalism, the virtual class christens the birth of technotopia by supressing the potentially emancipatory relations of production released by the Internet in favor of the traditionally predatory force of production signified by the digital superhighway. Data is the anti-virus of meaning—telematic information refuses to be slowed down by the drag-weight of content. And the virtual class seeks to exterminate the social possibilities of the Internet. These are the first lessons of the theory of the virtual class. (147)

> Refuse, then, nostalgia for the surpassed past of remaindered flesh, and hyper-text your way to the (World Wide) Webbed body: the body that actually dances on its own data organs, sees with multi-media graphical interface screens, makes new best tele-friends on the MOO, writes electronic poetry on the disappearing edges of video, sound, and text integrators, and insists on going beyond the tedious world of binary divisions to the new cyber-mathematics of FITS. The hyper-texted body, then is the precursor of a new world of multi-media politics, fractualized economics, incept personalities, and (cybernetically) interfaced relationships. After all, why should the virtual class monopolize digital reality? It only wants to suppress the creative possibilities of virtualization, privileging instead the tendencies of technotopia towards new and more vicious forms of cyber-authoritarianism. The vir-

tual class only wants to subordinate digital reality to the will of capitalism. The hyper-texted body responds to the challenge of virtualization by making itself a monstrous double: pure virtuality/pure flesh. Consequently, our telematic future: the wireless body on the Net as a sequenced chip microprogrammed by the virtual class for purposes of (its) maximal profitability, or the wireless body as the leading edge of critical subjectivity in the twenty-first century. [. . .] Always already the past to the future of the hyper-texted body, the virtual class is the particular interest that must be overcome by the hyper-texted body of data trash if the Net is to be gatewayed by soft ethics.

Soft ethics? Nietzsche's got a modem, and he is already rewriting the last pages of *The Will to Power* as *The Will to Virtuality*. As the patron saint of the hyper-texted body, Nietzsche is data trash to the smooth, unbroken surface of the virtual class. (153)

Until the very end, Kroker and Weinstein, while appearing to be open to creativity and innovation, whenever they expose evidence of a paranoid delusion about the supposedly exploitative intentions of the virtual class, they inevitably reveal their own pathological and viral condition. Therefore, when looked at from the perspective of the virtual class, Kroker and Weinstein also generate and appear to identify themselves as an anti-virus program. That is, their article as well generates metaphors of disease along the innovative stances they profess. Therefore they simultaneously draw their own free-riding radical individualism towards a more moderate middle ground. The myth of the land carries onto moderation and legitimization by seemingly professing the destructiveness of all innovation.

During its evolution and change this positioning of technology on a global setting invites a redefinition of the self along the intermediary of the diverse uses of blogs. How far can blogs define themselves as autobiography within the context of cyberspace? Or would they share the mythical codification as both cure and disease? This will constitute the following inquiry.

Blogs as Cyber-Autobiography in Hypertext Format

Autobiography under a most generic definition needs a definite author writing about him- or herself. The usual formats for autobiographical writing, diaries, memoirs and other versions of this genre are discussed in depth in Sidonie Smith and Julia Watson's *Reading Autobiography: A Guide for Interpreting Life Narratives* (see especially appendix A [183-207]). The blog, however, is a diary generated on the web and of the web. It is an online, cyber-recording in hypermedia format of words, animations, voice and music recordings compiled by the individual author of the web page. Because of its sequential and non-linear aspect, it is also up to the reader of the blog to form a meaningful whole of it.

Normally a diary or a memoir would have a limited audience or none at all for long years since it is considered to be a rather private contemplation of the individual. Devoted believers use diaries as a log of their good deeds with a view to appreciation and recognition sought ultimately from God. The founder of Mount Holyoke College, Mary Lyon, saw to her students' religious disciplining through biblical reading and self-examination, especially by writing resolutions over keeping diaries and journals (Cole 103-104).

In most of its versions memoir and diary writing also has a *healing effect* since it is a form of *confession* recorded for reconsideration and reevaluation on future visits. The writing of diaries and memoirs is also a *displacement* of *excess information* from the interiors of the human body onto another plane, again for reconsideration at different times and places. These future visits to the past in the form of diaries or logs may or may not be a measure to acquire new perspectives of analysis over time. The *self's temporary distancing away* from the individual content at issue also provides an opportunity to reevaluate and analyze recorded moments of past feelings and observations with varying levels of complexity. In this respect diary and memoir may be considered as a do-it-yourself version of confessing and thus a search for healing, recognition and appreciation of the individual by him- or herself.

What distinguishes the blog from conventional confession is that it does not seek postponed recognition and appreciation to be gained from God at an indefinite time, or from the gradually accumulated experiences of the do-it-yourself author of the diary or memoir over an extended period. The blog seeks a similar level of recognition from unidentified, or semi-identified strangers in a relatively shorter span of time. Therefore it is not so important who the other is who will provide relief through recognition or distress through rejection.

In this regard blogs, in comparison to private diaries, involve a high level of deliberate self-exposure to the others out there. The blog page can almost be compared to a tattooed or pierced body participating in a convention where the involved parties consist of like-minded persons. In other words, the blog world is a community of performing and shape-shifting alikes looking for different and more interesting ways of accomplishing the act of blogging. Blogging in this respect is just another artifact like tattoo or piercing to be added to the endless list of material culture analysts. Louise Krasniewicz and Michael Blitz, in their study titled "Morphing Identities," where they make use of internet e-mail communication between researchers as a means of constructing meaning around the media image of Arnold Schwarzenegger, claim that writing on the net is somewhat equivalent to tattooing:

> Talking is like skywriting. The sounds and phrases vaporize almost before they are fully comprehended. But writing across the Net is like a tattoo; the image of the message remains—somewhere. The typists write themselves into the ar-

chive, onto the skin of the network potentially for all to see. Their texts are unremovable except by a surgical erasure. Even so, trace versions remain embedded within the software, the mainframe, or another hard drive. And of course, the traces and the by-products of those remain forever, now, in me. (106)

However, blogging is also different from e-mail messaging, if complemented by the techniques of e-mail messaging. E-mail messaging is limited to the conversation of a limited selection of parties: E-mailing occurs between two people or with the use of distribution lists may expand its area of influence. It is also possible for correspondents to meet and communicate through blogs and initiate e-mail messaging. This happened during the preparation of this paper when I inquired about the source and its citation of the slide show on blogging titled "Blogg Blogger Kültürü ve Entegre Uygulamalar" (Blogg Blogger's Culture and Integrated Applications) on Barış Erkol's web site ("işitsel görsel"). Erkol in his response to my e-mail query expressed his pleasure about being asked for permission to use the slide show (14 Apr. 2006). The free use of intellectual property with proper citation on the blog page is permitted by the author's note "some rights reserved." This Turkish blog page with links to quite a lot of other sites globally offers new venues in the arts, advertising and the design world. The above-mentioned blog page *Blog kardeşliği* (fellowship of the blog), another Turkish blog page, defines itself by the following motto: "Blogger en asil duygunun insanıdır" (The blogger is a human being of the noblest feeling"). The fellowship of the blog offers to bring together different blog pages.

Designing blog pages as a marketing strategy has become a must for organizations addressing those who choose to live by the blog. Contrary to what many think, the blog world is living their everyday lives with a high level of security and privacy. It is known that anything written on the cyberspace is recorded or leaves traces either on the hardware or on the web. For this reason some people transform the ASCII codes (Soulie; see also <http://triple-double-u.com>) and traces left on the cyberspace, after stripping them of their content, into patterns that are later woven into carpets for sale over the internet (see the link on Barış Erkol's işitsel görsel blog site). This is the most playful and performative manifestation of what can be done with traces. The cyberspace is in this sense a confident world which is at peace with the traces it leaves and with itself; yet it is also always aware of the viral potential lurking as a prevailing myth of the land.

Works Cited

"Are there web sites for writing and storing diaries online?" *Ask Yahoo*. 6. Oct. 2006 <http://ask.yahoo.com/>.
"Blog." *Webopedia*. 6 Nov. 2006 <http://www.webopedia.com/TERM/b/blog.html>.
"Blog." *Wikipedia*. Apr. 2006 <http://en.wikipedia.org/wiki/Blog#How_blogs_differ_from_traditional_sites>.
Blog Kardeşliği. 1 Apr. 2006 <http://www.blogkardesligi.com/>.
Cole, C. Arthur. *A Hundred Years of Mount Holyoke College: The Evolution of an Educational Ideal*. New Haven: Yale University Press, 1940.
Erkol, Barış. Blogg Blogger Kültürü ve Entegre Uygulamalar. 14 Apr. 2006 <http://www.labtr.com/blogger_kulturu.pps>.
___. *Buzdolap*. Fotoğraf paylaşım ortamı. 6 Nov. 2006. <http://buzdolap.blogspot.com/2005_11_06_buzdolap_archive.html>.
___. işitsel görsel dokunsal sanatsal dijital inovatif provokatif blog. 6 Nov. 2006 <http://www.isbn9760806.com>.
Graham, Gordon. "Neo-Luddites versus Technophiles." *The Internet: A Philosophical Inquiry*. New York: Routledge, 1999.
Hafner, Katie. "For Some, the Blogging Never Stops." *New York Times on the Web* 27 May 2004. 1 Apr. 2006 <http://www.nytimes.com>.

Hayles, N. Katherine. "The Seductions of Cyberspace." *Rethinking Technologies.* 1993. Rpt. in Trend, ed., 305-321.
Kay, Alan. "Computer Software." *Scientific American* 251.3 (Sept. 1984): 52-59.
Krasniewicz, Louise, and Michael Blitz. "Morphing Identities: Arnold Schwarzenegger—Write US." *Getting A Life: Everyday Uses of Autobiography.* Ed. Sidonie Smith and Julia Watson. Minneapolis: University of Minnesota Press. 1996.
Kroker, Arthur, and Michael Weinstein. "The Theory of the Virtual Class." *Data Trash: The Theory of the Virtual Class.* 1994. 4-26. Rpt. in Trend, ed., 144-153.
Landow, George. "Hypertext and Critical Theory." Excerpt from *Hypertext: The Convergence of Contemporary Critical Theory and Technology.* 1991. 2-12. Rpt. in Trend, ed., 98-108.
Laurel, Brenda. "Computers as Theatre." Rpt. in Trend, ed., 109-114. Rpt. of "The Nature of the Beast." *Computers as Theater.* Reading, MA: Addison-Wesley, 1991.
"Online Diary." *Wikipedia.* 6 Nov. 2006 <http://en.wikipedia.org/wiki/Online_diary>.
Ronell, Avital. "A Disappearance of Community." *Immersed in Technology: Art and Virtual Environments.* 1996. 119-127. Rpt. in Trend, ed., 287-293.
Smith, Sidonie, and Julia Watson. *Reading Autobiography: A Guide for Interpreting Life Narratives.* Minneapolis: University of Minnesota Press, 2001.
Soulie, Juan. "Ascii Codes." *C++ Resources Network,* 2. 12. Nov. 2005 <http://www.cplusplus.com/doc/papers/ascii.html>.
Trend, David, ed. *Reading Digital Culture.* Malden, Mass.: Blackwell, 2001.
triple-double-u.com / ascii carpet/?s mailia. 4 Nov. 2006 <http://triple-double-u.com>.
"What are Blogs, and how did they become so popular?" *Ask Yahoo.* 15 Nov. 2002. 4 Oct. 2006 <http://ask.yahoo.com>.

A Historical Approach to Turkish Women's Autobiographies

Nazan Aksoy
Istanbul Bilgi University

Abstract: This paper is an attempt to survey the historical tradition of female autobiographical writing with particular emphasis on how the tradition has been shaped by certain key assumptions vis-à-vis Turkish modernization and westernization. As the writers of autobiographies were leading intellectuals of Turkey (Halide Edip, Sabiha Sertel, Afet İnan, Samiha Ayverdi), they ascribed to themselves also a pioneering role in the modernization process which is reflected in their autobiographical writing. However, in the 1980s Turkish political and cultural climate underwent a series of transformations, partly due to the introduction of new ideas. Among these new ideas feminism was particularly influential. Hence, literature as well as autobiography moved towards the representation and narration of more personal experience.

Autobiography's being a recent phenomenon in Turkish literature can be largely accounted for by the insufficient development of the written culture in our country. To put it another way, memories were shared orally both in family circles and among acquaintances and have been retained in the memory of audiences without being recorded in writing. The second reason for the late emergence of the genre is that people who wished to write their autobiographies were discouraged by pressure from the state and the society, fearing that what they wrote might violate the principle of privacy. The belated emergence of individualism in Turkey seems to have contributed most to the relegation of the autobiographical genre to the background for autobiography, by definition, is an account of individual lives—a subgenre of life-writing. Women's autobiographies written during the first half of the twentieth century were also influenced by the above-mentioned conditions.

In the nineteenth century the decline of the traditional structure of the Ottoman society declined and the same century also marks the beginning of modernization. The Ottoman élite who looked to modernization for their rescue thought that women's liberation was at the core of this project. The ideas on and reforms concerning women's issues were the most important signs of the severing of the ties with the past. In the process of modernization woman was the crucial symbol both domestically and abroad. In the construction of the nation state women needed to be integrated in the political and economic structure since they gained a visibility both through the support of the war of independence and their active role in economic production. Nevertheless, the acceptance of women into the public sphere did not preclude women's emancipation. Within the process of constructing a nation state women's rights gained considerable momentum by the aid of the bureaucratic élite and the state itself, but these rights were part of the politics alongside individual rights and civil rights. These changes in the public sphere could not prevent the continuation of the patriarchal system in the private life. A point worth mentioning here is women's own acceptance and internalization of modernization.

The first awakening in the woman's world revealed itself in the newly opened schools and newly published journals between the mid-nineteenth century and the beginning of the twentieth century. This new vision soon led to significant progress in literature. After the proclamation of the Second Constitution in 1908 more women started to write and several journals appeared. During this period two main approaches became apparent: All these journals were products of the modernization process, therefore they all agreed on the view that women should change, although the envisioned change was conceived in different ways. Some of the journals advocated from the very onset that women should be educated and should take part in public life while others wanted women to modernize themselves as mothers and wives. In both types of journals the common denominator was nationalism. Many women who wrote for these magazines were also members of nationalistic political organizations. This is especially important in understanding the women who wrote their autobiographies. As seen by these women themselves woman's issues were closely interwoven with the nationalistic discourse.

The mentality of the women who were brought up in those years was shaped by the nationalist discourse of the time. Those of these women who later came to write their autobiographies participated in the modernization process and gained powerful positions in the public sphere. Yet the crucial question is how much of their private life which they infrequently mention in their autobiographies they were able to change.

These women were brought up in the earliest phases of Turkish modernization. While telling the story of their *Bildung* they voiced the painful experiences resulting from polygamy, they advocated the right of education for women and called for the eradication of gender discrimination—a demand which was in line with the ideas of progressive men of the period.

Halide Edib, Sabiha Sertel, Müfide Ferit Tek, Samiha Ayverdi, Halide Nusret, Cahit Uçuk and İsmet Kür are some of the autobiographers who were born before the foundation of the Republic. They all came from the Ottoman élite living either in Istanbul or Thessaloniki and they were all professional writers. Although they displayed different inclinations in terms of political and ideological positions, they were all products of the modernization and westernization process, and this characteristic they had in common is revealed in their autobiographies. Hence, in order to see how the modernization project was received by women it would be interesting to evaluate their life stories with regard to the years in which their books were published.

Within this framework it would be very appropriate to begin with Halide Edib, who was the pioneering figure of the women's movement, a social thinker and a celebrated novelist. She was of the opinion that women should play a leading part in the social progress of a nation. Her reformist ideas about women's life show the influences of the leaders of Turkish nationalism, especially the sociologist Ziya Gökalp. Like Gökalp, Halide Edib refrained from adopting Western feminist ideas and believed that the Arab version of Islam should be reformed. She came to the conclusion that the core ideas for the reform of women's issues were to be found in the customs and mores of old Turkish communities in central Asia where women enjoyed a particular social priority. She referred to a model motherhood, which she called the "enlightened" motherhood that was supposedly inherent both in the Turkish and Islamic tradition. This type of motherhood was not limited to giving birth to and bringing up children but prescribed a "national duty" of bringing up new generations. Thus she writes: "The liberation of Turkish women differs them sharply from Western feminism because their emancipation is based on their being socially useful individuals. In Turkey the women's movement has not been primarily a resistance to male hegemony" (*Conflict* 197). Halide Edib's ideas are not basically different from those of men who supported women's reform, yet it is undeniable that her autobiography displays a completely peculiar aspect of her identity.

Halide Edib's compiling her autobiography coincides with a very special phase of her life. The first part of the autobiography (*Memoirs of Halide Edib*) was published in 1926 and the second part (*The Turkish Ordeal*) in 1928. The second volume came out upon the publication of Atatürk's *Nutuk* (speech) in 1927, in which Halide Edib had been introduced almost as a traitor about which she could not remain silent. She then decided to retell the story of the War of Independence from her point of view placing her own life story into this narrative. Here it is worth pointing out that Halide Edib had to publish her memoirs in English which enabled her to reach a larger reading public. The memoirs came out in Turkish as late as the 1960s.

The first volume begins with her childhood as in Western autobiographies. After the death of her mother in her early childhood her father remarried, so Halide spent the greater part of her childhood in her grandmother's home. The home where she was brought up was marked by the oriental atmosphere of Ottoman urban culture and Sufi tradition. Yet her father, who wanted her daughter to be educated as a European, sent her to an American high school and Halide became one of the first Muslim girls who graduated from this school. Being quite different from the children around her, Halide started reading and dreaming at an early age. Immediately after her graduation from high school she married a professor, Salih Zeki Bey, a well-known mathematician. Although in her autobiography she describes her childhood and early years of her youth extensively, her private life after her marriage gradually disappears from the text. Her marriage and career as a writer begin simultaneously. She writes on social problems and women's issues and her husband encourages her to write by introducing her to Turkish intellectual circles. Salih Zeki Bey plays a constructive role in her life and widens her horizon. In the Turkish edition of her memoirs she writes as follows: "While I was writing for *Tanin* and other papers Salih Zeki used to receive letters of threat urging him to prevent me from writing, but he supported me with all his heart" (*Mor* 122). Surprisingly enough, Salih Zeki Bey deceives her and wants to take a second wife during the same days. Halide Edib divorces her husband with her two children after nine years in marriage. Her father and husband had a most positive role in encouraging her to reading, thinking and writing, yet it was the same men who maintained the institution of polygamy in their private lives and hurt her feelings very deeply. Her father by letting her spend her childhood with her grandparents made her feel lonely and her husband by taking a second wife wounded her female pride. After divorce her private life retreats to the background. But the great love she felt for her first husband becomes apparent in the second volume of her autobiography in English. After reading in the newspaper the news of Salih Zeki's death at the front in the in the middle of the war Halide Edip recollects her past with Salih Zeki: "How many times the man in the brown cap and the poor little girl vowed in earnest that they would die together and be buried in the same grave" (*Turkish Ordeal* 265). However, Halide did not want to share these intimate feelings with the Turkish reading public most probably because she wanted to remain a public figure in the common memory of the Turkish nation. Moreover, this unfulfilled love might have been perceived as a weakness in a politically powerful woman.

Halide Edip's autobiography can also be read as the story of a woman's transition from the private to the public sphere. She narrates this change in her life like this: "Nothing mattered to me from that moment to the time of the extraordinary march to Smyrna in 1922. I suddenly ceased to exist as an individual. I worked, wrote and lived as a unit of that magnificent national madness" (*Turkish Ordeal* 23). Indeed her two-volume autobiography ends on the day Izmir (Smyrna) was recaptured by the Turkish army.

Halide Edib's life story has been placed within the very framework of history. In the midst of political and military struggles a woman's world is also revealed in the book. However, as she acquires her historic identity her private life, her female identity gradually disappears. She leaves her children and leaves them in her elder sister Mahmure Hanım's care. Leaving her children in Istanbul she goes to Ankara to join the national struggle. The following sentences reveal her feelings at the time she leaves for Ankara: "Nor did I allow myself to face the fact that there was only one chance in a million that I would see or touch them [her children] again. But I wanted them to have an account of me. I wanted them to understand how circumstances and my too large and greedy heart had led me to be more than a mother" (*Turkish Ordeal* 191). In Ankara her life changes, as she admits "now [. . .], the Halide not of flesh and blood was going to turn her back on the physical Halide" (168).

Although throughout her autobiography Halide Edib states repeatedly that she repressed her feminine identity, nevertheless she is very proud to be the only woman to be present in this history-making process. Her description of a meeting in Istanbul at the beginning of her political career reveals her paradoxical presence:

Then I was asked to join the meeting of the National Block. To this day I cannot make out why. Anyhow, in the rather small and shabby room I saw the most stately looking council of thirty that has ever existed, and if I live a hundred years more I will never have a chance to see a more dignified body of men. All seemed above six feet, all were finely dressed and all had some past pages of Turkish history attached to their records in some way or other. [. . .] And I, the pygmy, in a black charshaf, earnestly tried to find a corner where I would not be seen—my presence seemed so incongruous and out of place. (*Turkish Ordeal* 37)

Halide Edib's autobiography reflects how Turkish modernization affected the life of a woman. This woman is on the one hand an authority with her pen in the male-dominated public world, and one who had to give up her private life on the other. As a woman she is not willing to become prominent, wanting to remain a rank-and-file member of the struggle, which is an attitude expected by men from women who are accepted to the public sphere. Yet she is quite aware of the fact that if she ever remained silent she would definitely be erased from history by a man, by Atatürk. She thus composes her autobiography and claims her contribution to history to be acknowledged.

As a matter of fact, Halide Edib under the impact of Ziya Gökalp's nationalist and solidarist ideology defended in her articles the idea of male-female equality as a point of departure yet reduces female presence only to motherhood and wifehood. Yet parodoxically enough, by renouncing her role as mother and wife, she has transgressed the horizon of male-dominated reforms of women's issues and constructed an identity far beyond male anticipation.

Another autobiography of historical significance was written by Sabiha Sertel who was born in 1895 in Thesselonika, 13 years after Halide Edib. Her autobiography was published a year after her death in 1969. Her story is also a story of struggle during the Republican era. Sertel also dedicated her life to political struggle. After completing her secondary education she married at an early age the journalist-writer Zekeriya Sertel. She found herself deeply involved in the political struggle in occupied Istanbul. After her husband's arrest she became the editor-in-chief of the opposition newspaper which was actually published by her husband. She was only 22 at the time. Sertel's autobiography differs from the autobiographies of other women in that she starts her story not with her childhood but with the time when she began working for her husband's newspaper. The following is the only childhood memory in her book: One evening her mother comes home late and her father immediately divorces her after which her mother is left alone with her kids. Sertel relates this childhood memory only to explain why she dedicated her life to writing on women's issues. The autobiography ends in 1950 when extreme nationalists set fire to her husband's printing press, Tan, and the couple has to leave Turkey. The writer does not talk about her 18 years in exile. Like Halide Edip and her second husband, Sabiha and Zekeriya Sertel choose to go into exile since they are afraid of being killed in Turkey. Sertel's main motivation in writing her autobiography is not to be forgotten, to make a place for herself in public memory. She is apparently a dedicated socialist who has written throughout her life for political purposes. This time she decides to write her own story and she considers this her last chance to reach out to the public. Possibly for this reason she does not share the memory of her struggle with anybody and she barely mentions her husband's name. However, her husband is not the only one who is left out of the book: her private life, her children are also omitted. She refers to them only a few times like many other women who work alongside men in the public sphere. Sertel seems to have left the domestic world to other women. Her husband's niece, Ayşe, takes care of her children: "I used to leave home at 8 in the morning and come back at 10 in the late evening. I did not see my children" (*Roman Gibi* 110).

The fact that she hardly talks about her private life may be attributed to her intention to show to what extent she sacrificed her private life for her political struggle. However, from a different perspective this shows how a woman who takes part in public life regards home life as a waste of time. At a time when she was forbidden to write for the newspaper she says: "In order not to waste my time at home I decided to write a book" (122).

Sertel's autobiography is entitled *Roman Gibi*, which literally means "Like a Novel." In this "novel" the protagonist's inner life is revealed to such a small extent that it is as if we are introduced to a one-dimensional political woman. However, her daughter Yıldız Sertel must have noticed this deficiency in her mother's self-portrait because she finds it necessary to interpolate the following remark in the biography of her mother: "Referring to the portrayal of my mother my father used to say, 'Sabiha could bring together three different identities: those of a good house-wife, a wonderful mother and a serious writer. She merged these identities harmoniously without allowing one to predominate the others. Her being a good journalist and writer did not harm her presence as a mother and housewife" (*Annem Sabiha* 192).

There is an episode mentioned in both Sabiha Sertel's autobiography and her daughter's biography of her. One day the daughter falls ill; while Sabiha Sertel is waiting for her recovery at the head of her bed she blames herself for not being able to give enough care to the child. At that moment the mother claims that the housemaid has stolen the silver spoons and says that she must be sent away. Sabiha Sertel, who for many years has defended women's rights, immediately dismisses the woman without even looking for evidence. The woman denies stealing anything and curses her (Yıldız Sertel, *Annem* 33). Sabiha Sertel gets mad and pushes the woman from the staircase on the fifth floor. The inclusion of this specific event by both mother and daughter may simply be attributed to feelings of guilt, it also shows how relationships between women were in reality complicated.

Though Sertel advocates women's rights with her pen, she does not know the actual significance of female solidarity or how to treat a woman from the working class when faced with a concrete situation.

To recapitulate, although her husband and daughter try to depict Sertel as a woman who succeeds in combining the three identities of mother, wife and professional woman, Sabiha Sertel presents herself in her book as a career woman concentrating on her public duties.

There are also female autobiographies written in the same period which shed light on different aspects of contemporary life. Halide Nusret Zorlutuna is the author of one of them. She was born in 1901 and published her autobiography in 1973. It focuses on the formation of her identity rather than on her public significance. She composed her book not to create a place for herself in public memory but to share her reminiscences as a female poet and teacher with her readers. Her autobiography entitled *Bir Devrin Romanı* (The Story of an Era) differs from the others in that it highlights those external forces which determine women's position in society and still continue to exist in the modernization era: the parents, husband and finally the state. The mother will draw the borders of her imagination, the husband will give her permission to work in the public sphere as long as her external appearance is decent enough, and the state will decide for her on her social behavior, telling her how to dress. In her youth, although old and established traditions still existed in society, in the world of literature a communication between men and women was possible through writing. At the time, the intimacies formed through writing were a way of resisting tradition. Traditions are such an integral part of the social make-up that Zorlutuna's mother bans her daughter from reading novels. She does not stop there. She even decides whom Zorlutuna cannot marry. This is the picture at home. In the outside world too, at the end of the 1920s, the behavior of men and women is monitored by higher authorities. "One day we were told that an order came from Ankara that the veil was forbidden, that on the independence day etc there were to be formal balls, and the government officials were to attend these balls with their wives and dance. Teachers, both male and female, were ordered to participate" (*Bir Devrin* 236). The author learns of the dress code reform on a working trip to Bulgaria. "While we were there, hat reform was issued at home. We did not forget to buy a hat" (265).

Zorlutuna later becomes a teacher and marries an army officer. An interesting conversation takes place between Halide Nusret Zorlutuna and her husband on their wedding day:

> "One of your virtues that I very much approve of is the fact that you do not wear make-up. I hate women who paint their faces, eyes and lips. Especially the lips. They seem to me like man-eating cannibals [. . .]." Actually, I was very envious of the women who wore lipstick. When I was a young girl I could not wear it because I was afraid that they would call me a husband-hunting flirt if I did. I thought, if I ever marry I will get a lipstick and paint my lips, but now this became an impossibility. (275)

The autobiography of this conservative writer is interesting in its description of the social pressure imposed upon women. Although Zorlutuna is a dedicated admirer of the nationalistic ideals of the Republic, she still is skeptical about the authoritarian application of the reforms. And her husband, an officer of the Republic, is ready to accept the reforms as long as they remain within the framework of male authority and control. Her autobiography reveals the fact that the freedom and liberty given to women through state-sponsored reforms did not actually take women's real expectations and aspirations into consideration.

In the 1980s and 1990s women's issues began to be discussed at a scope going beyond the immediate horizon of the modernization project. After the *coup d'état* of 1980 and the subsequent depoliticization of Turkey feminism appeared as the first democratic movement. In those years books on modern feminism were translated into Turkish leading to more intensive debates on women's problems. This intellectual climate did affect autobiography writing. Indeed, the number of autobiographies increased considerably in the 1990s. Most of the writers of these books were born either before the foundation of the Republic or shortly after it, but all were born into the Republican ideals.

However, it must be noted that a deeper awareness of women's issues first appeared not in theoretical essays and autobiographies but in Turkish fiction. This process can be traced as far back as Halide Edip's earlier novels such as *Handan, Seviyye Talip, Raik'in Annesi*. In her novels Halide Edib tried to analyze the female soul although her female outlook did not go beyond that of her time. The novelists of the post-1970 era have dealt with women's issues more freely questioning the established norms and conventions of female ideology. The common aspect of these novelists is their emphasis on female sexuality. Yet it is still a new step for the writer to move from the fictional world of the novel to the world of autobiography. Even in a novel displaying autobiographical features, the novelist has the chance to disguise herself behind fiction. However, the "autobiographical pact" which assumes identification of the writer, the narrator and the protagonist of the story, makes such an escape impossible in an autobiography, hence it becomes difficult to maintain privacy. In the autobiographies that appear after 1990, we clearly observe that the veil of privacy has been gradually removed. Within this context the autobiographies of Cahit Uçuk and İsmet Kür add to works cited gain special significance since both writers were born at the beginning of the twentieth century, before the foundation of the Republic. It would have been impossible to expect from them to produce the same autobiographies in the 1950s or 1960s.

Cahit Uçuk's book entitled *Erkekler Dünyasında Bir Kadın Yazar* (A Female Writer in a Man's World) was published in 2003. Uçuk was born 1909 in Thessalonica and spent her childhood in several places in Anatolia before she moved to Istanbul in her twenties. She never had a formal education. She was enthusiastic in reading and writing and as she needed to make a living, she decided to publish her writings. Most female writers do not state that they have been writing to make a living, they consider writing a personal calling beyond financial concerns. But Uçuk believes that real independence of women can only be achieved through economic independence.

Uçuk overtly states that she is a beautiful woman. The two male poets who read her work first, Abdülhak Hamit and Nâzım Hikmet, introduced her into the world of literature. The question of whether she was accepted into Babıali because she was a beautiful woman or because she was a good writer is a complex issue. For Cahit Uçuk beauty is a central problem. A beautiful woman faces all sorts of dangers in the man's world. For Cahit Uçuk there is a strong link between morality, virtue and beauty. Beauty threatens virtue. Although Uçuk often talks about preserving her virtue, she does not choose to repress her sexuality. She talks about the day when she takes her writing to Abdülhak Hamit for the first time and she explains in great length how smart and elegantly she was dressed on that particular day. She wants to attract the old poet's attention both as a woman and as an intelligent writer. The author who publishes her first writing in the journal *Yarımay* in 1935 and introduces her as a promising young writer is Nazım Hikmet. She changes her name from Cahide Üçok to Cahit Uçuk as several of her predecessors in Western literature had done hoping that a male name will help her in her literary career. Although Uçuk tells us that gender is of no importance in literature, she believes that writing as an occupation is part of the male realm. In Uçuk's opinion a career woman should put her sexuality aside while she is working alongside men. And yet her autobiography shows that she does not practice what she preaches.

That she is obsessed with her beauty and questioning her talents as a writer may be ascribed to her doubts about her adequacy as a writer. This also might have been due to the fact that she was not considered a significant writer in the 1980s in Turkish literary circles. In fact, her autobiography becomes a milestone in her literary career. Her novels and children's stories are no longer remembered, but her autobiography revives her name. Her life story is much more interesting than are her schematic, moralistic, didactic stories. In her autobiography, she addresses the problem of being a female writer in a male society in 1940s Turkey by exhibiting the private aspects of her life and she widens the scope of self-writing. Yet on the whole her autobiography remains within mainstream male-dominated ideology.

In İsmet Kür's autobiography, published in 1995, the public and private spheres are interconnected. The taboos of private life, particularly the restraints on sexuality, are discussed boldly. İsmet Kür is aware that Turkish modernization had created and reinforced sexual hypocrisy. Thus she writes:

> Talk of sexual matters was not tolerated in our home. Yet it was not something never to be mentioned. My mother and her friends used to talk about men and sexual affairs, though indirectly and unwillingly. Virginity was one of such things that had been mentioned deliberately, when I was in the vicinity. It was about a membrane and this membrane was the symbol of female chastity. (93)

As a mother and housewife Kür has difficulties in fulfilling her own professional aspirations. Her private life hinders her from working for herself, i.e. she cannot write the books she wants to write. As she cannot actualize her professional expectations her desire for her husband, whom she describes as responsible and loving, diminishes gradually. Ismet Kür quite openly admits her own mistakes and shortcomings and displays the complicated problems that confront a woman who tries to be successful as mother, wife and career woman. Her autobiography reflects the difficulties of the newly-emerging professional women in Turkey in the 1940s and 1950s; women's expectations and aspirations increase drastically as they take their place in the public sphere.

Everything considered, in Turkish women's autobiographies we observe a development similar to that in the West in the twentieth century, a development moving gradually from the public sphere to the private. Autobiographies manifesting the conventional attitude, for example those which introduce only scenes from public life, still continue to come out. The writers of such books are either professional women or wives of men holding important positions in society, consequently they partly relate the success story of a woman and partly the different phases of the political and ideological struggle in Turkey. Since all these women are products of the modernization process their lives are interwoven with the political and social life of the country. However, in the recently published autobiographies, even in the most political ones, we find that private life occupies a far more substantial place. Unlike the women writers of the early Republican period, almost all of the contemporary female writers emphasize their female identity in their self-writing.

Furthermore women's autobiographies have assumed a central position in the cultural and social history of Turkey because they reflect the history of women's liberation and their integration into the public sphere in a male-dominated society from the viewpoint of women. According to their autobiographies, in spite of the differences in their approach to the Republican ideology, these women share a common goal, namely that they should be useful to the society and to the country. They consider their service for their country to be a moral duty incumbent upon themselves in return for their emancipation. Consequently their public lives play an important role in their autobiographies.

Works Cited

Adıvar, Halide Edip. *Conflict of East and West in Turkey*. Jamia Millia Extension Lectures. Lahore: S. M. Ashraf, 1935.
___. *Handan*. İstanbul: Atlas, 1967.
___. *Memoirs of Halide Edib*. London: John Murray, 1926.

___. *Mor Salkımlı Ev*. İstanbul: Atlas, 1985.
___. *Raik'in Annesi*. İstanbul: Atlas, 1967.
___. *Seviyye Talip*. İstanbul: Atlas, 1967.
___. *The Turkish Ordeal*. London: Century, 1928.
___. *Türkün Ateşle İmtihanı*. İstanbul: Atlas, 1987.
Akşit, Elif Ekin. *Kızların Sessizliği*. İletişim: İstanbul, 2005.
Kür, İsmet. *Yarısı Roman*. İstanbul: Yapı Kredi, 1995.
Lejeune, Philip. "The Autobiographical Contract." *French Literary Theory Today: A Reader*. Ed. Tzvetan Todorov. Trans. R. Carter. Cambridge: Cambridge University Press, 1982.
Sertel, Sabiha. *Roman Gibi*. İstanbul: Belge, 1987.
Sertel, Yıldız. *Annem*. İstanbul: Yapı Kredi, 1995.
___. *Annem Sabiha Sertel Kimdi, Neler Yazdı?* İstanbul: Belge, 2001.
Uçuk, Cahit. *Erkekler Dünyasında Bir Kadın Yazar*. İstanbul: Yapı Kredi, 2003.
Zorlutuna, Halide Nusret. *Bir Devrin Romanı*. İstanbul: L&M, 2004.

Reception and Audience in Life Writing and Healing

Wendy Ryden
Long Island University

Abstract: Trauma and illness narratives constitute important sub-genres for investigation within the study of life writing, and the research on the healing effects of narrative is interdisciplinary. James Pennebaker's seminal work, for example, has shown us that writing privately has salubrious effects, and we need not share what we write with anyone for such benefits to accrue. And yet much of the scholarship on writing and healing speaks in terms of witnessing and testimony and the implied role of audience in the process of narrative formation. Under what circumstances does sharing one's story with an audience stand to benefit both teller and hearer by uniting them in empathetic discourse, and under what circumstances does the telling constitute disempowering confession where agency is relinquished to a dominant, oppressive narrative?

"It is probably no exaggeration to say," writes Walter Slatoff, "that the single most common subject of art is some form of human suffering" (233; qtd. in Morris 194). Thus it is not surprising that an important trajectory in the study of life writing is the interdisciplinary scholarship on writing and healing and its accompanying theoretical considerations regarding narrative subjectivity in relation to bodily and lived experience. Illness narratives, for example, what Anne Hawkins has labeled "pathographies," have become a focus of scholarship as evidenced by such work as Arthur Frank's (*Wounded*) taxonomy of illness stories and Arthur Kleinman's study of patient narratives where such stories attempt, to use Kleinman's words, "to give coherence to the distinctive events and long-term course of suffering" (49). Similarly, trauma testimonies as well as other narratives dealing with emotional upheaval constitute important sub-genres of nonfiction writing, and physicians, psychologists, social scientists, and literary scholars have claimed that storytelling has the power to effect emotional and physical healing. In her emphasis on audience, Sunwolf tells us that this healing can be accomplished through storytelling, for both teller and listener, by creating "a tolerable narrative for what appears to be inexplicable" (2). Arthur Frank, in his discussion of illness narratives, locates the healing potential of narrative in the idea that "[s]tories are the ongoing work of turning mere existence into a life that is social, and moral, and affirms the existence of the teller as a human being" ("Enacting" 43).

Indeed speculation about what determines and explains the healing nature of writing is an important part of the scholarship in this field. As Judith Harris asks in her book *Signifying Pain*, "What are the linkages between the creative writing process and therapeutic catharsis of pain or suffering? When does writing alleviate pain for the writer or for the reader?" (7). With regard to the question of when writing becomes healing for the writer, much of the speculation centers around narrative subjectivity and what we might regard as some of the problematic aspects of first person writing in relation to the power dimensions of so-called confessional writing as well as issues of essentialized identity steeped in romantic notions of the self. In confronting these questions, scholars use the insights of post-structuralist narrative perspectives to shed light on how writing can produce healing. From this point of view, where textual subjectivity is seen as conditional, fragmented, performative and constructed, the writer's text and the writer's life are not one and the same, and personal narrative heals not because it is a unified declaration of truth but rather because the text becomes a strategy of discourse intervention where writers have the chance to confront and revise dysfunctional narratives which interpellate them. We see the prevalence of this idea in such statements as Barbara Kamler's when she indicates that through writing one can "transform the text and the way experience is viewed" in order for writers to "reconstruct and renegotiate their identities" (54) or in Louise DeSalvo's notion that "through writing, we revisit our past and review and revise it [. . .]. [W]e use writing to shift our perspectives" (11).

Charles Anderson highlights this idea of the "perspective shift" in his discussion of student writing and healing. In his article, "Suture, Stigma, and the Pages that Heal," Anderson discusses student texts that he sees resisting through narrative strategy what he calls "suturing" discourses of disempowerment; dominant cultural narratives that rob subjects of agency by writing them into passive positions. The student writers that Anderson discusses manage to create in their stories what he labels "contracontextual" space, by which he means places where the writers oppositionally write back against dominant narratives rather than allow themselves to be written, and through this process produce healing narratives. As a rhetorician and writing teacher, he, like Louise DeSalvo, sees this act specifically being accomplished through rhetorical tropes and strategies of revision that allow students to revise through their texts their victimized subjectivity to create new subject positions for themselves in the narratives of their lives. As Anderson and his coeditor Marian MacCurdy say, "Through the dual possibilities of permanence and revision, the chief healing effect of writing is thus to recover and to exert a measure of control over that which we can never control—the past" (7).

Thus for these scholars healing subjectivity is engendered when narratives function as the equivalent of therapeutic holding spaces where the writers can interrogate their subjectivity. This view of narrative allows for psychoanalytic explanations of writing's healing function, especially creative writing that is envisioned as tapping into the unconscious. Judith Harris explains that "Both psychoanalysis and literature are interested in the therapeutic process of bringing disorder into order, the chaos of the inner self into control and coherence. Language is the medium that mirrors the struggle, and the interplay between subjectivity and objectivity" (31). The notion of narrative order is another idea that comes up frequently in rationales for healing, thus linking the therapeutic and composing processes through language.

Support for this belief comes from physiological explanations of trauma that depict the traumatic memory as being stored in a part of the brain that does not encompass language function. Writing thus can help integrate and order the traumatic experience through language. Anderson looks for what he calls gaps in the text, where the narration is not complete, and urges writers to fill in the lacunae. Likewise, psychologist James Pennebaker, whose seminal research established empirical links between writing and improved health, urges the craft of story construction as part of a therapeutic program of writing. And Kleinman speaks of patients "ordering their experience of illnesses" through "plot lines, core metaphors, and rhetorical devices that structure the illness narrative" (49).

While the creation of narrative order is seen as a means of gaining control, it is also associated with the subject obtaining ironic or critical distance from the experienced suffering, which is viewed as essential to opening up the contracontextual space necessary for revision of the disempowering narrative. "Because art," Harris tells us, "demands a certain amount of detachment [. . .] artistic activity accelerates the therapeutic process" (31). Louise DeSalvo expresses this idea of detachment too when she says, "A healing narrative doesn't just narrate what happened to us and how we feel. It is a way for us to reflect upon the significance of what happened" (60). But the question of what constitutes narrative order in the healing story is a complex one, as many critics acknowledge the fragmentary nature of trauma memories and illness experiences. Laura Gray-Rosendale, for example, sees the fractured time-line as an important textual strategy in the structure of sexual abuse narratives. And Miriam Marty Clark argues, in her discussion of Hemingway's work as illness narratives, that "the illness narrative advances and coheres not by contiguity and causality but by metaphors that mark the outfolding of the body's traumas into cultural narratives and the infolding of the cultural trauma into bodily symptoms" (170).

The post-structural trajectory of much writing and healing criticism as described above locates, ironically perhaps, writing's healing effects in and through a kind of new critical textual analysis irrespective of audience and reception. But Clark's remark about "cultural trauma" reminds us of another key component in the discussions of when and how narrative becomes healing. In addition to the interdependent issues of subjectivity, resistance, and order, another connected strand that emerges in rationales for writing and healing is the question of community and social engagement. David Morris tells us that "[t]he modernist narrative of suffering as a quintessentially private state is not the last word or the only word on suffering" (199). Suffering, trauma, pain can be understood as having social dimensions. Indeed, rather than something that isolates us, suffering can be seen as linking us to the rest of humanity. "Pain," writes Judith Harris, "is an individual experience, but pain is also what we understand about ourselves, and through other people with whom we empathize" (5). David Morris tells us that "pain is always subjective" but with "sharable intersubjective dimensions" (109). He goes on to say that suffering and pain exist in part beyond language: "One function of narrative is to bring this deeper silence to awareness, to make such silences 'speak'" (196) and in so doing remove the perceived isolation of suffering. Thus the structure of narrative order mentioned above, although sometimes approached from merely a perspective of textual analysis and function, links the writer through the communal localities of genre and language. In this view, to write about pain, or any subject, even in private, is to join with and make the experience part of a discourse community and a greater phenomenon than what the individual alone must bear.

The distinction of private versus public writing is precisely the question I want to engage with regard to the healing text. But before I turn to that question, I want to explore further how some critics see the public text as being crucial to the possibilities of healing. References to the ideas of witnessing and testimony in relation to healing are ubiquitous. As Laura A. Milner writes, "Theorists in trauma studies, psychoanalysis, medicine, history, composition, narrative, and literacy describe the dynamic, though sometimes painful benefits of naming, knowing, and re-visioning our experiences in the presence of an empathetic reader or witness" (23). Harris, in her psychoanalytic approach to healing writing, observes a parallel process between the act of writing for an audience and therapy when she notes that "a relief exists concomitant with unburdening one's self to an/other [. . .]. Transferring pain, with the belief that an objective observer, analyst, or reader can shoulder pain seems very much at the heart of [healing] writings" (31). For Harris, then, the cathartic moment implies a witness to the pain, and indeed it is through the ideas of witnessing and testimony, as the explanation for the healing significance of stories for listeners and readers, that we move in a different direction than the psychoanalytic model. As David Morris points out, "Support groups—the post-modern social equivalent of one-on-one modernist psychoanalysis—provide evidence that shared narratives of suffering, under the right conditions, can hold healing powers" (201). Relying on the trauma work of Cathy Caruth, Dori Laub and Cassie Premo Steele, Milner likewise cites the condition of feeling "safe enough to write and read our stories aloud" as being a prerequisite to the "knowing and valuing" that must accompany healing (24).

The question of audience here is a vexed one for several reasons. The first aspect of this difficulty that I will discuss concerns the power dynamics of the confessional situation that I mentioned earlier. Foucault famously problematized the telling of one's story by pointing out the hegemonic and coercive nature of the confessional. The sensationalized talk show format of confession that emerged in latter twentieth-century popular culture seemed evidence of Foucault's identification of the Western compulsion to confess. Rather than empowering the teller, the relating of one's story within confessional discourse seems instead to hand the story over to an outside mediating authority, as Gray-Rosendale identifies in her discussion of the appropriation of sexual abuse stories through talk show culture. The question then becomes: under what circumstances does sharing one's story with an audience function as the witnessing and testimony that stands to benefit both teller and hearer by uniting them in empathetic discourse and under what circumstances does the telling constitute disempowering confession where agency over one's experience is relinquished to remain sutured in a dominant oppressive narrative?

Perhaps the key in distinguishing between confession and testimony rests with the issues of coercion and agency. The genre of the confession relies on a subject apparently confessing freely, but the impetus of promised absolution, or rather the fear of *not* obtaining it, figures as a coercive element in compelling the story. In observing such a distinction, Ermien Van Pletzen describes testimony as a case where "the subject testifying is less caught up in the mechanisms of power and authority, in that he or she speaks not as transgressor, but as witness" (169). But this line between transgressor and witness frequently blurs within autobiography, especially if we allow the notion of "transgressor" a positive attribute of rebellion even as we acknowledge the coercive role of audience in narrative formation. Leigh Gilmore discusses the problematic dimensions of the power dynamics inherent in the project of self-representation in "the mechanisms of judging and assessment which inform its [self-representation's] production of knowledge." Implicit in Gilmore's analysis is the role of audience as she describes the "discursive demand" and "the knot of resistance" that self-representation requires where "one is both abjured to speak and exposed to scrutiny." But importantly, according to Gilmore, "the demand may be met with some degree of agency" (43). Thus although textual self-representation of the traumatic or the intimate may always contain an element of Foucault's "obligation to confess" (60), the act of witnessing through committed self expression also always concomitantly holds the possibility of self-empowerment and (or perhaps through?) cultural critique.

For Gilmore the distinction between the confessional and anti-confessional trauma narrative, as Foucault understood the latter, rests on the question of whether such narratives are "petitioning for belief from readers." If so, then they are not "anti-confessional" in the Foucauldian sense, as they relinquish authentication and validation to an outside authority. But Gilmore suggests we adjust our reading of such writers to see them not as petitioning for belief but rather "as asserting their speech" (37). In other words, storytellers require not so much that they be *believed* as that they make themselves *heard* in narrative acts of declaration.

This "assertion of speech" can take place, according to Judith Harris, when

> people who are in distress or crisis need the support of a community that will not shun them for exhibiting their intimate feelings. Without such a community, people are reluctant to bear witness to traumatic events, and the grieving process is halted or forestalled. (14)

Harris further explains the ambivalence with which testimony and witnessing are regarded, and in so doing turns us back to the issue of narrative and resistance when, as she says, "the [expressed] pain challenges authoritative beliefs" (10) at which point "[a] witness is both sought and shunned; the desire to hear his truth is countered by the need to ignore him" (14).

The possibility of being ignored—or misunderstood or censored or somehow silenced—or, to use Gilmore's terms, unable to assert speech, is a crucial question in considering the role of audience in the production of healing texts. For despite rhetoric's contribution to our understanding of the interpenetration of audience and author in text construction, the role of audience in the healing narrative is far from clear. Indeed there is good evidence to suggest that not only is the witnessing and testimony described above *not* necessary to produce the healing narrative but that in fact writing for others could impede this function. The research of James Pennebaker mentioned previously has shown us that writing privately has salubrious effects, both mentally and physically, and we need not share what we write with anyone for such benefits to accrue. In Pennebaker's initial study, which has received much follow up, participants were asked to write in an emotionally connected way about a traumatic event for 15 minutes each day in a four-day period without showing the writing to anyone. The results unequivocally showed benefits accruing in physical health (see, for example, *Writing* 5-7). Work done since this initial study continues to support the findings that writing privately is healing. Indeed, Pennebaker states, "The effects of writing are not related to the presumed audience" ("Telling" 6). According to a study by Gidron, Peri, Connolly, and Shalev, it is public scrutiny and critique of writing that may erode its healing function, in part, admittedly, because of the difficulty in fostering a group of empathetic listeners or responsible witnesses to testimony. Pennebaker tells us in 2004 that

> [a]lthough the expressive writing paradigm has generally produced positive health outcomes, a recurring puzzle concerns how and why it works. No single theory or theoretical perspective has convincingly explained its effectiveness. This may be attributable to the fact that expressive writing affects people on multiple levels—cognitive, emotional, social, and biological—making a single explanatory theory unlikely.
> ("Theories" 138)

Pennebaker's and other clinical psychologists' attempts to explain the phenomenon of the healing narrative are not mutually exclusive of those offered by literary and writing scholars. Indeed many of the latter rely on Pennebaker's precepts as he advocates constructing complete narratives, although his reason for doing so can sound quite different than the rationale offered by literary critics. He is in agreement with the idea that a coherent narrative makes trauma more meaningful, but the healing function derives from the fact that writing "boosts working memory" (*Writing* 9) so that the experience can then be, to use his words, "summarized, stored, and forgotten more efficiently" ("Telling" 8-9). Studies that build on Pennebaker's work use, of course, discipline-appropriate concepts and language such as 'habituation' and 'extinction' to theorize the healing effects of writing and expression rather than ideas about oppositional narrative and witnessing. While it may be counterintuitive for us literature and writing folks to downplay ideas such as the role of audience in helping the subject locate herself in a cultural narrative or create oppositional discourse, it behooves us to look more carefully at how and under what circumstances audience affects, if in fact it does, the healing narrative. More ethnographic studies of writing groups would be useful in this regard to help us see when the role of audience is enabling and when it is debilitating.

For example, in my own practice, I have experienced both of these situations—where writing groups function as witness to testimony in a way that appears to benefit both writer and audience, but also where what I'll call 'freedom from audience' seems far more generative not only in terms of writing's healing function but in terms of producing cultural critique. In a class on writing the personal essay, many of the pieces that students submitted to me privately were far more probing than what they submitted for workshop. One student, who wrote a glib piece about cell phone use for class critique, turned in to me privately another far more complex essay where she discussed the dysfunctionality of her family in terms of class and regional affiliation, producing exactly the kind of healing essay that many teachers hope the empathetic writing group will help elicit. Most writing teachers are familiar with this complication to our ideas of public and private, and it problematizes a monolithic understanding of audience in relation to personal writing. Students may not share with the class what they will share with the instructor—in both cases the texts are by definition "public" but in different degrees. And to what extent is it enabling (and do we want to encourage) the semi-private texts communicated between teacher and student when such a power dynamic begins to resemble suspiciously the disempowering confessional structure mentioned previously? In a class specifically devoted to writing and healing, many students found that they could write texts that could be read by other students but that they themselves could not read aloud, suggesting that an identification of the text with the body was problematic for them. The idea of the anonymous audience is an extension of this—students could write narratives about deeply personal issues that they could send, say, to the unknown editor of a literary magazine but that they could not read to their friends in class. In this case, the anonymous audience was a more enabling witness than the writing group. Such scenarios help demonstrate the continued need to assess the relationship of audience to the healing text.

Works Cited

Anderson, Charles. "Suture, Stigma, and the Pages that Heal." Anderson and MacCurdy 58-82.

Anderson, Charles and Marian MacCurdy, eds. Introduction. *Writing and Healing*. Urbana: NCTE, 1999. 1-22.

Clark, Miriam Marty. "Hemingway's Early Illness Narratives and the Lyric Dimensions of 'Now I Lay Me.'" *Narrative* 12.2 (2004): 167-177.

DeSalvo, Louise. *Writing as a Way of Healing: How Telling Our Stories Transforms Our Lives*. San Francisco: Harper, 1999.

Foucault, Michel. *The History of Sexuality*. Vol. 1. *An Introduction*. Trans. Robert Hurley. New York: Random House, 1978.

Frank, Arthur. "Enacting Illness Narratives: When, What, and Why." *Stories and their Limits*. Ed. Hilde Lindeman Nelson. New York: Routledge, 1997. 31-49.

___. *The Wounded Storyteller: Body, Illness, and Ethics*. Chicago: University of Chicago Press, 1995.

Gidron, Y., T. Peri, J. F. Connolly, A. Y. Shalev. "Written Disclosure in Post-Traumatic Stress Disorder: Is it Beneficial for the Patient?" *Journal of Nervous and Mental Disease* 184 (1996): 505-507.

Gilmore, Leigh. *The Limits of Autobiography: Trauma and Testimony*. Ithaca: Cornell University Press, 2001.

Gray-Rosendale, Laura. "Constraining Our Talk Show Culture: Narrative, Identity, and Truth in Compositions by Survivors of Sexual Assault." *The Personal Narrative*. Ed. Gil Haroian-Guerin. Portland: Calendar Islands, 1999. 142-159.

Harris, Judith. *Signifying Pain: Constructing and Healing the Self through Writing*. Albany: SUNY, 2003.

Hawkins, Anne. *Reconstructing Illness: Studies in Pathography*. West Layayette, In: Purdue University Press, 1993.

Kamler, Barbara. *Relocating the Personal*. Albany: SUNY, 2001.

Kleinman, Arthur. *The Illness Narratives: Suffering, Healing, and the Human Condition*. New York: Basic, 1988.

Milner, Laura. "On Writing, Healing, and Wholeness: Personal and Cultural Benefits of Naming What Remains." *Intertexts* 8.1 (2004): 23-35.

Morris, David. *Illness and Culture in the Postmodern Age*. Berkeley: University of California Press, 1998.

Pennebaker, James. "Telling Stories: The Health Benefits of Narrative." *Literature and Medicine* 19.1 (2000): 3-18.

___. "Theories, Therapies, and Taxpayers: On the Complexities of the Expressive Writing Paradigm." *Clinical Psychology: Science and Practice* 11.2 (2004): 138-142.

___. *Writing to Heal: A Guided Journal for Recovering from Trauma and Emotional Upheaval*. Oakland: New Harbinger, 2004.

Slatoff, Walter J. *The Look of Distance: Reflections on Suffering and Sympathy in Modern Literature: Auden to Agee, Whitman to Woolf*. Columbus: Ohio State University Press, 1985.

Sunwolf. "R$_x$ Storysharing, prn: Stories as Medicine. Prologue to the Special Healing Issue." *Storytelling, Self, Society* 1.2 (2005): 1-10.

Van Pletzen, Ermien. "Mine is the Speech that Cannot be Silenced: Confession and Testimony in *Heart of Darkness*." *Conrad in Africa: New Essays on Heart of Darkness*. Ed. Attie de Lange and Gail Fincham with Wieslaw Krajka. Conrad, Eastern and Western Perspectives 11. Boulder: Social Science Monographs, 2002. 153-176.

II CASE STUDIES

Henry James' *Autobiography* (1913-1915): Creating "The Master"

Laurence Raw
Başkent University

Abstract: By focusing on selected passages from Henry James' three volumes of autobiography, *A Small Boy and Others* (1913), *Notes Of A Son And Mother* (1914) and *The Middle Years* (1917), this paper will argue that James himself was largely responsible for constructing his reputation as a "difficult" author. The reason for this was obvious; ever since the failure of his stage play *Guy Domville* (1895), James had become more and more aware that he would never enjoy commercial success. After publishing his last completed novel, *The Outcry* (1912), to poor reviews, he began writing his autobiography, in which he deliberately sought to address educated rather than popular readers.

I will subsequently show that this purpose emerges through the style of the autobiographies. On the one hand James demonstrates strict control over his material as he recounts how he discovered and subsequently developed his artistic talent. I will argue that this control was entirely deliberate, prompted by the author's need to justify, in some way or other, his vision of his earlier life. On the other hand the autobiographies are written in a style reminiscent of the late novels; every detail is carefully constructed, every reaction carefully planned in advance. Without any impetuous drive of narrative, or the accumulation of incidents to divert the reader's attention, the autobiographies reveal James' modernist preoccupation with the process of vision, of making sense of the world.

Henry James' *Autobiography*—comprising the three works *A Small Boy and Others* (1913), *Notes of a Son and Brother* (1914) and the unfinished *Middle Years* (1917)—can be regarded as a classic example of what F. O. Matthiessen described long ago as "a record of experience" combined with "the maturing of thought and emotion that comes from intense living" (394-95).[1] Written right at the end of the author's life, it began as a small work dedicated to his brother William. What he fi-

---

[1] The title *Henry James: Autobiography* was actually created by F. W. Dupee for his 1956 edition—the first time all three works had been reprinted since their original publication (Dupee vii).

nally produced was an extended account of his early development—an account in which William James figures occasionally, but scarcely at all as an objective character. Instead Henry James wrote an account of his discovery of a vocation for writing, a true "calling"—a trade which was also a way of life. The experience is a sacrificial one, a bitter triumph at best; it may end happily—with James achieving his desired profession—but the path towards that goal is fraught with difficult, often nightmarish experiences. These include the all but overwhelming impact of Europe on Henry as a boy, the Civil War with its terrible losses, and an experience in the Galérie d'Apollon on the Louvre, when the young James turns upon and violently routs a pursuer who threatens to destroy him. James writes his autobiography as if his present self was continuous with his past self, combining immediacy of impression with maturity of judgment and so remain faithful to the experiences he recounts. Hence the peculiar intimacy of the book; it almost seems as if the author is talking in a "stream of consciousness" style, trying to describe the manifold impressions going through his mind on any given occasion.

This paper will situate the *Autobiography* in context, and subsequently show how it played a major part in establishing James' literary reputation—a reputation that continues to this day. It will suggest that James wrote it at a time when his fiction had little popular appeal; the reissue of his popular works in the New York edition of 1908 had failed to cause much impact, while his later novels raised scarcely a critical murmur. Autobiography's ultimate purpose is to fix the self for all time; to put forth the idea that the autobiographer matters and that his life is significant in the supposed order of things. With this in mind, James set out to create a work that would consolidate his reputation as a writer of distinction—someone associated with a difficult, resistant style of writing that frustrated general readers and opened him to claims of literary ancestorship by modernist and/or postmodernist writers and critics.[2] He is more preoccupied with the mind rather than objective detail, enticing the reader into an unbendable process of supplementation and (over-)reading. The *Autobiography* is based on a contradictory premise; on the one hand it shows the author demonstrating strict control over his material, limiting the small boy to a single activity—the discovery of his own vocation as a writer. On the other hand it is clear that such control is designed to encourage us to participate actively in the reading process—to write as we read, to make our own text and thereby participate in the same process of self-discovery as James himself recounts (Stowe 193).

The second part of this paper will argue that the *Autobiography* more than succeeded in its purpose of installing James at the very center of the canon of literary value and esteem. His achievements were not only recognized by critics and/or reviewers, but the book itself was instrumental in contributing to his posthumous image as an artist of the esoteric, preoccupied with the internal realities of his characters and how they respond to given situations. I will demonstrate this by showing how "Henry James" has appeared as a character in adaptations of his work (ranging from television productions such as *The Golden Bowl* [1972] and *The American* [1998] to a variety of BBC radio documentaries and dramas), as producers and/or directors have tried to recreate the experience of his novels by re-invoking him as a controlling presence, encouraging viewers and/or listeners to engage in an active process of interpretation.

James' reasons for writing the *Autobiography* have been convincingly outlined by his biographer Fred Kaplan:

> The project seemed more vivid, more challenging, more pertinent than any ideas for fiction that came to mind. It offered

---

[2] Susanna Egan remarks that this is characteristic of many American autobiographies after the Civil War where "the self is an object of history. [. . .] Even at his most personal, in other words, the autobiographer sees fit to make himself most universal" (78).

him an alternative at a time when he felt hesitant about his powers as a novelist, fearful that his illness had drained him of some of the imaginative energy he would need for fiction. [. . .] If he were interrupted by momentary bafflement or even by prolonged illness, he imagined that it would be easier to resume an autobiography where he had left off than it would a novel (540).

As the writing progressed, he gradually discovered that the center of attention had to be his own consciousness; in his version of the family romance, through the power of artistic shaping, James made himself both bearer and firstborn, father and brother, the giver and maker of life to the entire family. He saw the work as one last opportunity to "have one last sustained expression [of talent] and triumph of himself as an artist" (Kaplan 542). The second volume—*Notes of a Son and Brother*—further traced the growth and development of his artistic consciousness at a time of national turmoil. It was criticized by some of his acquaintances for being somewhat narcissistic; James responded in a letter to Henry Adams that he wrote it because he still found his consciousness interesting: "It's, I suppose, because I'm that queer monster, the artist, an obstinate finality, an inexhaustible sensibility" (*Life* 533). In another letter to the author Hugh Walpole, he emphasized the fact that this was the kind of image he wanted to create of himself in the minds of his readers: "An extraordinarily impudent attempt surely, that of regaling the world with the picture of my rare consciousness [. . .] & aggravated by the fact that when I began to tap the fount I found it come, the crystal stream—& *liked* the way of its coming" (*Life* 522-23). Some readers grasped his purpose—even though they had to make considerable mental effort to do so: James congratulated Edward Emerson (son of Ralph Waldo Emerson) in another letter for being one of "but three or four [readers], at the most, who have known what most of groping Notes so much as mean. You have been able to recognize what they supposed themselves, as they went on, to be talking about—& the mode of your recognition deeply touches me" (*Life* 541).

James' controlling presence is evident throughout the work. Consider, for instance, the following passage, where he tries to make sense of a childhood experience in France:

> This a reminiscence that nothing would induce me to verify, as for example by any revisiting light; but it was going to be good for me, good, that is, for what I was pleased to regard as my intelligence of my imagination, in fine for my obscurely specific sense of things, that is, that I should so have hung about. (*Autobiography* 261)

He reflects on his past self through the prism of the present, and tries to see how the experience contributed to the development of his consciousness (or "the intelligence of my imagination"). There is also a deliberate attempt to distance himself from the general populace as someone possessing an "obscurely specific sense of things." This is something he expects readers to identify with. Later on James attempts to describe the process of writing his autobiography in more detail. It seeks to trace the development of the young writer's artistic consciousness, which is not only dependent on the imagination but also on memories

> too fine or too peculiar for notation, too intensely individual and supersubtle—call them what one will; yet which one may thus no more give up confusedly than one may insist on them vainly. Their kind is nothing ever to a present purpose unless they are in a manner statable, but is at the same time ruefully aware of threatened ridicule if they are overstated.
> (*Autobiography* 426)

However it is his responsibility to communicate them in some way to the reader, even though he might render himself liable to "threatened ridicule." Once again James sets himself apart as someone with an acutely developed sense of memory—so acute, in fact, that many people might not be able to understand his purpose. It is only those who are prepared to engage with his concerns that will be able to appreciate the significance of what he writes.

Some experiences are given particular prominence as being essential to the formulation of the artist's consciousness. One of these takes place in the Gallérie d'Appollon in the Louvre, an occasion that James himself recalled.

> To this hour, with the last vividness, what a precious part it played for me, and exactly by that continuity of honour, on my awaking, in a summer dawn many years later, to the fortunate, the instantaneous recovery and capture of the most appalling yet most admirable nightmare of my life. The climax of this extraordinary experience [. . .] was the sudden pursuit, through an open door, along a huge high saloon, of a just dimly-descried figure that retreated in terror before my rush and dash. [T]he great point of the whole was the wonder of my final recognition. Routed, dismayed [. . .] he sped for *his* life, while a great storm of thunder and lightning played through the deep embrasures of high windows at the right.
>
> (Autobiography 196-197).

To those familiar with James' early work, this moment may remind us of *The Turn of the Screw*, where the governess' moment of extreme terror—as she encounters the ghost of Peter Quint—also represents a moment of self-discovery, as she realizes the presence of powerful sexual desires within her. On this occasion James recalls that the moment of chasing the apparition down the corridor proved so "educative, formative, fertilizing, to a degree which no other 'intellectual experience' our youth was to know could pretend, as a comprehensive, conducive thing" (*Autobiography* 197). The author is here firmly in control, trying to make sense of his experience, while helping readers to understand the workings of his conscious mind, both in the present and the past.

However what renders this *Autobiography* most interesting is that, while the narrative is dominated by a controlling presence, readers are left to make their own decisions about how to respond to it. James describes himself as a "man of imagination," who had discovered his talent "from within rather than meet him [the imaginative talent] in the world before me. [. . .] It wasn't what I should have preferred, yet it was after all the example I knew best and should feel most at home with" (*Autobiography* 455).[3] Yet within a sentence he is suggesting that "it is of course for my reader to say whether or no what I have done *has* meant defeat" (455). In a sense he anticipates what his readers might be thinking about his choice of profession; perhaps it does represent a defeat, in the sense that it leaves him with fame but very little money. Or perhaps other readers might think that it condemned him to a life of contemplation rather than action—something which might be rather inappropriate during the time of the Civil War. The narrator himself might believe that the choice of profession enabled him to bring up "from the deep [of his imagination] many things probably not to have been arrived at for the benefit of these pages without any particular attempt" (455). But that does not mean that readers have to agree with him. As with many late works, the *Autobiography* expects us to engage in an active process of reading; to consider the material set before us and to draw our own conclusions—in other words, to create a text of our own which might be very different from that set forth by the narrator. However, as we have already seen, James is well aware that only those readers competent enough to understand his "obscurely specific sense of things" will engage in this process of meaning-making.

When *Notes from a Son and Brother*—the second volume of the *Autobiography*—was first published in 1914, the *New York Times* re-

---

[3] James also says the same thing about Hawthorne in the *Autobiography* (409-412). For a fuller discussion of this, see Caramello 21-56.

viewer acknowledged the fact that perhaps it was not intended for general readers, but for those "with sufficient leisure and application" to make sense of his dense prose. However if they were prepared to make the effort, they could feel "particularly intimate with the author, to feel, in fact, that one has become a member of his family" (Kilmer BR1). On his death in 1916, the same newspaper published an obituary describing him as a someone sharply distinguished from the novelists of his own day by "the abundance of his thought and his conscience for mental labor." He was a master "at the highly specialized game of making literature for adult minds"; for those readers who could appreciate it, his work revealed a "richness and fullness of spirit" ("Henry James" SM7). The final volume of autobiography, *The Middle Years*, appeared in 1917: William Lyon Phelps remarked in a review that, while James' style was undoubtedly difficult to understand, it nonetheless repaid the reader's efforts "more highly than others atone for your expenditure of time. Henry James is definitely worth reading" (47). He had a "wonderful style that none but a master of English could have designed; but it is so carefully constructed that it is opaque, and the reader beholds the style as a barricade rather than a medium" (47). Such opacity, I would argue, was entirely deliberate, as James sought to reestablish his reputation towards the end of his life. The task clearly proved a successful one.

The notion of Henry James as "The Master" has proved a powerful one ever since. It has become a staple theme of literary criticism since his death—something that has exerted both positive and negative effects, as readers have either confessed to finding him a "difficult" author, or someone who requires a great deal of effort to be understood. This idea has been thoroughly explored in histories of James criticism, and need not concern us now. What appears more interesting to me, however, is the way in which "Henry James" as a *persona* reappears in film, television and radio adaptations of his work, exhibiting much the same kind of characteristics that appear in his autobiography. In the National Sound Archive at the British Library in London, there exist recordings of several radio programs devoted to his work; one of them, a series of "Memories of Henry James," first broadcast in 1958, consists of a series of anecdotes about James from contemporaries who knew him, interspersed with readings from his work by Carleton Hobbs (billed in the *Radio Times* as "Henry James"). This deep, rich-voiced actor—a member of the BBC Radio Drama Company for many years—suggested a controlling presence, as he delivered James' words in a sonorous tone, inviting listeners to take note of his every word. In several radio adaptations of his novels—notably *What Maisie Knew*, and *The Wings of the Dove*—"Henry James" once again appears as a narrator, reading out passages to link dramatized scenes and encouraging listeners to form their opinions about the action that follows. Once again he is characterized as "The Master," while the listeners, to extend the metaphor, are the "pupils."

In James Cellan Jones' television adaptation of *The Golden Bowl* (1972), "Henry James" does not appear as a character, but many of his lines are read out by Bob Assingham (Cyril Cusack) direct to camera. On one occasion Bob likens Maggie to a bird who "had flapped her little wings as a token of wanting to fly a little, not merely as a plea for a more gilded cage" (*Golden Bowl* 355; slightly rewritten). The result, according to Bob's patriarchal view of the world, was that Maggie "felt suddenly immensely alone." This summation is undermined by the events that follow, as Maggie admits that Charlotte has "always been so good, so perfect, to me—but never as wonderfully as just now. We have somehow been more together—thinking for the time almost only of each other; it has been quite as in old days" (*Golden Bowl* 365). Cellan Jones emphasizes the closeness of their relationship by means of a split-screen image, with Charlotte on the left of the frame, and Maggie on the right. Such contradictory impulses—where Charlotte chooses to remain close friends with someone who suspects her of having an affair with her husband—are beyond the scope of Bob's imagination. In this particular instance, viewers are encouraged to make up their minds for themselves; not to take Bob's words at face value but rather to engage as active participants in the process of watching the program. Bob/Henry James might seek to be a controlling presence, but paradoxically he expects viewers to look at what he says with a detached perspective.

By contrast the character "Henry James" (Alec McCowen) in Paul Unwin's 1998 BBC adaptation of *The American* seeks to be a controlling presence alone, setting the scene for the story at the beginning of the film, and offering a concluding statement about Christopher Newman (Matthew Modine), who leaves the Bellegarde household for good, but "at what cost?" For this "Henry James," Newman's behavior might seem logical (in terms of the plot), but it also causes him emotional pain—a pain which, as the final phrase "at what cost?" implies, has left him with a perpetual emotional scar.

This presentation has tried to show that, while the study of an autobiographical text might tell us a lot about how authors construct their own personae—which may or may not be "factual" or "fictional" (it doesn't really matter which)—perhaps we should also look at the ways in which such autobiographies have been received in different contexts, to understand how that persona (as expressed in the autobiography) has impressed itself on readers, critics and (in the case of James) adaptors of his work. Particularly in the case of canonical authors such as James, I think that the *Autobiography* tells us a lot about James himself in his late 60s, at the end of his career, as he looks back on his past years, and tries to reconstruct his public persona. But more significantly, I would argue that the way in which the *Autobiography* was received—especially in the *New York Times*, as well as in more scholarly journals—exerted a profound influence over the way in which the author's posthumous reputation as ("Henry James" the Master) was established, and continues to this day. Moreover, I would suggest that the fact that this persona reappears not only in literary criticism, but in media adaptations of his work, demonstrates how effective James was in accomplishing his task.

Works Cited

Caramello, Charles. *Henry James, Gertrude Stein and the Biographical Act*. Chapel Hill and London: University of North Carolina Press, 1996: 21-56.

Dupee, F. W. "Introduction." *Henry James: Autobiography*. New York: Criterion, 1956. vii-xiv.

Egan, Susanna. "'Self'-conscious History: American Autobiography After the Civil War." *American Autobiography: Retrospect and Prospects*. Ed. Paul John Eakin. Madison and London: University of Wisconsin Press, 1991. 70-94.

"Henry James, Interpreter of American Types." *New York Times* 5 Mar. 1916: SM7.

James, Henry. *Autobiography*. Ed. F. W. Dupee. New York: Criterion, 1956.

___. *The Golden Bowl*. Ed. Patricia Crick. Harmondsworth: Penguin, 1987.

___. *A Life In Letters*. Ed. Philip Horne. Harmondsworth: Penguin, 2000.

Kaplan, Fred. *Henry James: The Imagination of Genius*. New York: William Morrow, 1992.

Kilmer, Joyce. "Henry James at School: Delightful Volume of Reminiscences of a 'Son and Brother' in an Important Autobiographical Series." *New York Times*, 15 Mar. 1914: BR1.

Matthiessen, F. O. *American Renaissance: Art and Expression in the Age of Emerson and Whitman*. London and New York: Oxford University Press, 1941.

Phelps, William Lyon. "The Last Words of Henry James." *New York Times*, 9 Dec. 1917: 47.

Stowe, William. "James' Elusive *Wings*." *The Cambridge Companion to Henry James*. Ed. Jonathan Freedman. Cambridge: Cambridge University Press, 1998. 187-204.

Samuel Beckett's Trilogy: The Picture of the Artist Trying to Represent the Self

Oya Berk
Haliç University

Abstract: Samuel Beckett's trilogy (*Molloy, Malone Dies, The Unnamable*) is a key text which contains all the distinguishing features of his writing. It comprises most of the major Beckettian themes and provides the best example of the mode of writing Beckett has devised for exploring self or being. Moreover, standing in the centre of Beckett's oeuvre, it offers a thorough commentary on Beckett's previous work and at the same time anticipates the predominant themes and narrative techniques on which his mature fiction is based. In this sense, it is a metatext or metanarrative through which Beckett comments on his own work and revisits as a source throughout his later oeuvre. In fact, Beckett's later work can be viewed as a "re-presentation" of the trilogy in a different narrative mode.

The purpose of this paper is to provide an in-depth analysis of Samuel Beckett's *Trilogy* as autobiographical writing with a focus on Beckett's search for the self, the unattainable "core of the eddy" (*Proust* 65), as he himself calls it and his quest, as a writer, for a proper form or means of self-expression that will enable him to tell a story in the likeness of his life as the maker of the trilogy.

The quest for the self, for the unattainable "core of the eddy," as Beckett describes it in *Proust*, his book on literary criticism, is a central theme in his entire work (65). As Martin Esslin puts it,

> For Beckett's characters [. . .] the ultimate quest is the quest for their own self or rather the pursuit of the unity of that self: attainment of a moment when the split between the thinker of the thought and the observer who hears that thought as the voice that eternally drones on within the consciousness might be transcended. ("Samuel Beckett" 121)

For Beckett self is a dimensionless and timeless entity that exists in the void outside the world of time and space and is therefore by definition unattainable in this world. In his own words, "At any given moment our total soul, in spite of its rich balance sheet, has only a fictitious value. Its assets are never completely realizable" (*Proust* 41).

Given the impossibility of knowing and defining the "I" or self, the artist's effort to represent it is doomed to failure. The anguish and suffering of the impotent artist trying to narrate a story with no means of expression and with nothing to express lies at the core of Beckett's work. A formless figure crawling in the dark, falling, resting, and trying to crawl once more; a disembodied voice talking to itself in the void; the crucified writer-martyr who will never reach the death and silence he desires and finally a foetus that cannot be born out of the labor of writing, and thus cannot finish its own creation are among Beckett's favorite metaphors for the impotent artist striving in vain to find a form or means of self expression, a narrative of the "I" or the self he can grasp and put to use.

The trilogy, comprising *Molloy* (1950), *Malone Dies* (1951) and *The Unnamable* (1952), is a key text which contains all the distinguishing features of Beckett's writing. It comprises most of the major Beckettian themes and provides the best example of the mode of writing Beckett has devised for exploring the self. Moreover, standing in the center of Beckett's oeuvre, it offers a thorough commentary on Beckett's previous work and at the same time anticipates the predominant themes and narrative techniques on which his mature fiction is based. In this sense, the trilogy is a meta-text or meta-narrative through which Beckett comments on and revisits his own work as a source throughout his later œuvre. In fact, Beckett's later creations can be viewed as a "re-presentation" of the trilogy in a different narrative mode, reminding us of the hero's words in *Watt*, one of Beckett's earlier novels, named after its protagonist: "[T]his seemed rather to belong to some story heard long before, an instant in the life of another, ill told, ill heard, and more than half forgotten" (46).

The trilogy starts out with a quest for the narrator's roots and origins and moves towards total disintegration and nullity. The last volume, *The Unnamable,* brings Beckett to the brink of the cessation of the creative act beyond which it may be impossible to continue. As Beckett himself puts it: "In *L'Unnomable*, there is complete disintegration. No 'I,' no 'have,' no 'being.' No nominative, no accusative, no verb. There is no way to go on" (qtd. in Shenker 148). However, as "I can't go on" is always balanced with "I must go on" in Beckett, after *The Unnamable,* Beckett does go on writing for a long and prolific period of more than a quarter of a century, saying to himself, "Ever tried. Ever failed. No matter. Try again. Fail again. Fail better" (*Worstward Ho* 7).

As the trilogy reflects the enactment of the writing process and the traveling author-heroes of the three volumes are associated with Beckett himself, it can be read as autobiographical writing, or more specifically, as Beckett's quest as a writer for a proper form or means of self-expression that will enable him to tell a story in the likeness of his life as the maker of the trilogy. In fact, not only the trilogy but Beckett's entire work can be described, to borrow James Olney's words, as "a representation of the writer's life as writer" (342).

The first novel of the trilogy, *Molloy,* is divided into two sections related by two different narrators, Molloy and Moran. Both Molloy and Moran are writers who are now writing about a journey they have just completed. Both narratives are written in first person and linked together by a series of similar characters, incidents and peculiarities. As the physical journeys of the two narrators are linked with the artist's quest for a proper means of self expression, their failure to attain the objectives of their journeys reflects the plight of the artist who is doomed to failure.

The first narrator, Molloy, is an old man with a stiff leg who walks on crutches. He is toothless and he does not smell good. Molloy writes with great difficulty; writing is sheer torture for him: "What I'd like now is to speak of the things that are left, say my goodbyes, finish dying" (9).

Before beginning to relate his journey, Molloy identifies himself with his creator when he says: "I'll manage this time, then perhaps once more, then perhaps a last time, then nothing more" (10). As the author of the trilogy, he will first finish writing *Molloy*, then he will perhaps write *Malone Dies* ("perhaps once more") and then *The Unnamable* ("perhaps a last time").

After having identified himself with the author of the trilogy, Molloy begins to relate his journey towards his mother in first-person narration. The connection between one's point of origin and self is a time-honored analogy frequently encountered in the myths of the past, e.g. those surrounding Oedipus and Odysseus. Freudian psychology also maintains that an oedipal connection exists between self and mother—the source of one's origins and roots. In the light of these interpretations, it can be said that on one level, Molloy's journey to his mother represents a descent into the psyche, into the void of the self.

Throughout his narrative, Molloy poses ontological questions relating to the nature of the self, reality and human existence. He feels that his self is enveloped in a darkness that cannot be pierced: "My sense of identity was wrapped in a namelessness often hard to penetrate" (30). He describes his self as "all that inner space one never sees" (11) where "nothing stirs, has ever stirred, will ever stir" (38). Molloy's vision of the self is fragmented because he realizes that since the self exists in time, it is not a continuous and static entity. It is in fact in constant flux, changing with time and contingencies. Consequently, the essential components of one's own psyche or those of another can never be fully perceived or comprehended. In short, he realizes that the concept of a unified self is only a delusion: "Perhaps there is no whole, before you're dead" (27).

Molloy is painfully aware that given the impossibility of piercing the void that lies beyond human experience, the writer has nothing to say, and yet is still condemned to write to affirm his existence: "Not to want to say, not to know what you want to say, not to be able to say what you think you want to say, and never stop saying or, hardly ever, that is the thing to keep in mind, even in the heat of composition" (27). This passage is almost a pastiche of Beckett's enunciation of the artist's dilemma in *Three Dialogues with Georges Duthuit*: "The expression that there is nothing to express, nothing with which to express, nothing from which to express, no power to express, no desire to express, together with the obligation to express" (103). Even the rhythm of the two passages is similar.

In the course of his journey, Molloy's condition deteriorates rapidly. He cannot walk on crutches any more and begins to move on his stomach. The image of Molloy moving on his belly—a dim figure crawling in the dark—is one of Beckett's favorite metaphors for the impotent artist who is condemned to write in agony and desperation. By way of this image, it is also indicated that both the solitary wanderer's quest for self-actualization and that of the artist for his art will end in failure.

As Molloy's narrative progresses, we observe that fragmentation, contradiction and non sequitur constitute the stylistic norm of the text. Molloy continually interrupts the narrative to comment on either the fictional process or to express his thoughts and feelings which have no direct connection with the narrative being told. Hence, it becomes very difficult for the reader to make linguistic or narrative inferences. Contradictions which become more prevalent in the second part of *Molloy* set up another interpretive hurdle for the reader. When what is said is immediately contradicted, the reader tends to lose his way. One of the most striking contradictions in *Molloy* is Molloy's description of his journey or quest for his mother, which constitutes the gist of the text, as "unreal": "And this [the cries of the corncrakes] enables me to know when that unreal journey began" (17). This contrast is further reinforced and the reader is even more baffled when Molloy later says that he has never left his hometown: "I am in my town, after all, I have been there all the time" (56). The voice within him also confirms that he has never been on a journey: "Molloy, your region is vast, you have never left it and you never shall" (61). Contradictions such as this one undermine the intelligibility of the text through self-effacement or self-erasure. The overall effect then is one of uncertainty, confusion and a babble of words which do not mean much. As Michael Valdez Moses puts it: "By means of a dialectics without progression the text ultimately decomposes itself, announcing only to renounce, asserting only to deny" (670). In view of the above, it can be said that in *Molloy*, as in contemporary autobiography in general, the writer's split and fragmented self which lacks a central core is reflected in an equally fragmented and discontinuous discourse which further widens the gap between the self that writes and the self that is written.

The chronicle ends with the sentence, "Molloy could stay, where he happened to be" (84). This sudden shift from the first-person pronoun to the third-person pronoun accentuates Molloy's movement away from the self, the "I" that he set out to find and sought desperately throughout his narrative.

In part 2 of *Molloy*, the narrative voice shifts without any explanation or transition to another speaker, Moran Jacques, who is writing about his journey in search of Molloy. Moran is very apprehensive about his mission because he realizes that Molloy, far from being a stranger, was present within him before he began his search: "Molloy or Mollose was no stranger to me [. . .] Perhaps I had invented him, I mean I found him ready-made in my head" (103). He locates Molloy within the dark region of his mind where there is "finality without end" and where everything moves slowly: "All is dark, [. . .] From their places, masses move, stark as laws. Masses of what? One does not ask. There somewhere man is too, vast conglomerate of all nature's kingdoms, as lonely and as bound. And in that block the prey is lodged" (102).

The relationship between Molloy and Moran is obscure. Is Molloy Moran's repressed antithetical self which he is expected to seek and assimilate into his conscious apparent self? This question is raised throughout Moran's narrative but is left unanswered. The issue is further complicated when Moran realizes that, in fact, there are more than two Molloys: "The fact was there were three, no, four Molloys. He that inhabited me, my caricature of the same, Gaber's and the man of flesh and blood somewhere awaiting me" (106). As Molloy's self is disintegrated and dissolved into plurality, the presumed unity of the flesh-and-blood Molloy with a distinct personal identity is seriously challenged.

In Moran's story, many events and incidents in Molloy's journey are evoked and the two accounts become mirror images of one another, futilely reflecting the same episodes themselves in an endless chain of repetition. Moreover, as the point of view shifts from Molloy to Moran, and later as the two protagonists seem to be identical, the notion of a unified subject and the reality of subjectivity are contested. Moran's narrative finishes with: "It is midnight. The rain is beating on the windows. It was not midnight. It was not raining" (162). The last two sentences obliterate both Molloy's and Moran's stories of their journeys through direct negation. Consequently, their narratives are effaced and dismissed as fiction, artifice and lies.

As the quests of Molloy and Moran are linked with their quests as writers, their failure to attain the objectives of their journeys reflects the failure of the artist in quest of a form of expression. Faced with a world that resists interpretation, and with selves that cannot be pierced through, the two writers become, to borrow Beckett's words, "non-knowers or non-can-ers" (qtd. in Shenker 148) who can only succeed in pushing their narratives to the point of impossibility.

The protagonist of the second volume, *Malone Dies*, who is also a writer, is alone in a room, confined to his bed because he is paralysed from the waist down and unable to move more than a few inches. Like all the author-heroes in Beckett's fiction, he gropes in the dark, searching for words, phrases and images that would allow him to capture his selfhood. However, the "long blind road" he travels on has ended at an impasse (167) and he has fallen back into the darkness which shrouds the self. Malone describes the process of writing as "shapelessness and speechlessness, incurious wandering, darkness, long stumbling, [. . .] hiding" (166). "What tedium," "no, that won't do" and "no, I can't do it" are among the expressions Malone frequently uses. He urges himself to continue his stories with the help of his motto "We are getting on." As James Olney puts it,

> Malone as narrator is both a demonstration and the effect of the impossibility of narrative as experienced in Beckett [. . .] How can we locate ourselves in this farrago of stories, coming from we know not where and refusing to form themselves into a single story with a subject and a subjectivity—stories that will not cease nor cease proliferating but that will not offer us any focus of being either. (278)

As Malone tries to unfold the plots of his stories about the Saposcat family, the Lamberts and Macmann, the intricate relationship between writing and self-discovery turns out to be one of the major themes of the book as is the case in Beckett's entire fictional work. In Ruby Cohn's words: "Through the years, Beckett has hacked at his plots and characters; he has decimated his sentences and the number of his words, until he is left with a single protagonist in the generalized human situation, an 'I' in quest of his 'I' through fiction" (299).

Malone realizes that his efforts to create a fictional character independent of himself are futile. This is made clear when he says, "And on the threshold of being no more I succeed in being another" (178). He is also aware that in addition to his failure to depict the "other" without projecting himself onto him, he has not been able to locate his real, elusive self in any of his fictional characters: "After the fiasco, the solace, the repose, I began again, to try and live, cause to live, be another, in myself, in another" (179).

What Malone would really like to do is recreate his real self—as opposed to his pseudo-self which exists as Malone in the outside world—in writing: "My concern is not with me, but with another, far beneath me" (179-180). However, he is painfully aware of the impossibility of capturing his own self or the self of the other in the writing process: "Of myself I could never tell, any more than live or tell of others" (180). Realising that the "I" has no narrative, Malone resigns himself to what Beckett terms the "fidelity to failure" (*Three Dialogues* 125) which is the inevitable end for the writers who recognize the impossibility of ever piercing through the void that lies beyond their existence. Thus, Malone writes "no longer in order to succeed, but in order to fail" (179). He feels compelled to hold on to his motto, "Live and invent" (179), because the creative act is his only means of existence, that is, only through writing can he suspend the end of fiction and the end of Malone.

Malone uses Beckett's recurrent image of the artist as a foetal figure in the womb waiting to be born to describe himself: "Yes, an old foetus, that's what I am now, hoar and impotent [. . .] I shall never get born and therefore never get dead" (207). As he labors to be delivered, he both records his fragmentary memories of the past and writes stories that together provide material for his ceaseless monologue which seems to lead nowhere.

Malone Dies extends beyond itself to include Beckett's earlier fiction. Molloy is constantly evoked and there are also occasional references to the protagonists and secondary characters in the earlier *Murphy* and *Watt* interspersed throughout Malone's narrative. For example, he makes sporadic references to *Murphy* which imply that he existed under the persona of Murphy in the past (169, 170, 200). However, when Malone remembers the old butler in *Murphy*, who had committed suicide by cutting his throat with his razor, and maintains that he has killed him, he goes beyond identifying himself with Beckett's earlier characters; he claims to be their creator and thus merges into Beckett himself: "There was the old butler too, in London I think, there is London again, I cut his throat with his razor [. . .] It seems to me he had a name" (217).

In Malone's last story, one of the nurses of a mental hospital named Lemuel takes five inmates for an outing to the islands. The privileged inmates who are chosen to go on the excursion bear strong resemblances to Beckett's heroes, namely to Murphy, Watt, Molloy, Moran and Macmann and Malone describes them as "his creatures": "My creatures, what of them? Nothing. They are there, each as best he can, as best he can be somewhere" (262).

In the final part of the story, Lamuel murders the two sailors who were going to accompany them on their journey with his hatchet, he and his patients get into the boat and set out from the shore. In detached and fragmented phrases which trail off without any punctuation, Malone merges into Lemuel, perhaps a play on Samuel, Beckett's first name, and Lemuel's bloody hatchet is transformed into Malone's pencil: "He will not hit anyone any more, [. . .] with his hammer [. . .] or with his pencil or with his stick" (264). The writer can kill as well as create characters as Malone does when he destroys his "creatures" with Lemuel's hatchet, hammer or stick. At the end of *Malone Dies*, Malone perishes with his story but another weary voice talking incessantly from beyond the grave continues the writer's doomed quest for the self and for an appropriate artistic expression in *The Unnamable,* the last novel of the trilogy.

In *The Unnamable*, unlike Molloy and Malone, the speaker who narrates the story does not even have a name, the minimal sign of identity. From the 13-page introduction we learn that the Unnamable's impotence is more marked than that of his predecessors. While Molloy and Malone could force themselves into some sort of narrative, the Unnamable continually wanders around a dead circle he cannot bring to life. Even beginning his narrative is an insurmountable problem for him. Seeking for a point of departure, he says: "What am I to do, what shall I do, what should I do, in my situation, how proceed?" (267). Confused but in need of a beginning, he concludes: "But I have to begin. That is to say I have to go on" (270). 11 pages later, he is still in the throes of his introduction, saying, "I hope this preamble will soon come to an end" (277). His inability to begin mirrors his basic dilemma: the inability to do or say anything at all.

The information the Unnamable can give about the physical features of his locale is scanty. It is neither hot nor cold and probably without limits. It is illuminated by a grey light, at first murky, then opaque. The other inhabitants of the zone are his predecessors. "They are all here at least from Murphy on," he says (270). The presence of the other deceased heroes of Beckett suggests that the Unnamable exists beyond reality, beyond life even, in a kind of post-mortem state, but even this is difficult to ascertain since he does not know whether he is alive or dead. At times he speaks of his life as if it is over; at other times he thinks he is still living and hopes that death will bring him peace and solace. Now and then, he doubts if he has ever lived at all: "I don't know if I ever lived, I have really no opinion on the subject" (365).

Throughout his narrative, the Unnamable expresses his total frustration with words and as his story proceeds, he becomes more and more disillusioned with his failure in verbal expression. He defines language as a string of disconnected words devoid of meaning and content, as empty signs or ciphers unable to convey anything:

> that's all words they taught me, without making their meaning clear to me. I use them all, all the words they showed me, there were columns of them, oh the strange glow all of a sudden, they were on lists with images opposite [. . .] these nameless images I have, these imageless names. (375)

With disconnected words without relation to any pattern, the Unnamable cannot bring himself into being; that is, he cannot proceed from disjunct words to connected narrative, from the internal mass of subjectivity to externalised form.

As in *Molloy* and *Malone Dies*, the impossibility of knowing and defining the self is made a central issue in *The Unnamable*. The Unnamable's inability to decipher his identity becomes an obsession which torments him, and his anguish is effectively captured in the phrase, "I, of whom I know nothing" (279), which becomes a leitmotif in the text. As the narrative progresses, the speaker's despair over his lack of identity is intensified and he desperately wonders if he will ever be able to attain self-knowledge. "Shall I come upon my true countenance at last?" he asks himself (311). His split and fragmented self which he cannot conceptualize as a unified whole is revealed in his utterances like "I talking to me about me" (363) and "I am waiting for me there" (381). The Unnamable's voice drowns in the profusion of empty pronouns with no referents: "[. . .] it's the fault of the pronouns, there is no name for me, no pronoun for me, all the trouble comes from that" (372). As his "I," the telling subject and "me," the told object, can never be reconciled, he remains "unbeknown" to himself (348) and wonders, "how can I recognize myself who never made my acquaintance?" (366).

Like Molloy and Malone, the Unnamable identifies himself with Beckett, his creator, at the beginning of his story. He refers to Beckett's earlier protagonists as "my troop of lunatics" (282) and bewails the time he has wasted in writing their stories: "All these Murphys, Molloys and Malones do not fool me. They have made me waste my time, suffer for nothing, speak of them, when [. . .] I should have spoken of me and of me alone" (278). Like Malone, he had created his characters with the hope of slipping into them and recreating his self in writing, but now he thinks that his surrogates or "vice-existers" (289) have distanced him further from his self by assuming his identity and trying to persuade him that he was "they": "I am neither, I needn't say, Murphy, nor Watt, nor Mercier, nor-no, I can't even bring myself to name them, nor any of the others whose very names I forget, who told me I was they" (299). By trapping him in an identity that is not his, they have prevented him from writing the story of his "I," one which will enable him to ascertain his own existence:

It is of me now I must speak, even if I have to do it with their language, it will be a start, a step towards silence and the end of madness, the madness of having to speak and not being able to, except of things that don't concern me, that don't count, that I don't believe, that they have crammed me full of to prevent me from saying who I am, where I am, and from doing what I have to do. (297-298)

The Unnamable refers to his characters using derogatory terms, e.g. "poor bastards" (289), "the old gang" (299), "dirty pack of fake maniacs" (338), because they have put their words in his mouth and "blown him up with their voices, like a balloon" (298). Seeing that his characters fail to bring him into being, he decides to dispense with them so that he can talk about himself, instead of "they" talking about him: "I'll scatter them and their miscreated puppets. Perhaps I'll find traces of myself by the same occasion. That's decided then (298)."

One of Unnamable's stories is about a character named Mahood who seems to be another replicate of Molloy, Moran and Macmann. Similar to his predecessors, Mahood goes on a journey, crawling and dragging himself on his belly with great difficulty. Towards the end of his journey, his body is imprisoned in a huge jar where it becomes completely motionless:

> For of the great traveller I had been, on my hands and knees in the later stages, then crawling on my belly or rolling on the ground, only the trunk remains (in sorry trim), surmounted by the head with which we are already familiar [. . .] Stuck like a sheaf of flowers in a deep jar, its neck flush with my mouth, on the side of a quiet street near the shambles, I am at rest at last. (300)

Michael Robinson maintains that Mahood, in his state of stasis, is "the culmination of his predecessors attempts to eliminate everything superfluous to the self" (*Long Sonata* 197). Indeed the image calls to mind the self eternally fixed and imprisoned in the body from which it seeks release. The torso seems to stand for the shrunken remnant of the narrative as well as the narrator, the Unnamable, who is reduced to a head on a limbless trunk.

Realizing that he is in danger of believing that Mahood's stories are about himself, the Unnamable abandons Mahood: "[. . .] he says I as if he were I, I nearly believed him, do you hear him, as if he were I, I who am far, who can't move, can't be found" (371).

In the last section of the volume, the Unnamable begins a new story with a new surrogate for his "I": Worm. He decides not to use the first-person pronoun "I" in Worm's story on the grounds that it presupposes an identification with its antecedent and therefore confirms existence: "But enough of this cursed first person, it is really too red a herring" (315). He soon realizes, however, that it does not at all matter which pronoun he uses, as the antecedents of all pronouns are non-existent: "[N]o sense in bickering about pronouns and other parts of blather. The subject doesn't matter, there is none" (331).

Realizing that he cannot locate his self in Worm either, the Unnamable leaves this story unfinished as well. In the last section of the book, the Unnamable continually vacillates between Mahood and Worm, hoping that by the friction produced in the struggle of the two, he can bring forth himself. Finally he gives up this ruse, too, saying, "I'm something quite different, a quite different thing, a wordless thing in an empty place" (356).

Having dispersed "his few puppets [. . .] to the winds" (267), the Unnamable is reduced to "the image of a vast cretinous mouth, red, blubber and slobbering, in solitary confinement" (359). Unable to proceed with his quest for self, he ends his monologue by pointing to the impasse he finds himself in: "I can't go on. You must go on, I'll go on, you must say words as long as there are any, until they find me, until they say me, strange pain, strange sin [. . .] you must go on [. . .] I can't go on, I'll go on" (381-382).

At the beginning of his essay "What is an author?" Michel Foucault quotes Beckett: "'What does it matter who is speaking'" someone said, 'what does it matter who is speaking'" (174), and claims that this *indifference* is one of the fundamental principles of contemporary writing which dissociates itself from self-expression and refers only to itself:

> [I]t is an interplay of signs arranged less according to its signified content than according to the very nature of the signifier. Writing unfolds like a game that invariably goes beyond its own rules and transgresses its limits. In writing, the point is not to manifest or exalt the act of writing, nor is it to pin a subject within language; it is rather a question of creating a space into which the writing subject constantly disappears.
>
> (197)

In the trilogy, Molloy, Moran, Malone and the Unnamable are "writing subjects who constantly disappear into the space they create" through writing. Each author-hero annihilates the characters he has created when they fail to replicate his self, and perishes with them to begin again with another name and another voice in the next volume. Consequently, the trilogy, reflects a work in progress, never-ending, perpetually going on to depict the exasperated observations of its creator about the chaos of the self and the impossibility of constructing it in writing. As the "I" of Beckett disappears behind the author-heroes of the trilogy who are only masks or "Not Is," the reader is left with the image of Beckett surrounded by his "troop of lunatics" revisiting his career as a writer, recalling what he has done so far, failing and going on.

Works Cited

Beckett, Samuel. *Proust*. Dublin: Hely Thom, 1967.

___. *The Beckett Trilogy: Molloy. Malone Dies. The Unnamable.* 1952. London: Picador, 1979.
___. *Not I.* London: Faber and Faber, 1973.
___. *Three Dialogues with George Duthuit.* 1949. Dublin: Hely Thom, 1967.
___. *Watt.* 1953. New York: Grove, 1959.
___. *Worstward Ho.* London: John Calder, 1983.
Cohn, Ruby. *The Comic Gamut.* New Brunswick: Rutgers University Press, 1962.
Esslin, Martin. "Samuel Beckett—Infinity, Eternity." *Beckett at 80/Beckett in Context.* Ed. Enoch Brater. Oxford: Oxford University Press, 1986. 110-123.
Foucault, Michel. 1988. "What is an Author?" *Modern Criticism and Theory.* Ed. David Lodge. New York: Longman, 1989. 196-210.
Moses, Michael Valdez. "The Sadly Rejoicing Slave: Beckett, Joyce and Destructive Parody." *Modern Fiction Studies* 4 (Winter 1985): 658-680.
Olney, James. *Memory and Narrative: The Weave of Life-Writing.* Chicago, London: University of Chicago Press, 1998.
Robinson, Michael. "Beckett: At Another Impasse." *Journal of European Studies* 5 (1971): 353-361.
___. *The Long Sonata of the Dead.* London: Rupert Hart-Davis, 1969.
Shenker, Israel. "An Interview with Beckett." *Samuel Beckett: The Critical Heritage.* Ed. Lawrence Graver and Raymond Federman. London: Routledge and Kegan Paul, 1979. 146-149.

Art and Artifice
in Sylvia Plath's Self-Portrayals

Richard J. Larschan
University of Massachusetts

Abstract: Biographers often ascribe considerable psychological significance to two auto-biographical essays Plath wrote toward the end of her life. Ignoring purely literary conventions and commercial considerations in favor of theories about trauma-induced neuroses, some critics have detected deep-seated sources of resentment of her mother and feelings of displacement at the birth of her brother. Such explanations, however, disregard the immediate context within which Plath was working as a professional writer in early 1960s London. I myself largely discount such "deep psychic structures" in favor of more fully crediting Plath's imaginative powers and commercial instincts. While both "Ocean 1212W" and "America! America!" incorporate childhood experiences into miniature self-portraits of the nascent artist, in the former Plath transforms factual circumstances into an imaginatively compelling narrative, whereas in the latter she adopts a largely unpersuasive guise as the alienated anti-hero much in vogue at the time. Rather than allowing her imagination free rein to pursue enduring mythic truths, Plath coerces her powers of invention in the service of the marketplace. In neither case should we read these self-portrayals as literal autobiography.

> Nearly all her earlier writings (and definitely all the prose she wrote for publication) suffered from her ambition to see her work published in particular magazines, and her efforts to produce what the market seemed to require. [. . .] This campaign of willful ideas produced everything in her work that seems artificial.
>
> —Hughes, foreword xiii

> Those first nine years of my life sealed themselves off like a ship in a bottle—beautiful inaccessible, obsolete, a fine, white flying myth.
>
> —Plath, "Ocean 1212W" 26

In two autobiographical essays commissioned toward the end of her life, Sylvia Plath incorporates childhood experiences into miniature self-portraits of the nascent artist. But whereas "Ocean 1212W" transforms factual circumstances into an imaginatively compelling narrative, in "America! America!" Plath adopts a largely unpersuasive guise as the alienated anti-hero much in vogue at the time. Rather than allowing her imagination free rein to pursue enduring mythic truths as she does in "Ocean 1212W," in "America! America!" Plath coerces her powers of invention in the service of the marketplace.

In his introduction to the prose miscellany, *Johnny Panic and the Bible of Dreams*, Ted Hughes (5) rightly notes that "painful subjectivity" was Sylvia Plath's "real theme, and that the plunge into herself was her only real direction." He further remarks that, "the themes she found engaging enough to excite her concentration all turn out to be episodes from her own life; they are all autobiography"; though, he concedes, often "the sheer objective presence of things and happenings immobilized her fantasy and invention." In other words, her imagination encountered difficulties transforming personal experience into art—a dilemma that was only compounded when she was writing for the marketplace.

Plath herself was quite aware of the problem and as early as 1952 spoke of conscious efforts to transcend her actual experiences, noting at the end of a *Mademoiselle* story (Plath, *Johnny Panic* 295-312) that her summer jobs had provided a "variety of characters who manage to turn up dismembered, or otherwise in my stories." This was true not just of her fictional works but also of autobiographical pieces like "America! America!" and "Ocean 1212W," where she frequently sought opportunities to activate her imagination by appropriating the experience of others to embellish her own. Aurelia Plath knew well her daughter's customary habit of "rearranging truth for the sake of art," of "violating actual circumstances," and of "fusing characters and manipulating events to achieve her artistic ends" ("Letter" 289). This so-called "triple dicta" often entailed incorporating events from other people's lives to produce an amalgam that satisfied both artistic and commercial purposes—though not always with equal success.

Plath's renowned practicality has been well-documented—most recently in Diane Middlebrook's *Her Husband: Hughes and Plath—A Marriage*, citing a 1961 BBC radio interview in which Plath spoke light-heartedly of being "a little more practical" than her husband Ted ("Two"; qtd. in Middlebrook xvi). No doubt it was the quite *im*practical decision to forgo teaching in favor of full-time writing that prompted Plath's decision to deposit her earnings in America and her pay stubs in a scrapbook. Methodical saving was a habit that dated back to childhood—as Mrs. Plath remarked to me regarding Sylvia's earliest publications:

> "Every Sunday she looked for the children's page in the Boston *Herald*, which I had shown her in the newspaper. And she thought she'd send her [poem] in."
> "So, in other words, it was self-initiated?"
> "It was self-initiated."
> "And this is at the age of...?"
> "Oh, about 8."
> "That's very interesting because she's taking initiative and trying to get public recognition, it seems to me, at the age of 8.
> "Uh-huh."
> "Why else would you print something?"
> [Several second pause]. "She wanted the dollar."[1]

"She wanted the dollar"! Contrary to Christine Jeffs' depiction in the recent biopic, *Sylvia*, Plath was not raised in manorial grandeur attended by liveried servants—but neither was she the scion of working-

---

[1] These remarks were made in a conversation that took place in my home in Wellesley, Massachusetts taped on 3 Nov. 1986 in preparation for Mrs. Plath's televised appearance in *Voices and Visions: Sylvia Plath*, Lawrence Pitkethly, Producer (New York, 1987).

class stock. Her family was solidly middle class, both parents professional educators. If commercial considerations influenced Jeffs' decision to portray Plath forsaking opulence in the service of her Art, "America! America!" equally exaggerates her blue-collar background to capitalize on an early 60s vogue for anti-Establishment rebels. But rather than helping further Plath's "artistic ends," such "viola[tions of] actual circumstances" actually undermine them.

Writings by the so-called "angry young men"—John Osborne (*Look Back in Anger*, 1956), Alan Sillitoe (*Saturday Night and Sunday Morning*, 1958, and *Loneliness of the Long Distance Runner*, 1959), John Braine (*Room at the Top*, 1959), and Arnold Wesker (*Chips With Everything*, 1962)—had all featured young, working-class men who disdained the hypocrisy and self-satisfaction of England's political, social and intellectual Establishment. As Diane Middlebrook reminds us, "playwrights such as [. . .] John Osborne, and Arnold Wesker were [. . .] writing social commentary on the failure of the Labour government to reform postwar English society. Hughes and Plath took a professional interest in this new arena for writers" (134). According to Peter Stead (198), in *Film and the Working Class*, it was a time when "television personalities, politicians, academics, writers, designers, and photographers clung on in a wholly unprecedented way to their regional accents and identities. Quite simply the message [. . .] was that you could be talented and successful although you came from an unfashionable region or working-class community" (198). In particular, films like Alan Sillitoe's "*Saturday Night and Sunday Morning* had above all succeeded in mythologizing that crucial moment when the successful person comes to terms with what was best about the family and community whilst at the same time appreciating that his individuality and talent would now have to be tested in a wider world."still page 198? This same general trend discerned by John Russell Taylor in *Anger and After* included "increasing recourse to personal myth, possibly in a quasi-historical framework" (158).

At almost the same time Sylvia and Ted were befriending Alan Sillitoe and his wife, Ruth Fainlight, Plath declared to BBC interviewer Peter Orr, "I am not very genteel and I feel that gentility has a stranglehold: the neatness, the wonderful tidiness, which is so evident everywhere in England is perhaps more dangerous than it would appear on the surface" (interview 168-169). Indeed, this was the very danger Plath's poetry had been directly confronting in the weeks preceding her BBC interview. Keenly attuned to this *zeitgeist*, she endorsed contemporary challenges to the Establishment from a perspective neither fully English nor altogether American but, in Peter Orr's words, "straddling the Atlantic": "You, as a poet, as a person who straddles the Atlantic, if I can put it that way, being an American yourself..." (168). Acknowledging that rather "awkward position," it was one she nevertheless "accepted" because it affirmed her professed anti-Establishment-arianism. Though she lacked true working-class *bona fides*, in "America! America!" Plath self-consciously portrays her upbringing as that of a non-conformist outsider thrice over: as American, working class, and nascent artist.

She begins by differentiating the American concept of "public school"—not in the Etonian or Harrovian sense, but "genuinely public. *Everybody* went:"

> [. . .] the future electronic scientist, the future cop who would one night kick a diabetic to death under the mistaken impression he was a drunk and needed cooling off; the poor, smelling of sour wools and the ruinous baby at home and polyglot stew; the richer, with ratty fur collars, opal birthstone rings and daddies with cars ('Wot does *your* daddy do?' 'He don't woik, he's a bus droiver.'). ("America!" 53-56)

That was sure some rough neighborhood: Novice schoolyard bullies practicing how to pummel victims of diabetic shock, while the barely washed lorded it over the Great Unwashed. Precisely how even supposedly "polyglot" inhabitants of the Boston bedroom community of Winthrop, Massachusetts acquired New York accents we never do learn; but the purported economic deprivation of Plath's childhood is her entrée into the company of fellow working-class refugees like Sillitoe's Arthur Seaton, Osborne's Jimmy Porter, and Braine's Joe Lampton. Like them, she had grown up amidst dispirited tenement-dwellers who "slumped dumbly after work and frugal suppers over their radios"—her particular world populated by "a great loud cats' bag of Irish Catholics, German Jews, Swedes, Negroes, Italians and that rare, pure mayflower dropping, somebody *English*" ("America!" 52). But the "infant citizens" of the "rowdy seaside town" of Winthrop making that journey in "steerage" were always assured that "[i]f we worked. If we studied hard enough. Our accents, our money, our parents didn't matter. Did not lawyers rise from the loins of coalheavers, doctors from the bins of dustmen? Education was the answer" (53)—even for the daughter of two university professors like young Sylvia.

Moving from downtrodden Winthrop to affluent Wellesley, teenage Plath was soon beset by full-time guidance counselors discussing "motives, hopes, school subjects, jobs—and colleges," constantly warning against "eccentricities" and "the perils of being too special," "too dangerously brainy." "All-Rounded"-ness, they insisted, was the key: "My high, pure string of straight A's might, without proper extracurricular tempering, snap me into the void." Nonconformity was to be avoided at all costs: "There was no uniform, but there *was* a uniform—the pageboy hairdo, squeaky clean, the skirt and sweater, the 'loafers,' those scuffed copies of Indian moccasins" ("America!" 54).

Eager to be "tailored to an Okay Image," Plath describes being subjected to such ego-annihilating humiliations of sorority initiation as wearing no make-up and neither bathing, combing her hair, nor changing clothes for a week. Speaking with boys also was forbidden—though not insulting passers-by or begging rotten grapes and moldy rice from shopkeepers; and "[i]f I smiled—showed, that is, any sense of irony at my slavishness, I had to kneel on the public pavement and wipe the smile off my face." But isn't it precisely a sense of self-irony that this autobiographical account lacks? Rather, Plath's tone alternates between heavy-handed sarcasm and smug self-congratulation:[2]

> Somehow it didn't take—this initiation into the nihil of belonging. Maybe I was just too weird to begin with. What did these picked buds of American womanhood do at their sorority meetings? They ate cake; ate cake and catted about the Saturday night date. The privilege of being anybody was turning its other face—to the pressure of being everybody; ergo, no one. ("America!" 55).

In her closing paragraph Plath describes "lately" visiting an American primary school where "all the anarchism, discomfort and grit I so tenderly remembered had been, in a quarter century, gentled away" (52), supplanted by antiseptic "child-size desks and chairs in clean, light wood, toy stoves and minuscule drinking fountains," and where "reading (my lot did it by age four off soapbox tops) had become such a traumatic and stormy art one felt lucky to weather it by ten." More ominous still, she glimpses in the First Aid cabinet, "a sparkle of bottles—soothers and smootheners for the embryo rebel, the artist, the odd." "Soma," perhaps, from *Brave New World*? Or "Plan B" Levonorgestrel to thwart implantation in the womb of the body politic "the embryo rebel, the artist, the odd"?

In allying herself with fellow nonconformists like Seaton, Porter and Lampton, already we see Plath taking imaginative liberties—as she does again here with chronology. Because she had not visited the United States in over three years, her glimpse of an American primary school could not have occurred "lately" ("America!" 55). As for other supposed reminiscences, poetic license is likewise fully operational, starting with her representation of Winthrop socio-economics. Unless

---

[2] This difficulty with tone is illustrated by the responses of two early biographers, Linda Wagner-Martin and Anne Stevenson. The former detects in "America! America!" a "scathing exposé of American public education" (236); while the latter characterizes the piece as "a humorous reminiscence [. . .] about her schooling" (280).

ethnic cleansing had occurred before that "polyglot stew" of working class "poor, smelling of sour wools and the ruinous baby at home" (52) were attending Winthrop High School, their near-total absence from the 1950 school yearbook for Plath's putative graduating class is difficult to explain. Indeed, except for a somewhat higher proportion of recognizably Jewish surnames than in Plath's actual yearbook, the ethnic and racial demographics reflected by these two tomes are almost indistinguishable.

This admittedly imprecise calculus, even when supported anecdotally by Plath's childhood friend Ruth Geisler (née Freeman) and Town Historian David Hubbard, is better confirmed in official town records like *The Winthrop Comprehensive Community Survey Project* (Gordon and Gyurina) and *The History of Winthrop Massachusetts 1630-1952* (Clark). According to the former, even during the Great Depression, residential triple deckers, "an ingenious, highly effective way to house working class families in a manner that was both cost effective and desirable from the stand point of aesthetics" that was "extremely popular" in low income South Boston neighborhoods, "never caught on in Winthrop. The few 'three deckers' that were built in the town tend to be located at Winthrop Beach" (Gordon and Gyurina 41). Another significant socio-economic index is the prevalence of contagious disease, and according to *The History of Winthrop* "in 1933, when the state began a program for early detection of tuberculosis, no town or city was found with a lower tendency than Winthrop to this disease" (Clark 264).

The Town's relative prosperity, even during the worst years of the Great Depression, is likewise indicated by teachers' salaries, which remained comparatively stable or underwent pay cuts "not so drastic as the cuts in some other communities" (282).

At the same time, the Town's academic standing remained highly competitive:

Local representatives won the 1935 state-wide spelling championships for ninth and tenth grades, and the next year for tenth and eleventh grades and the grand championship as well. Winthrop received still wider recognition in 'The Nation's Schools,' which published a full article on the official opening of the Shirley Street School, which was in January, 1937, the month when salaries were restored to the pre-depression basis. (Clark 282)

That same year, as Plath prepared to enroll full-time in the Annie F. Warren Grammar School, the town's weekly newspaper, *The Sun*, proudly announced, "Winthrop Students Make Progress: Many Senior High Graduates Advancing in Major Colleges." Of 167 graduates, the paper reported nearly 10% had been accepted by the country's most prestigious Ivy League universities, including Harvard, M.I.T. and Dartmouth ("Winthrop Students").

Nor does Plath's description of "the richer [Winthrop residents], with ratty fur collars, opal birthstone rings and daddies with cars" tally with accounts of the three yacht clubs that for over 100 years had "not only been prominent in matters maritime but also play[ed] a leading part in many civic and social affairs." Indeed, according to the official tercentennial history, "Winthrop would not be Winthrop without its yacht clubs" ("Winthrop Yacht Clubs," Clark 264), just as *Wellesley's Centennial Story* depicts Plath's subsequent home town as "a shining new suburb with the very best of everything" (Hinchliffe 89). For all intents and purposes, the "rowdy seaside town" and the "shining new suburb" were not so very different. Moreover, if Plath was "just too weird" to fit into Wellesley's social scene, her two smiling photos in the 1950 *Wellesleyan* give little evidence. In one she is seated front-and-center among 59 fellow writers and reporters for the school's newspaper, the *Bradford*, all but nine of them female (*Welleseyan* 64); in the other, her broad smile is no less evident among the 33 members of the National Honor Society, 19 of them female (76). Not one person of color can be found in either photograph—or, for that matter, almost anywhere else in both yearbooks.

Clearly, then, it was not that "the sheer objective presence of things and happenings immobilized [Plath's] fantasy and invention" in "America! America!" so much as that "violat[ions of] actual circumstances" were more strongly influenced by commercial considerations than "artistic ends." The problem is not that Plath's self-portrayal was noticeably distorted—that is to be expected, perhaps even admired—but that she tried much too self-consciously to capitalize on the contemporary vogue for working class heroes and alienated artists.

How very different is her other autobiographical essay, "Ocean 1212W," which likewise freely embellishes childhood recollections—as when she describes the after-effects of a hurricane that left behind "a dead shark filled [in] what had been the geranium bed" (26). According to her mother "Sylvia didn't actually get to see the shark" that had been swept ashore by "a storm before she was born" (Larschan). But who really cares whether the shark discovered in her grandmother's garden was something Plath herself had actually witnessed, or was in fact something her mother had recounted from her own childhood a quarter-century earlier? Hurricanes! Dead sharks in flower beds! That's the sort of violence on which Plath's imagination thrived. As she acknowledges explicitly at the conclusion of her BBC radio presentation, "those first nine years of my life sealed themselves off like a ship in a bottle—beautiful, inaccessible, obsolete, a fine, white flying myth." These "mythic" features of Plath's autobiographical reminiscences exhibit the workings of her imagination as a means to convey emotional truths without the least attempt to encase her self-portrait in a ready-made frame.

That is not to say Plath's choice of incidents to color "Ocean 1212W" was altogether original. Another mythic childhood reminiscence broadcast over the BBC nearly two decades earlier comes immediately to mind—namely, "A Child's Christmas in Wales." Indeed, one can hear in "Ocean 1212W" certain resonance of Dylan Thomas' lyrical account of idealized childhood. A great admirer of Thomas (with whom she happened to share her October 27th birthday), Plath has created her own version of life by the "carol-singing sea": "A Child's Mythical Massachusetts." It is, to be sure, characteristically a somewhat less exuberant vision of the bygone past. But, like Thomas, Plath conveys her retrospection through a series of imaginatively reconstructed incidents common to childhood everywhere: beach combing for "the shell of a blue mussel with its rainbowy angel's fingernail interior," resentment over the arrival of a new sibling ("I hated babies"), swimming for the first time ("I should have sunk like a stone, but I didn't") and winter storms ("the sea molten, steely-slick, heaving at its leash like a broody animal, evil violets in its eye" ["Ocean" 25]).

Un-doubting Thomas, for his part, "plunge[d his] hands in the snow [to] bring out" childhood memories of "Mrs. Prothero and the firemen," jolly postmen "[w]ith sprinkling eyes and wind-cherried noses," and long lists of Christmas presents—both the "useful" ones and, more importantly, the "useless" ones (Thomas 2-3). Round-bellied Welsh uncles snoring by the fireside and Welsh aunts with a fondness for port are his endearing counterparts to the over-protective mother and clichéd, bread-baking Grammy summoned forth from the "vision" Plath "picks up," "like the purple 'lucky stones' I used to collect with a white ring all the way round" ("Ocean" 20).

Plath clearly invokes Thomas for the more playful features of "Ocean 1212W." The same childhood imagination responsible for envisioning snowy footprints left by Wellington boots as evidence of Giant Sloths and produced coloring books populated by "sky-blue sheep" likewise engenders 3-year-old Sylvia's earnest refusal to hide her grandfather's pipe in the rubber plant—"to make it a pipe tree." And the young savant in Thomas' story who knew so much about Trolls because "he was always reading" (Thomas 5) re-surfaces in Plath's narrative as "Harry Bean," "who knew with absolute assurance what lay behind the sea that cupped the bulge of the world like a blue coat"—"'Spain,' said owl-eyed Harry Bean, my friend" ("Ocean" 24).

Ignoring such purely literary conventions in favor of theories about Plath's emotionally damaged childhood, critics like Edward Butscher in *Sylvia Plath: Method and Madness* and Linda Bundtzen in *Plath's Incarnations* have scoured "Ocean 1212W" for deep-rooted psychological implications: resentment of her mother ("I should, according to Mother, have sunk like a stone, but I didn't" ["Ocean" 25]) or feelings of displacement at the birth of her brother ("I would be a bystander, a museum mammoth. Babies!" [23]). Citing Freud, Butscher asserts: "No amount of analysis or sophisticated detachment could conceal the obsessive absorption with a spoiled paradise. As Freud has observed, 'The unwelcome arrival of a baby brother or sister is the oldest and most burning question that assails immature humanity'" (7-8). Bundtzen, for her part, subscribes to Melanie Klein's theory about "persecutory anxiety"; that fearing loss "of connectedness to a benevolent and lovable outside force," Plath associated her mother with "the retaliating, devouring, and poisonous [bad] breast" rather than the nurturing "good breast" (97).

Langdon Hammer, on the other hand, maintains in "Plath's Lives" that "she is always reinventing herself in her texts" because "her writing is not an abstraction that has meaning independent of the [social] conditions of her life" (68). Agreeing with Hammer, I likewise largely discount "deep psychic structures or early childhood experience" in preference to more fully crediting Plath's "imaginative power" and commercial instincts. Moreover, Butscher and Buntzen seemingly ignore Plath's self-conscious use of hyperbole for self-ironic purposes. Their readings imply that in the final months of her life Plath had so far regressed emotionally that she was unable to recognize the absurd petulance manifested by her childish alter-ego: "I flung the starfish against a stone. Let it perish. It had no wit. I stubbed my toe on the round, blind stones. They paid no notice. They didn't care. I supposed they were happy" ("Ocean" 121). Such a woeful lack of self-awareness is altogether inconsistent with whimsical recollections of hiding pipes in rubber plants to make them into pipe trees. Nor does the standard portrayal of sibling resentment appear any less self-ironic than Plath's arch depiction of literal-minded Harry Bean—something her mother equally failed to recognize:

> She says in 'Ocean 1212W' that she never knew the baby was coming. She helped me get the clothes, and we talked about the baby coming before he was born. That I'd like to have stressed. And every time, she'd say, 'Not today!' Because she knew that I was going away to get the baby. But it wasn't one of these instances where she was kept in ignorance and then her grandmother told her in her Victorian way. It wasn't that at all.

There again, there's misrepresentation.[3]

All the psychoanalytic inferences about "Ocean 1212W" and defensive literalizing by her mother finally overlook the essay's imaginative appeal as a coming-of-age narrative and thus diminish Plath's captivating portrayal of shared human experience—in particular, loss of innocence. To turn the essay into a mere gloss on Freud or Klein ends up saying almost nothing about Plath as an artist—someone capable of transforming her own experience into "a fine, white flying myth" ("Ocean" 26).

Indeed, imaginative self-mythologizing abounds throughout the essay, starting with the narrator's matrilineal descent: "I recall my mother, a sea-girl herself, reading to me Matthew Arnold's 'Forsaken Merman'[. . .] a spark flew off Arnold and shook me, like a chill." Besides Matthew Arnold, Plath's mythical ancestry evokes Charles Darwin and William Butler Yeats. As a Mermaid, she hearkens back to other amphibians: "I crawled straight for the coming wave and was just through the wall of green when [mother] caught my heels [. . .] if I had managed to pierce that looking glass [. . .] would my infant gills

---

[3] These remarks were made in a conversation that took place in Aurelia Plath's home in Needham, Massachusetts taped on 30 Oct. 1986.

have taken over, the salt in my blood?" In turn, the "spark that shook [her] like a chill" ("Ocean" 21) resembles the "sudden blow" and "shudder in the loins" that engendered Helen of Troy in Yeats' "Leda and the Swan." Thus, "The motherly pulse of the sea" coursing through her veins confirms Plath an immortal from classical mythology—part human/part deity: in short, that is, an Artist.

Looking to her sea-mother for a "sign of election and specialness," Plath discovers "out of a pulp of kelp, still shining, with a wet, fresh smell"

> [A] monkey made of wood. Heavy with the water it had swallowed and scarred with tar, it crouched on its pedestal, remote and holy, long-muzzled and oddly foreign [. . .] It looked like no monkey I had ever seen eating peanuts and moony-foolish. It had the noble pose of a simian Thinker. I realize now that the totem I so lovingly undid from its caul of kelp [. . .] was a Sacred Baboon. So the sea, perceiving my need, had conferred a blessing. ("Ocean" 24)

And what was that blessing if not the imagination's power to decipher in life's flotsam and jetsam encoded messages from the gods? Plath's myth of childhood thus celebrates the artist's ability to transform our lowly ape-ancestry into idealized representations of Man, like Rodin's "Thinker"—yet without all the self-conscious posturing of "America! America!"

The sea's "blessing" here can in some ways be compared to that conferred by the landscape on Wordsworth in "Tintern Abbey." Like Wordsworth, Plath is only too aware that age brings what she terms, "that awful birthday of otherness": "As from a star I saw, coldly and soberly, the *separateness* of everything"; "my beautiful fusion with the things of this world was over" ("Ocean" 23). Her depiction is, of course, so much more consistently violent than Wordsworth's. But the Myth of Childhood and subsequent realizations are at least somewhat comparable. In both cases the child's "clouds of glory" are all-too-soon dissipated; and only the artist's creative imagination can help restore that earlier oneness with the universe. Wistfully recalling his former state, Wordsworth in "Tintern Abbey" concedes, "I cannot paint / What then I was" (lines 75-76). "That time is past, / And all its aching joys are now no more, / And all its dizzy raptures" (83-85)—of bygone childhood. In "Ocean 1212W," Plath invokes a similar mythos of childhood, and to much the same purpose.

Immersed in the world's "getting-and-spending," their imaginative powers laid waste, adults in "Ocean 1212W" lack the artist's transcendent immersion in the life-threatening/life-affirming mythicised sea. Not seawalls, not whiskbrooms, not even maternal love—only the artist's imagination can transcend the chaos of human existence by creating again that oneness with the universe experienced in childhood. Thus, so far from "immobilizing" Plath's "fantasy and invention," as Ted Hughes once claimed, the "objective presence of things and happenings" in "Ocean 1212W" actually propels her triumphant imagination toward a re-telling of the Eden Myth. The crucial distinction between Plath's two self-portraits is that factual distortions in "America! America!" were more influenced by commercial considerations than artistic need. Self-consciously attempting to capitalize on a popular vogue for anti-heroes, Plath lost sight of the emotional truths she successfully conveyed in "Ocean1212W." To me, it is in the dynamic interplay between Plath's "fantasy and invention" and objective things and happenings that we can begin to understand characteristic workings of her imagination at its creative best. Rather than subordinating her powers of invention to the needs of the unsacred baboon marketplace, she uses them to "order, reform, relearn and re-love people and the world as they are and as they might be" (*Journals of Sylvia Plath*, ed. Kukil, 436)—a considerable blessing not just to Sylvia Plath but to anyone who reads her best work.

Works Cited

Bundtzen, Lynda K. *Plath's Incarnations: Woman and the Creative Process.* Ann Arbor, Michigan: University of Michigan Press, 1983.

Butscher, Edward. *Sylvia Plath: Method and Madness.* New York: Simon & Schuster, 1976.

Clark, William H., ed. *A History of Winthrop Massachusetts 1630-1952*, Winthrop, Mass: Winthrop Centennial Committee, 1952.

The Echo: Winthrop High School Yearbook. Winthorp, Mass., 1950.

Geisler, Ruth (née Freeman). Conversation in Plath's childhood home at 26 Elmwood Road. 7 Nov. 2005.

Gordon, Ed, and Stephen Gyurina. *The Winthrop Comprehensive Community Survey Project.* Winthrop, Mass., 1994.

Hammer, Langdon. "Plath's Lives," *Representations* 75 (Summer 2001): 61-88.

Hinchliffe, Elizabeth M. *Five Pounds Currency, Three Pounds Corn: Wellesley's Centennial Story.* Wellesley, Mass.: Town of Wellesley, 1981.

Hubbard, David. Telephone interview. 11 Oct. 2005.

Hughes, Ted. Foreword. *Journals of Sylvia Plath.* Ed. Hughes and McCullough. xiii-xv.

___. Introduction. *Johnny Panic* 1-9.

Larschan, Richard. Program 8: "Sylvia Plath and the Myth of the Monstrous Mother." Poets of New England (video series). Amherst: University of Massachusetts. Academic Instructional Media Services, 2001.

Orr, Peter, ed. *The Poet Speaks: Interviews with Contemporary Poets Conducted by Hilary Morris, Peter Orr, John Press and Ian Scott-Kilvert.* London: Routledge & Kegan, 1966.

Plath, Aurelia. "Letter Written in the Actuality of Spring." *Ariel Ascending.* Ed. Paul Alexander. New York: Harper & Row, 1985. 208-213.

Plath, Sylvia. "America! America!" *Johnny Panic.* By Plath. 53-56.

___. *Johnny Panic and the Bible of Dreams*. Ed Ted Hughes. New York: Harper and Row, 1979.
___. *The Journals of Sylvia Plath*. Ed. Ted Hughes and Frances McCullough. New York: Ballantine, 1982.
___. *The Journals of Sylvia Plath 1950-1962*. Ed. Karen V. Kukil. London: Faber and Faber, 2000.
___. Interview. Orr 167-172.
___. *Letters Home: Correspondence 1950-1963*. Ed. with commentary by Aurelia Schober Plath. London: Faber and Faber, 1975.
___. "Ocean 1212W." *Johnny Panic*. By Plath. 21-27.
Mademoiselle. Aug. 1952: College Number 87-95. Rpt. *Johnny Panic*. By Sylvia Plath. 295-312
Middlebrook, Diane. *Her Husband: Hughes and Plath—A Marriage*. New York: Penguin, 2003.
Stead, Peter. *Film and the Working Class*. London and New York: Routledge, 1989.
Stevenson, Anne. *Bitter Fame: A Life of Sylvia Plath*. Boston: Houghton Mifflin, 1989.
Taylor, John Russell. *Anger and After: A Guide to the New British Drama*. London: Methuen, 1977.
Thomas, Dylan. *A Child's Christmas in Wales*: New York: New Directions, 1954.
"Two of a Kind: Poets in Partnership." Ted Hughes and Sylvia Plath interviewed by Owen Leeming. 18 Jan. 1961. Transcript. British Library.
Wagner-Martin, Linda. *Sylvia Plath : A Biography*. New York: Simon & Schuster, 1987.
The Welleseyan: Wellesley High School Yearbook. Wellesley, Mass., 1950.
"Winthrop Students Make Progress: Many Senior High Graduates Advancing in Major Colleges." *Sun* 13 Feb. 1937: B: 6.

Auto/biography, Knowledge, and Representation: The Theory and Practice of Filial Narrative

G. Thomas Couser
Hofstra University

Abstract: In mid-life and in mid- to late career, I have undertaken two related projects. One is a survey and analysis of what I call narratives of filiation (memoirs of fathers by sons and daughters). (In North America, a significant number of these have been published since 1980 or so.) The other is a memoir of my own father, William Griffith Couser (1906-1975), with emphasis on discrete periods of his life before he had children.

In pursuing the latter project, I have worked from papers I found among his effects when he died thirty years ago. What I am writing is obviously a relational narrative, which grows out of my complicated relationship with a somewhat distant father. Yet it is not a memoir in the literal meaning of that word, since it is not based on memory. Rather, his experience is mediated primarily through the papers he left behind.

Through this complex process of mediation, I have come to know my father better some thirty years after his death than I did when he was alive and present to me. My paper will reflect on this process and what it may tell us about auto/biography not as a means of *representing* another but as a way of *knowing* that person—an aspect of life writing that I think is ripe for discussion.

In mid-life and in late career, I have undertaken two related projects. One is a survey and analysis of filial narratives (that is, memoirs of fathers by sons or daughters) produced in North America in the last 25 years. The other is a memoir of my own father, William Griffith Couse r, with emphasis on discrete periods of his life before he married and had children.

The academic project grew more or less organically out of my interest in relational life writing—hence the slash in "auto/biography" in my title, indicating the double focus of this kind of life writing. The personal project is a total departure for me; I have never done any sustained life writing, and I never thought I would. However, for reasons I probably do not fully comprehend and therefore will not try to articulate here, I recently retrieved from my attic a cache of paternal papers that I discovered when my father died in 1975 at the relatively young age of 69. Most of these papers—and the most interesting of them—are letters that he wrote. One significant batch of papers includes letters, saved by his family, that he sent home from Syria, where he taught English at Aleppo College in the early 1930s, not long after he graduated from college. Another significant batch comprises letters he wrote to my mother from the South Pacific, where he served in the U.S. Navy during World War II. I read through all of these papers with fascination shortly after his death; I then laid them aside, not to look at them again for fully thirty years.

Not long after my father died, I began writing my dissertation; my subject was American autobiography, and I made that my academic specialization, broadening my scope eventually to include other forms of life writing as well. A few years ago, I began to notice an emerging corpus of contemporary memoirs: narratives of fathers, or filial memoirs. I quite quickly worked up a bibliography of nearly 100 such narratives published since about 1980. Despite the increasing currency of such memoirs, some of which have been prominently reviewed, the phenomenon as a whole has gone largely unnoticed by critics of life writing.

So I have begun to survey them. The American fathers whose lives have been represented by their offspring are diverse in race, ethnicity, and social class. And yet, as is usually the case with published autobiography, there are significant demographic patterns within the literature. A primary factor in much published filial narrative is, not surprisingly, the father's celebrity, which, after all, creates a potential reading audience and thus, from a publisher's point of view, a market. Perhaps the most prominent (but not the largest) cluster of texts, then, comprises those devoted to fathers who were also famous public figures. These include the psychologist Erik Erikson (Bloland), the comedian Bob Elliott of the comedy team Bob and Ray (Elliott); the painter Philip Guston (Mayer); the movie star Yul Brynner (Brynner);

the movie star and U.S. President Ronald Reagan (Davis and Reagan), and the architect Louis Kahn—in this case, appropriately, in the form of a documentary film (Kahn). Infamous fathers have also prompted filial narratives; for example, in variants of apologia Alger Hiss' and Julius Rosenberg's sons (Tony Hiss and Robert Meeropol) have defended them post-humously against charges of treason and espionage. Whether famous or infamous, these fathers are "biography-worthy" in their own right, and this set of texts foregrounds relations among filial loyalty, historical truth, and ethical judgment.

Another prominent cluster comprises narratives about well-known *writers*; these include John Cheever, James Dickey, Dashiell Hammett, J. D. Salinger, and Bernard Malamud (Smith). Because writers may achieve celebrity without leading public lives, their sons and daughters have more freedom to define their subjects. But writing their lives may entail a degree of public exposure that the fathers may not have desired and may in fact have resisted. (This is most obvious in the case of Salinger, who managed to squelch a biography by Ian Hamilton but could not prevent his daughter Margaret from publishing her memoir of him.) Thus, although these writers were public figures, these memoirs raise questions as to the seemliness of breaching their privacy. It is one thing for a professional biographer to do this; it's another for a son or daughter.

A complementary cluster of filial narratives consists of memoirs *by* famous writers; these writers include Philip Roth, Mary Gordon, Paul Auster, Sue Miller, Calvin Trillin, John Edgar Wideman, and the Wolff (half-)brothers—Tobias and Geoffrey. Rather than growing up in the shadow of famous fathers, these sons and daughters endow a kind of second-order celebrity on their otherwise obscure, and thus not biography-worthy, fathers. Among the most self-reflexive examples of filial memoir, these narratives expand the formal repertoire of the genre, setting a literary standard to which it may aspire.

Another cluster, narratives of senile fathers (e.g. Cohen), reflects another underlying demographic factor in the emergence of this form of narrative around the turn of the twenty-first century: the ageing of the baby-boom generation. As their parents grow old, dependent, and die, baby-boomers confront their own mortality and ponder their parenting. This sub-genre raises perplexing ethical issues: how much of a parent's decline into senility is it decent to reveal? How does an adult child avoid gratuitously patronizing a demented parent?

Still another significant cluster emerges from sons and daughters who narrate their fathers' wartime experiences (mostly during World War II but recently also the war in Viet Nam). This is where my academic project most obviously overlaps with and stimulates my personal project. Although my father rarely talked about his experience in WW II when I was growing up, I sensed that it was one of the most important, and gratifying, episodes in his life. Whether those wars occurred before or after the birth of the children, those children have no direct knowledge of that stage of their fathers' lives; thus, these narratives foreground epistemological issues inherent in the genre as a whole: how can a "memoir" recount experience of which the author has no personal memory? Indeed, how, and how well, can a child know a father in any case?

My research so far suggests that the predominance of narratives of fathers is a result not of the domination of mothers by fathers, but rather of the relative inaccessibility of fathers to their children. When children write a parent's life, it seems, they feel compelled to write memoirs of the more distant parent. This explains why my working title for this project is "Claiming Paternity": I see the writing of the narratives as a way of enacting a relationship with the parent who seemed less available to the author. Thus, although I see the genre as a product of patriarchy, it is hardly a patriarchal genre.

The genre interests me in part because of challenges peculiar to it as a distinctive form of life writing. Sons and daughters usually have personal, private, and often intimate knowledge of their fathers; in any case, they have a direct (usually biological) connection with them that patriarchy and patrilineality endow with great significance. This first-hand experience and this (usually) genetic connection motivate and justify their memoirs. And yet children come to exist only after a good portion of their fathers' lives is over; thus, children have no direct experience of their fathers' formative, and sometimes most interesting, years. In any case, they know their fathers first as their fathers; only late in their fathers' lives, if at all, are children able to interact with and assess their fathers as fellow adults. Much of the lure of the genre, both for its writers and its readers, has to do with this inherent aporia, which tantalizes and defies children. That is, built into the genre, and to a large degree motivating it, is the discrepancy between the apparently direct and intimate connection between fathers and their children, on the one hand, and the adult children's sense of the fundamental inaccessibility of key features of their fathers' lives and selves, on the other. The genre can be seen as emerging from, and attempting to fill in or close, that gap.

That is certainly the case with me. In beginning my own narrative, I have certainly been seeking to come to terms with a man who baffled me in many ways and from whom I felt quite distant from puberty on; if it is possible to repair a relationship with a dead parent, I suppose I am trying to do that as well. What I am writing, then, is a narrative that was belatedly stimulated by my complicated relationship with a distant father. Yet it is not simply a memoir in the literal meaning of that word. What I have written so far is not based on memory in either of the usual two senses: I have no personal memory of the two periods that concern me initially (the early 1930s and the early 1940s) since I did not exist then; furthermore, since my father did not speak frequently or extensively of those times, I cannot even claim to be passing along his memories. Rather, my sense of his experience is mediated primarily through the papers he left behind when he died. My method is thus more that of biography than that of memoir. The papers represent a somewhat miscellaneous, but by no means random, selection; in effect, my father was his own archivist, and he clearly kept only documents that were significant to him. Although I have no sense that he was compiling a dossier for me to discover—that he intended to communicate with me through these documents—I feel that they are in effect my patrimony, my most significant inheritance from him. And, as I have hinted, I suppose I am, at least indirectly, seeking to understand my self as well as my father—my self through my relationship with my father. To coin a phrase: my father, my self. So while my *method* may be biographical, my *motives* are not: hence "auto-slash-biography."

To some extent this method sidesteps problems of memory. My father's epistolary testimony is in a sense "im-mediate"; it was produced in the midst of the events in question, rather than recounted retrospectively. At the same time, however, his letters are undeniably shaped by his sense of his audience (usually his parents). Thus, his contemporary testimony is always already relationally mediated; he was at pains to represent himself as a dutiful son, a role that he probably felt more intensely as the oldest child and the first to leave home.

Fortunately, I have not had to rely solely on his letters; I have used other sources as well. Although I sometimes wish I had embarked on this project decades earlier, when I might have been able to interview people who have since died (including three of his four younger siblings), I realize that I did not do so in part because I was not emotionally ready. I turned to this project only when I sensed I was personally, as well as professionally, prepared. One unanticipated benefit of my procrastination has been the advent of the internet, which makes it possible to trace individuals and identify place names and other obscure references with relative ease and amazing speed. Using the internet—googling with glee—I have been able to track down information that I would never have had the patience or skill to locate using conventional research aids. Even where the internet does not allow direct access to the information I need, it often helps to locate non-electronic resources; using it, I have identified valuable archives that I would otherwise not have been aware of.

Primary-source research, assisted by the internet, then, has been a great help in enabling me to contextualize, and thereby better understand, my father's time in Aleppo. For example, I managed to locate and read an obscure memoir by a former president of Aleppo college, Alford Carleton—a man I remember visiting our home when I was growing up; though his memoir does not mention my father, it helped me understand the mission of the college and thus my father's experience there. I say "mission" advisedly, for Aleppo College (along with the American University of Beirut, which was originally known as Syrian Protestant College) was run by the American Board of Commissioners for Foreign Missions (ABCFM), an organization founded by New England protestants in the early 1800s.

Although I had known from childhood that my father had taught at Aleppo College—in large part because as a family we socialized with the families of several of his students, who had emigrated to New England—I had not been aware that he had been, at least nominally, a missionary. It was only after he died that I discovered that fact, and at the time I had trouble reconciling the term 'missionary' with my sense of my father as a not particularly religious man, certainly not a man with an evangelical passion. When I was growing up in the 1950s, we were a church-going family, like so many other suburban middle-class families. But neither of my parents, both secondary school teachers, seemed overtly religious. They seemed impelled not by deep piety but by the desire, in the formula of the day, to be a family that stayed together because it prayed together.

It was clear from my father's letters that he found teaching in Aleppo highly gratifying, but it was not immediately clear why. It is only in exploring his life as a biographer that I have come to understand what he and his colleagues spoke of reverentially as "the work." The ABCFM was not, at least from the late-nineteenth century on, a proselytizing institution; rather, it focused on founding, staffing, and developing educational and humanitarian institutions, especially schools and hospitals. And therein lies the resolution to the conundrum of my father the missionary, whose duties were purely academic and athletic, teaching and coaching. Three distinctive features of the College help to explain why he found teaching there so gratifying—indeed, far more so than the teaching he did in the States before and after his Syrian sojourn. One was that Aleppo College considered itself an "Opportunity College"; that is, it was oriented to students of limited financial means. (Indeed, when my father was there, the student body consisted overwhelmingly of Armenians who had been displaced during World War I.) Second, its educational philosophy was very progressive. Rather than the standard lecture and recitation method, which emphasizes the transfer of information from teacher to student, the basic instructional method at the College was "supervised study." According to its bulletin, the goal was a "constant, continuous, co-operative, democratic, friendly, and human relationship between teacher and student." Third, and most significantly, the religious curriculum was, for a "mission school," very ecumenical. Although students in this era were compelled to take a religion class, the course bulletins reveal that the curriculum covered not only the Old and New Testaments (or Hebrew and Christian Scripture) but an introduction to the Qur'an. Knowing this, I can better reconcile my sense of the man I knew as my own secondary school English teacher with the young "missionary" in Syria.

In addition to Carleton's memoir, I came across two memoirs by an Anglo-Armenian woman, Taqui Altounyan, who grew up in Aleppo and who, it turns out, knew my father. Taqui Altounyan's father and grandfather were Armenian physicians who practiced in Aleppo; indeed, her grandfather had founded the hospital there. At the core of a small Anglophone community, the Altounyans had befriended my father, who became an occasional dinner and holiday guest. Reading Taqui's memoir *In Aleppo Once*, I was startled, but quite delighted to learn that, as a teenager, she had developed a crush on my father. Here is a passage from her memoir in which she cites the diary she kept in 1930, when my father was 24 and Taqui was in her early teens:

That autumn there was also Mr. C., a new teacher in the boys' school, who, of course, came under our microscope, or rather, our distorting magnifying glass. [My sister] and I agreed that he was "Abstract noun. Common gender. Objective case. Very intransitive verb. Most passive voice." But he was very probably an ordinary, perhaps rather shy, young man, who was not particularly interested in girls of fourteen and under. My diary is full of scathing remarks about "grown-ups"—the clothes and hats they wore, the things they said. Everyone was either a friend or an enemy, and there were no half-tones. Young men were usually silly, but I was interested in Mr. C., the games master. I could usually catch sight of him in the distance, from our tennis court, drilling the boys in a neighbouring field. My diary is severe: "After the Christmas party charades Mr. C. came out of his shell amazingly. He even dared to bang on the table." Whenever we met I would be aggressive. He did not know how to take me, having no idea what I was feeling. Later I sent him cards from boarding school and he sent me one, which I treasured for a long time. (154-155)

How interesting that the man who taught me all the grammar I know should be sized up by a teenaged admirer in a grammatical code! While I am relieved to learn that my father was *not* interested in teenaged girls, I am glad that he made such an impression, happier that Taqui recorded her impression—first in her diary, then in her memoir—and thus endowed him with a kind of cryptic immortality some thirty-five years after they met. I only wish my father had come across the passage himself. All of this is to say—and, I hope, to show—that my research, initially stimulated by my father's "dead letters" but going well beyond them, has enabled me to flesh out a narrative, or at least a portrait, of this formative phase of his life.

My work *on* life writing has mainly focused on issues of representation and, especially lately, on ethical issues in the representation of vulnerable others. These issues continue to interest me. But my work *at* life writing has helped me, or perhaps forced me, to understand it differently: not as a means of *representing* someone, but as a means of *understanding* someone—a related but distinct activity. I, and many other critics of the genres that make up life writing, have probably been insufficiently attentive to the extent to which life writing is undertaken as a means to this relational end; that is, as a way of *knowing* the other. In any case, through the complex process of mediation involved in my own life writing project, and in ways that I neither expected nor as yet fully understand, I feel I have come to know my father better some thirty years after his death than I did when he was alive and present to me.

Works Cited

Altounyan. Taqui. *In Aleppo Once*. London: J. Murray, 1969.
Auster, Paul. *The Invention of Solitude*. New York: SUN, 1982.
Bloland, Sue Erikson. *In the Shadow of Fame: A Memoir by the Daughter of Erik H. Erikson*. New York: Viking, 2005.
Brynner, Rock. *Yul: The Man Who Would Be King: A Memoir of Father and Son*. New York: Simon and Schuster, 1989.
Carleton, Alford. *Vagaries of a Missionary Career: Recollections and Reflections*. United Church Board, 1983.
Cheever, Susan. *Home Before Dark*. Boston: Houghton, 1984.
Cohen, Elizabeth. *The House on Beartown Road: A Memoir of Learning and Forgetting*. Random House, 2003.
Davis, Patti. *The Long Goodbye*. New York: Knopf, 2004.
Dickey, Christopher. *Summer of Deliverance: A Memoir of Father and Son*. New York: Simon and Schuster, 1998.
Elliott, Chris. *Daddy's Boy: A Son's Shocking Account of Life with a Famous Father*. With Rebuttals by Bob Elliott. New York: Delacorte, 1989.

Gordon, Mary. *The Shadow Man*. New York: Random, 1996.
Hammett, Jo. *Dashiell Hammett: A Daughter Remembers*. Ed. Richard Layman, with Julie M. Rivett. New York: Carroll and Graf, 2001.
Hiss, Tony. *The View from Alger's Window*. New York: Knopf, 1999.
Kahn, Nathaniel, dir. *My Architect: A Son's Journey*. New Yorker Video. 2003.
Mayer, Musa. *Night Studio: A Memoir of Philip Guston*. New York: Knopf, 1988.
Meeropol, Robert. *An Execution in the Family: One Son's Journey*. New York: St. Martin's, 2003.
Miller, Sue. *The Story of My Father: A Memoir*. New York: Knopf, 2003.
Roth, Philip. *Patrimony: A True Story*. New York: Simon and Schuster, 1991.
Reagan, Maureen. *First Father, First Daughter: A Memoir*. Boston: Little, Brown, 1989.
Salinger, Margaret. *Dreamcatcher: A Memoir*. New York: Washington Square, 2000.
Smith, Janna Malamud. *My Father Is a Book*. Boston: Houghton Mifflin, 2006.
Trillin, Calvin. *Messages from My Father*. New York: Farrar, Straus, Giroux, 1996.
Wideman, John Edgar. *Fatheralong: A Meditation on Fathers and Sons, Race and Society*. New York: Pantheon, 1994.
Wolff, Geoffrey. *The Duke of Deception: Memories of My Father*. New York: Penguin, 1986.
Wolff, Tobias. *This Boy's Life: A Memoir*. New York: Grove, 1989.

Anglo-American Women Travellers Writing on the Self and on Oriental Women

Tea Jansson
University of Tampere

Abstract: Late nineteenth-century British and American women travel writers of the Orient represent nationality in distinctive ways which are affected by the gendering of nationality and the differences and interconnections between Britishness and Americanness. They construct Britishness and Americanness simultaneously as they construct the Orient and Orientalness. In women's travel writing, the expectations for the genre and the expectations placed on women's writing are combined, and writers need to accommodate themselves both to the genre and to gendered expectations. Women have a differently gendered position within the masculine genre of travel writing than men, and thus they apply specific strategies in legitimising their writing, involving for example the qualities of femininity and domesticity.

Introduction

In this article I will discuss the ways Anglo-American women travel writers participate in producing nationhood, Britishness, and Americaness while constructing the Orient and Orientalness; thus, the main theme that runs through my treatment of the representations of the self are these national and cultural differences. The definitions of West and East in the American and British contexts are permanently in flux: there are significant differences between the positions of the United States and Britain in the imperial, colonial and Oriental discourses.

I will focus on travelogues written in the late nineteenth century, and analyse briefly Sophia Poole's *The Englishwoman in Egypt: Letters from Cairo Written During a Residence There in 1842-46* (1848), Mary Eliza Rogers' *Domestic Life in Palestine* (1862), and Caroline Paine's *Tent to Harem: Notes of an Oriental Trip* (1859).

According to its preface, Poole's *The Englishwoman in Egypt* focuses on the feminine side of the Orient and Oriental women,[1] and was written as a companion to her brother's, the well-known British Arabist, Edward William Lane's, *Account of the Manners and Customs of Modern Egyptians*. Rogers, who was the sister of the British consul in Palestine, kept a journal of her stay, which she later on edited into the published volume *Domestic Life in Palestine*. The American traveller Caroline Paine's only published text is *Tent to Harem*, in which she depicts her travels across Egyptian North Africa and Turkey in 1850 and 1851. The mid-nineteenth century was a particularly important time in travel writing, because after the 1830s international travel started to become accessible owing to the use of steam liners and railroads, and acceptable for upper- and middle-class women (Schriber 2).

Women writers' gendered position sets them apart within the masculine genre of travel writing, and thus they apply different strategies in writing their travelogues. In this article, I will look at some of these strategies women utilise to legitimise their writing. In women's travel writing, the expectations for the genre and the expectations placed on women's writing are combined, and women writers need to accommodate themselves both to the genre and to gendered expectations. The discourse of Orientalism is closely connected with the genre of travel writing: there were many travelogues on the Orient and they were considered influential in producing knowledge on the East within the Western discourse of Orientalism. Thus, women writers need to situate themselves in relation to Orientalism as well. Discourses such as Orientalism need to be considered from two viewpoints: those of subjects as discourse users and of subjects as structured by discourse (Gough and McFadden). I also acknowledge that subjects are always to some extent constrained within the authoritative hegemonic discourses.

---

[1] This feminine side of the Orient is often linked with the domestic sphere and domesticity.

Representations of Nationality and Femininity

The often-used term 'Anglo-American traveller' is ambiguous, since there is no such unified concept: there are national and cultural differences between British (English) and American travel writing. The tradition of British women's travel writing seems to be more researched and the number of writers larger than in the American tradition.[2] However, the three women travel writers discussed in this article have not been studied extensively: it is illustrative that, although there is only some research on Poole and Rogers, virtually nothing is known about Paine.

The concept of Anglo-American has its relevance in emphasising the relation between the American and English travellers, their definitions and self-definitions. It should be borne in mind that the cultural contexts of the USA and Britain differ in relation to imperialism and colonialism, but the position of American travel writers is defined in many ways in relation to the English. According to Christopher Mulvey, who takes nationality as the main point of reference,[3] there was a fundamental difference between the American and English traveller in the nineteenth century: the English had a globally unique position as the most successful nation during the previous century. This refers to the commercial success of the British, but also to their imperial control. However, this also leaves room for another nation being even more successful in the future. Because of this situation, the American traveller felt both "admiration and contempt" for the English (Mulvey 3). In general, a distancing from England as the former coloniser was important when forming a new national identity through, for example, literature. Thus the American traveller had to oscillate between identification with the English and distinction from them. Mulvey adds that

---

[2] Mary Suzanne Schriber's *Writing Home: American Women Abroad 1830-1920* is one of the few comprehensive analyses of American women travellers. She has counted at least 195 travelogues written by women between 1830 and 1900.

[3] Mulvey does not address the question of gender when discussing the national differences between British and American travellers.

the American traveller also experienced cultural inferiority in comparison to the Europeans, because of the relatively meagre history of American culture (4, 6). In the colonial context, the English were doubtlessly in the hegemonic position as the colonisers, whereas historically America, although now independent, had been colonised, and controlled by the mother country. Within the American context, the colonisation of Native Americans by the white European settlers, and the history of slavery hierarchically position the white population as the superior and privileged part of the nation. Thus it is interesting to see in what kind of position the American traveller can situate him/herself in relation to the Orient and Orientals, the British and other Europeans. This ambiguous relationship between Americans and Europeans manifests itself occasionally in the American traveller Caroline Paine's writing. When she writes that the consular houses in Cairo are "too European to suit my fancy" (ch. 12) she represents Europeanness as a difference from Americanness. Mulvey sees the American traveller's expression of superiority in general as a masked fear of American inferiority, in contrast to the Europeans, and English in particular. Despite this paradoxical position of combined superiority and inferiority, the American traveller did not want to be confused with an English traveller (Mulvey 6).

In the context of a foreign country membership in the imagined community of a nation (Anderson) can be seen as an important aspect of identity and the self. Mulvey calls this "fictionalisation of nations and peoples," a "mythopoesis" that takes on when "nations and national characters" are described as a mixture of scientific discourse and "imaginative expression" (7). This applies both to the representation of one's own nationality and that of foreign peoples. The constructions of nationhood and cultural identity, whether British or American, are reflected through difference and the cultural other. Intertwined with the aspects of nationality are racial, ethnic, religious, and gender concerns. The interconnections of the historical perceptions of gender and nationality influence self-representations in autobiographical travel writing. Nationality is gendered in a way that defines male and female nationalities differently. As Yuval-Davis writes, women are primarily seen as the reproducers of nation, at the levels of biological, cultural, and symbolic reproduction. When considering the women travel writers under consideration here, cultural reproduction through the essentialised markers of nationality such as dress, behaviour, customs, religion and language is most significant. In the colonial context, women in particular were expected to maintain and reproduce the virtues associated with their nationality (see McClintock). These national virtues were gendered, but also connected with certain historical periods. The Victorian values, especially the expectations of silence, restraint, and virtue placed on femininity, represented by what Sara Mills calls "the well-behaved self," still reign strong in the texts of British and American women writers in the mid-nineteenth century (Mills; Foucault, *History*).[4]

Nationality can be represented in various ways in the writing of women travellers. Although Sophia Poole adopted Egyptian clothing while living in Cairo, there were certain instances, such as visits to the homes of the Egyptian élite, when she dressed in English clothes. Poole's adopting a position of Englishness through her dressing as an Englishwoman during these visits is an example of her awareness of the constructedness of national identity, since it is through clothing that she signalled Englishness to her Egyptian hosts. This emphasised representation of nationality is significant in constructing a hierarchy of nationalities as well. Poole writes:

> In visiting those who are considered the noble of the land I resume, under my Eastern riding costume, my English dress; thus avoiding the necessity of subjecting myself to humilia-

---

[4] In the American and European cultural contexts, the transformation from the Victorian to the Modern Period began at the end of the nineteenth century. The women travel writers discussed in this article, traveling as they did in the 1850s and 60s, should still be classified as Victorian.

tion. In the Turkish in-door costume, the manner of my salutations must have been more submissive than I should have liked; while as an Englishwoman, I am entertained by the most distinguished, not only as an equal, but generally as a superior. (102)

Poole is surprisingly conscious of her choices when utilising nationality for her own means and of the performativity of national identity. Emphasising her nationality by exterior markers, Poole is able to enforce a hierarchical distinction between English and Egyptians, which even surpasses social hierarchies of class: as an Englishwoman Poole is superior to Egyptian royalty.

Men Legitimising Women Travel Writers

In general, the canonised Western tradition of travel writing is a tradition of European male travellers writing about the rest of the world, especially the countries they colonised. In the West travel literature became more and more popular since the late eighteenth century, but until the mid-nineteenth century, the peak period of imperialism and colonialism, travelling was associated not only with upper-class privilege but also with masculine freedom of mobility.[5] The discourses of colonialism share several aspects with the tradition of travel writing: especially British travel literature has been marked by exterior goals of colonial preoccupation and territorial ambition (Lowe 31). The Western tradition of science and exploration motivated several writers of travelogues, and travelling was often perceived as an adventurous masculine conquest, and the traveller an explorer or a scientist who discovered and observed unknown (or misinterpreted) characteristics of foreign peoples and countries. In this sense travel can even be

---

[5] See for example Mary Louise Pratt who sees the 1750s as the starting point for (British) imperialist travel writing in the Americas and Africa. See also Mills; Birkett; and Melman.

called "a technology of gender" that constructs and reconstructs gender, and masculine gender in particular (Schick 90).

In Orientalist travel writing there seems to be a particularly strong connection with the masculine positioning of the writer. According to Said, within this masculine tradition of Orientalist travel writing, there is a continuum which extends from scientific writing, with little or no authorial self visible, to the personal pilgrimage, in which the Orient is exploited to justify the writer's personal "existential vocation." As examples of these extremes Said mentions Sophia Poole's brother Edward William Lane as a typical scientific Orientalist, whereas he sees French writers such as Nerval as typically representing pilgrims (168-170). Women travel writers write in relation to this continuum, but they have to negotiate their position within it. Neither the position of pilgrim, nor that scientific masculine Orientalist is easily available for women.

Women have produced travelogues in relation to the masculine standards of the genre: as Mills notes, the context of production and reception was similar to that of male writers, however, simultaneously pressure was exerted on female writers though a different discursive framework—the discourse of femininity (6). Combining the contradictory expectations of genre and gender was not easy for women travel writers, and they applied different strategies to compensate this incompatibility. Ali Behdad claims that women travellers often require a male legitimisation for their Orientalist authority (94). Thus some women discursively aligned themselves with the masculine colonial force and legitimised their texts through the authority of brothers, husbands or male travel writers, or what Said calls "the restorative citation of antecedent authority" (176).[6] This male authorisation mani-

---

[6] Both men and women travel writers refer to earlier travellers, but men more often try to manifest their own knowledge of the field, and to contradict earlier accounts to enforce the originality and importance of their own text. Within the Orientalist discourse, it is common to refer to preceding authorities even if the author has first-

fests itself in the prefaces as the editorial authority and guidance offered by husbands and brothers of the women writers: Poole, Rogers and Paine all legitimise both their travelling to the Orient and their writing of it through male authorities. Rogers formed a part of her brother's household in Palestine, and also dedicated her journal to him. Poole accompanied her brother, the well-known Arabist Edward William Lane, on one of his various field trips to Egypt, and wrote *The Englishwoman in Egypt* in accordance with the arrangements Lane had made with his publisher and as a complimentary book to his work. Poole's text is clearly produced under her brother's supervision, since in addition to providing the idea of a book on the Orient "accessible only to a lady," he suggested the form of genre she should choose, supplied her with material, and edited and selected the published texts (Poole 11). Poole quotes her brother word for word in several passages of her book, often resorting to his superior authority and expertise in the field of Oriental studies. Similarly, Paine refers to male travellers as reliable sources of knowledge on the Orient, and cites such well-known names as John Gardener Wilkinson and John Lewis Burckhardt (quoting the latter directly for 11 paragraphs in a row), while discrediting another female travel writer, Harriet Martineau, by labelling her as "most erroneous" (ch. 18). Such references, which Manfred Pfister in his contribution to this volume calls "textual traces, i.e. the accounts of previous travellers distilled into maps, guidebooks or travelogues" (2) intertextually anchor the women travellers' texts to the tradition of the genre. Behdad (94) sees that the hegemonic masculine voice of discursive authority interpolated in the woman writer's text highlights the unequal relationship female and male travellers occupy in relation to the Orient and its scientific control. It seems that to conform to and enforce the position of masculine power over the Orientalist discourse, the female travellers let the male travellers speak (almost) unmediated through their texts, making these

---

hand experience of the phenomenon described, so this is not unique to female writers, although they seem to resort to antecedents more often.

textual traces clearly visible. Thus, women strive to express conformity between their own experience and the male authorities' representations (Pfister).

Another strategy applied by women travellers was to enforce their femininity to compensate for the breach between gender and genre, by writing on the feminine Orient and by, as Reina Lewis phrases it, adhering "to feminine dress and decorum" (22). Poole, Paine, and Rogers refer to femininity and aspects associated with women already in the titles of their books. Poole's femininity is enforced by the publisher who named her 'the Englishwoman' in the title. In Poole's own suggestion for a title, "Letters from an English Hareem in Egypt," Oriental domesticity is enforced more explicitly. Similarly, Oriental domesticity is central in the names of Rogers' and Paine's books. Where men control the scientific knowledge of the Orient, women, according to their gender, have access to the knowledge of the Oriental domestic sphere.

Domesticity of the Feminine Orient

Despite the general convention of men legitimising the accounts of nineteenth-century women travel writers, women have one area of expertise in which they can claim an unequalled authority—the so-called feminine Orient. Behdad sees women travellers' first-hand experience of the Oriental domestic sphere and its inhabitants, the Oriental women, legitimised by experience which according to him "equals discursive authority" in Orientalist discourse (100), especially since men had to rely on women's accounts or other second-hand information in their representations of Oriental women. The domestic and feminine parts of the Orient are exceptionally important themes for women travellers, since this is the only field in which they can be the experts and even legitimise male writers' representations of Oriental women. In addition, the feminine Orient is seen as a proper and suitable topic for women writers.

Poole, Paine, and Rogers write on Oriental women in particular and that is the main theme of their books as they themselves claim. There are two reasons for this: firstly, Oriental women and the harem fascinate the Western reading public, and secondly, as women they had access to the private sphere. These women are aware of the Western interest in Oriental women and the cult of the harem, and they take a stance in relation to them, either enforcing or challenging these apprehensions. As Rogers notes of the English: "[M]y countrymen would like to have further insight into the mysteries of Eastern life" (vii).

Women travel writers mostly represent middle- and upper-class harems,[7] since lower-class women are not as confined to the domestic sphere as other women but move more freely and thus can be observed more easily. As Rogers writes, "The seclusion in which Moslem girls are kept is more or less strict, in accordance to their rank or position—the poor having unavoidably more liberty than the wealthy" (358). Although these women travellers were primarily interested in the upper-class harems, not all of the harems they visited were strictly speaking of the élite: especially in the rural areas, even the harems of the local governor or sheik were rather plain and did not correspond to the Orientalist image of the luxurious harem. When visiting a rural harem, Rogers describes the three wives as "more simple, frank and innocent-looking [. . .] young and rather fair, stout and ruddy, and cheerful and bright as happy children" (238). Rogers' depictions of rural harems strike a contrast to her portrayals of the upper-class harems of the city of Haifa, where surroundings are depicted as richer and the women as more beautiful and in closer correspondence to the image of the sensual and beautiful Oriental woman. Rogers depicts one of these harem

---

[7] In the nineteenth century travelling was becoming possible for a larger part of society; not only aristocrats, but also the middle classes were able to travel. Poole and Rogers can be defined as at least middle class because of their travelling. As the sister of the British consul, Rogers can be categorised as upper class, whereas as the widow of a barrister and the sister of a scholar, Poole is not strictly upper class. Very little is known of Paine's background, but her traveling as a tourist suggests upper-class privilege.

women during a feast as follows: "She looked delicate, but prettier than ever, and was very gaily dressed. She had rosebuds and strings of pearls in her hair" (370). Thus it can be said, that the Orientalist image of the harem and Oriental women is present in the women travellers' writing on the local élite. However, often the domesticity of women travel writers' depictions of the harem undermines the Oriental eroticism and exoticism: women represent the harem as "tame and domestic" (Lewis 134).

Orientalism and the cult of the harem were familiar themes in the American context, but still Paine is less interested in the harems than her British colleagues. She seems to regard the harem as a tourist attraction, if an essential one: "We were repeatedly invited to dine there [in the harem] afterwards, but our occupation of sight-seeing allowed us no time for it" (ch. 21). She does not discuss harems as much as the title of her book would lead one to believe.

Oriental homes and harems are perceived as suitable topics for women travel writers, since such a choice enforces the connection between women and domesticity, and thus alleviates the gender breach between travel and femininity. The domesticity of the topics of women writers writing of the Orient is manifest in their writing of the Oriental home in particular. According to Terry Caesar, women travellers either intentionally or often also unintentionally reproduce the domesticity of women in their writing (128).[8] Women are associated with the home even when travelling and breaking the boundaries of the domestic sphere. In addition to writing about topics associated with domesticity, there are other ways domesticity can be enforced: according to Schriber even emphasising the feminine gender can be seen as one (Schriber 2; Caesar 129). Poole, Rogers, and Paine enforce domesticity actively in their writing by referring to their gender

---

[8] Domesticity, as a common theme, particularly in nineteenth-century American literature but also British Victorian writing, manifests itself also in the writings of women travellers. The cult of domesticity enforces sentimentality, religion, and the association between women and the the domestic sphere.

on different occasions, by choosing to write on the domestic sphere of the feminine Orient, and through the way they represent themselves as sisters, mothers, and women travellers, emphasising their gendered position in relation to others. The domesticity of Poole's and Rogers' travels is enforced through their belonging to a family and a household even during their stay in the Orient. They were more bound to the domestic sphere than their brothers, who participated more in public life. In addition, the local custom of gender segregation reinforces the domesticity of women travellers. Women travellers did venture to break the practice of sexual segregation by meeting also local men, and thus were not completely restricted to the feminine sphere in the Orient. Rogers illustrates this in a passage where she converses with two "learned Muslim friends" (100-101). She asks if there is a law on the segregation of the sexes, and when she receives the answer that "it is the law of custom only which immures the women in their harims," she decides she can continue interacting with men, as well.

Both Poole and Rogers were (a part of) the family and household of their brothers, whereas Paine, although travelling as an unmarried woman, legitimised her position through "a family" that accompanied her. Paine describes the company consisting of "Mr. and Mrs. ---," "three [unmarried] ladies," and "a young man" as "a very harmonious family" (ch. 23). Although Paine travelled on the Nile more like a tourist than an explorer, her constant travelling posed a challenge to feminine domesticity. To alleviate this breach, Paine and her American companions retained a western domesticity in the boat by de-orientalising it "with all the luxuries that could be furnished by English bazaars at Cairo" (ch. 23). In this context, the English paraphernalia act as a domestic prop even for the American traveller in comparison to the Oriental surroundings. In addition to the need to enforce her domesticity to keep up her own appearance, a woman travelling with a man can also act as a "domesticity prop" domesticating and enforcing the Britishness (or Americanness) of the household. Poole's British femininity balanced the Orientalness of Edward William Lane's household, which would otherwise have consisted only of his Greek-Egyptian wife.

Conclusion

Several factors, such as the genre and topics of writing, affect women travel writers' gendered representation of the self. English and American women represent a gendered group in relation to male travellers and emphasise national feminine virtues associated with gendered nationality. American travellers distinguish themselves from European and English travellers in particular.

The relation of these women travellers to the Orient and Orientals differs according to nationality. They all can be superior in relation to the Orient through their whiteness. However, in certain situations, English women travellers can enforce their Englishness in order to transgress even class boundaries, so that they can be superior to the Oriental élite and royalty. On the other hand, American women cannot depend on such an ideological construction of a superior "Americanness." The position of American (women) travel writers is defined in relation to, not only the Orientals, but particularly the English.

The Saidian continuum of travel writing which extends from scientific objectivity to personal pilgrimage is constructed on the masculine premises of travelling, and women travel writers cannot position themselves in the very ends of this continuum; thus they have to negotiate their place in relation to these male norms of travel writing. To legitimise their position as travellers in this continuum, women travel writers use male travel writers' texts or rely on the authority of male family members. This relational position enforces the femininity and domesticity of female travel writers as well.

The topics women writers can write about are already predefined to some extent by the discourse of femininity, but woman travel writers' choice of topic is directed by the expectation that women can reveal a different side of the Orient and provide information men cannot.

Women can be experts on the feminine Orient because of the gender segregation and gendered access to the Oriental domestic sphere. In particular, this is related to representing (Islamic) middle- or upper-class Oriental domesticity. Unlike male travel writers, women focus on representing the harem as a home. The domesticity of the harem descriptions undermines the Orientalist sensuous perception of Oriental women so common to the Western cult of the harem.

Works Cited

Anderson, Benedict. *Imagined Communities: Reflections on the Origin and Spread of Nationalism.* Oxford: Oxford University Press, 1991.

Behdad, Ali. *Belated Travellers: Orientalism in the Age of Colonial Dissolution.* Durham: Duke University Press, 1994.

Burckhardt, Johan Ludwig [aka John Lewis]. *Travels in Nubia.* London: J. Murray, 1819.

Caesar, Terry. "Writing Home: American Women Abroad, 1830-1920; Edith Wharton's Travel Writing: The Making of a Connoisseur." *South Atlantic Review* 63.2 (Spring 1998): 128-132.

Foucault, Michel. *The Archaeology of Knowledge.* Trans. A. M. Sheridan Smith. New York: Pantheon, 1972.

Foucault, Michel. *The History of Sexuality,* Vol. I. *An Introduction.* Trans. Robert Hurley. New York: Pantheon, 1978.

Gough, Brendan, and Majella McFadden. *Critical Social Psychology: An Introduction.* Basingstoke: Palgrave, 2001.

Lewis, Reina. *Gendering Orientalism: Race, Femininity and Representation.* Gender, Racism, Ethnicity Series 3. London: Routledge, 1996.

Lowe, Lisa. *Critical Terrains: French and British Orientalisms.* Ithaca: Cornell University Press, 1991.

McClintock, Anne. *Imperial Leather: Race, Gender and Sexuality in the Colonial Contest.* New York: Routledge, 1995.

Mills, Sara. *Discourses of Difference: An Analysis of Women's Travel Writing and Colonialism.* London: Routledge, 1991.

Melman, Billie. *Women's Orients: English Women and the Middle East, 1718-1918: Sexuality, Religion and Work.* London: Palgrave Macmillan, 1991.

Mulvey, Christopher. *Transatlantic Manners: Social Patterns in Nineteenth-Century Anglo-American Travel Literature.* Cambridge: Cambridge University Press, 1990.

Paine, Caroline. *Tent to Harem: Notes of an Oriental Trip.* New York: D. Appleton and Company, 1859. Women's Travel Writing Digitization Project. Transcribed and encoded by Karen Roggenkamp. Ed. Miranda Beaven Remnek. Electronic Text Research Center, Minneapolis: University of Minnesota, 1998. 1 Sept. 2006 <http://erc.lib.umn.edu/dynaweb/travel/paintent/@Generic__BookTextView/;uf=0>.

Pfister, Manfred. "Travellers and Traces: The Quest for One's Self in Eighteenth- to Twentieth-Century Travel Writing." This vol. 1-13.

Poole, Sophia. *The Englishwoman in Egypt: Letters from Cairo Written During a Residence There in 1842-46.* Cairo: American University in Cairo Press, 2003.

Pratt, Marie Louise. *Imperial Eyes: Travel Writing and Transculturation.* London and New York: Routledge.

Rogers, Mary Eliza. *Domestic Life in Palestine.* London: Kegan Paul, 1989.

Said, Edward W. *Orientalism.* London: Penguin, 1994.

Schick, Irvin. *The Erotic Margin: Sexuality and Spatiality in Alterist Discourse.* London: Verso, 1999.

Schriber, Mary Suzanne. *Writing Home: American Women Abroad 1830-1920.* Charlottesville: University Press of Virginia, 1997.

Yuval-Davis, Nira. *Gender & Nation.* London: Sage, 1997.

Wilkinson, John Gardener. *Manners and Customs of the Ancient Egyptians, Including Their Private Life, Government, Laws, Art, Manufactures, Religions, and Early History; Derived from a Comparison of the Paintings, Sculptures, and Monuments Still*

Existing, with the Accounts of Ancient Authors. Illustrated by J. G. Wilkinson. London: J. Murray, 1837.

Istanbul: Edouard Roditi's Mirror of the Self?

Clifford Endres
Kadir Has University

Abstract: Edouard Roditi derives from one of the old Sephardic Jewish families of the Ottoman empire. A surrealist author in French and English, he also translated Turkish authors Yunus Emre and Yaşar Kemal. An interesting part is played in his work by the city of Istanbul. The urban landscape is characterized by strange fusions of history and memory and a Babel of peoples and languages. Here a modernist sense of alienation is the norm: everyone is in a state of exile, everyone is at home in this exile. But the city is also a surrealistic paradise where the never-ending eruption of chance, dream, and the *hasard objectif* creates a fabulous labyrinthine alternative to the physical city—an alternative in which "normal" identity slips its moorings and a hitherto unsuspected self can emerge. It is thus a locus of historical and psychological depth that serves as an implicit foil to the flattened surfaces of industrial and commercial modernism.

Edouard Roditi (1910-1992) was born in Paris of a father who was an American citizen but whose family possessed deep roots in the Byzantine civilization of the Eastern Mediterranean. When he was sixteen, in 1926, Edouard met the Surrealist poet Georgette Camille, and, through her, Robert Desnos, René Crevel, René Daumal and other young French Surrealists, and began to try his own hand at "automatic writing." A year or so later he became ill and, while convalescing in a Swiss nursing home, translated St. John Perse's *Anabase*, unaware that T. S. Eliot was engaged in the same task, the difference being that Eliot had the author's permission. Roditi's translation, though remaining unpublished, brought him to the attention of Eliot and other Anglophone modernists in Paris such as Joyce, Pound, and Beckett, who were associated with the avant-garde journal *transition*. It may be remembered that Joyce was then publishing in *transition* chapters of what would become *Finnegan's Wake*, and at the same time pursuing a French translation of the novel—a project in which the young Roditi was now enlisted. At the same time T. S. Eliot was editing *The Criterion*, which was devoted to what we now call high Modernism. Roditi would publish work in both journals.

Indeed, Roditi would go on to publish more than 20 volumes of poems and prose poems, in addition to countless articles, essays, and translations. These include the first English translation of French surrealism, André Breton's *Jeunes cerisiers garantis contre les lièvres*, published as *Young Cherry Trees Secured Against Hares* (1946), with drawings by Arshile Gorky; Yaşar Kemal's *Ince Mehmed* (*Memed, My Hawk*, 1961); and, with Güzin Dino, a selection of Yunus Emre's poetry, *The Wandering Fool*, illustrated by Abidine Dino (1987). As for the main body of his creative work, it may be described as oscillating between French Surrealism and Anglo-American Modernism, drawing at the same time on Jewish, Christian, and Sufi mysticism. In this corpus the *topos* of Istanbul/Constantinople makes some interesting appearances, and it is these that I want to look at here.

The roots of Edouard's association with the city are not entirely clear, but the Roditi name has been well known among the Sephardic Jews of Istanbul and the Levant for a couple of centuries and probably more; Roditi once described himself to Gregory Corso as deriving from "an old Byzantine Venetian family" (unpublished letter). But while the Roditis are indeed remembered in the city as "an old banking family," and there is a "Roditi Apartman" in the Tepebaşı district, I've not been able to gather much biographical information. Still, as a child Edouard must have imbibed family stories about life in the Empire along with his dose of *The 1001 Nights*. It would not be at all surprising if the city of Istanbul had become a locus of exoticism in his imagination. Moreover, as the Turkish poet Lale Müldür observes, on the Surrealists' map there were only two capitals—Paris and Istanbul (Nemet-Nejat 359).

Actually Roditi became a wanderer early on, heading to Oxford at the age of 18 to study classics, then, two years later, in 1930, continuing his student life in Germany, where he was dismayed by the rising tide of anti-Semitism. Perhaps it was owing to this shock that, on returning to Paris, he developed an interest in Jewish mysticism and composed, in 1931, his *Journal of an Apprentice Cabbalist*, which among other things is a meditation on the nature of love. In 1935, at the age of 25, Roditi moved to the USA to attend the University of Chicago, and then to graduate school at the University of California at Berkeley. By 1940, with war declared in Europe, he was in Kansas City; meanwhile, his friends and relatives in Berlin and Paris were struggling for their lives. It was in Kansas, the heart of the American heartland, that Roditi, an American citizen suffering pangs of exile from his European home, finished his long war poem, "Cassandra's Dream."

An amalgam of autobiography and allusion, "Cassandra's Dream" is an apocalyptic poem that approaches the looming conflagration of World War II through the prism of history and the persona of Cassandra. It traces the destruction of Troy, of Rome, and finally of Constantinople. The last was of course a double destruction—first by the Crusaders and then by the Sultan's army—which brought an end to the line of descent that had run from Troy to Rome to Rome's heir. Each catastrophe felt to its survivors like the end of history:

> All those who watched aghast the fall
> Of lofty-towered Ilion, Rome
>
> Believed eternal, Byzantium poised
> Between two continents, each time did think
> That history now must stop, appeased
> In pity and fear. (372-377)

But history did not stop; it "blindly rages on" (378). The poet foresees a juggernaut that will take down not only London but Manhattan, which must fall "as low / as Priam's city" (345-346). "New York, New York, oh city, city" (352), he eulogizes, echoing the historian

Ducas' lament for the fall of Constantinople in 1453; but from his position of exile he can only rail as helplessly as Cassandra:

> A dead man, in a world dead, to the dead
> I speak, not knowing who lives, who hears,
> Deaf to my words, shrill twitter of ghosts.
>
> I know not yet which friends are dead,
> Which maimed, whose mangled bodies
> Gape at the sky through yawning wounds
> And laugh in death's distorting mirror
> Which makes such a mockery of life. (388-395)

"Death's distorting mirror": the image demands our attention. As mentioned earlier, it is not clear when Roditi first visited Istanbul. However, another poem on the topic of death, in which the mirror image plays a significant role, appears to have been written there around or somewhat prior to 1960, judging from internal and external evidence. Called "Experience of Death," it is dedicated to "Thilda and Yashar Kemal." As Roditi's translation of Kemal's *Ince Mehmed* was published in 1961, it is probable that Roditi was in the city shortly before then to work with the author. Indeed, in an unpublished and undated (but probably 1958) letter to Gregory Corso, Roditi writes that he is leaving London for Istanbul "to work with my Turkish cousin Yashar Kemal on the revisions to the English translation of his novel, which has been disastrously translated by some goon who knows Turkish alright, but has no idea of English style, not being a writer but just some poor teacher who taught english [sic] for a while in a college in Turkey and picked up Turkish while he was on the job there."

Section I of "Experience of Death" is titled "THE IDIOT IN A TEA-ROOM," followed by, in parentheses in somewhat dubious Turkish, "DIVAN PASHTAHANESI, ISTANBUL." The speaker first casts a scornful eye at the patisserie's bourgeois clientele, who are there for nothing more than vicious gossip and loveless flirtation. Not even great sinners, they are doomed

> To inspire no pity, no fear,
> Only contempt, amazement
> At their folly, at the emptiness
> Of their lives, their minds, their chatter. (57-60)

Although the speaker is a man who is "out of place" and suffering in his own hell—his "built-in catastrophe"—he is nevertheless happier than his neighbors, who "all perform their dance / Of death" in petty ways, too banal to be worthy of Dantean allegory. But even though the tea is "nectar" and the pastries "ambrosia," he is terrified, for he has been suffering epileptic seizures and wonders how many more he can survive:

> A sick man, fearing death,
> I inspect my face in a mirror
>
> And meet a stranger, no double.
> Who am I? Have I ever seen
> Myself or any other man before?
> I'm dead again. Can I survive
>
> Another fit? (63-69)

Roditi was an epileptic. As he explains in his preface to *Thrice Chosen*, it is an old belief that people who are subject to epileptic seizures belong in a way to the elect, since it is thought that they are visited, while in their fits, by visions that transcend the understanding of other mortals (5). Moreover there is an apparent connection between epilepsy and artistic inspiration: the references to "nectar" and "ambrosia," the food and drink of the gods, are meant to remind us of the link between inspiration and divine possession. This link, which Roditi explores in *The Disorderly Poet*, was also recognized by Dostoevsky, the epileptic author of *The Idiot*, whose protagonist too is an epileptic and clearly the subject of Roditi's allusions (section II of the poem is called "FROM THE IDIOT'S DIARY"). Both Dostoevsky and Roditi speak of a state of heightened perception immediately preceding a seizure, during which the world appears as an allegory. This however is a level of intensity that the scene in the Divan Pastanesi fails to reach. The poet proceeds to associate his creativity with the disease ("two fits and three poems in a week" [73]) and to compare his experience of a seizure to death. For him, a fit is the experience of nothingness: "Last night this world was here, then gone, / Then here again" (108-109). But is the world that appears afterward the same as the one there previously? Perhaps death, large or small, possesses more valences than the uninitiated are accustomed to see.

Hence the importance of the mirror as an aid to the poet in confirming his identity. It is not a good sign, however, that the face it reflects is no "double." In *Journal of an Apprentice Cabbalist*, Roditi had discussed the importance of the double in the progress of the soul:

> Sometimes I feel that if I fail to become my own double I must die of frustration and loneliness. [. . .] I must wait for my double as the ideal lover who alone can break the monotony of the vast expanses of solitude where I still live. [M]y double or second self must inevitably come, though [. . .] the [. . .] destructive fire of my joy would consume both me and my double and, together with both of us, everything else, thus reducing the whole world to a joyful reconciliation of all contraries in a new and eternal harmony, one everlasting moment in the timeless peace of fulfillment. (26-27)

Such a reconciliation, or identity, of contraries is a suprarational concept that is important both to Surrealism and to traditional mysticism, though perhaps for different reasons. "The meeting of an umbrella and a sewing machine on a dissecting table" was the image famously bequeathed by Lautréamont to the Surrealists. The notion of the Surrealistic image as a yoking of opposites was adduced by Pierre Reverdy in *Nord-Sud* (1918) and further elaborated by André Breton in the *First Surrealist Manifesto* (1922). As Mary Ann Caws reminds us, "The spark struck by the meeting of opposites clarifies by its brilliance the dullest of everyday perceptions, infusing it with the light of the marvelous" (x). As the world is re-seen, so it is re-made. Now, just as the Surrealists hoped to break out of the "normal" into the experience of the marvelous—which is really the experience of a new self—so does the mystic strive to go beyond apparent contraries to the truth, as we see in the poetry of St. John of the Cross or of Yunus Emre, some of whose *tekerlemeler* ("riddles") Roditi has translated. For instance:

> Into the cauldron I put clay
> and set it to boil.
> To all who asked me, "What's cooking?"
> I gave a taste of my brew.
> [. . .]
> In the blind man's ear I whispered
> but the deaf man grasped my meaning
> while the dumb man sang and spoke
> the words that lay on my lips.
> (*The Wandering Fool*, I, 9-12, 37-40)

But we may take Roditi's own words:

> In our mind's distorting mirror
> We see night or day, man or woman,
> Never the whole, the union of both
> In the full identity of contraries.
> (*Thrice Chosen*, "Shechinah and the Kiddushim" 11-14)

Thus we may see that for Roditi both death and the mind are "distorting mirrors"—presumably because they represent only one side of the story. But the Divan mirror is perhaps more accurate: it is an object that reflects a stranger, neither a familiar nor a double. In short, it reflects the poet in a state of alienation from "normality"; it is precisely because of this that he feels more real than his fellow café-goers—"no puppet / In their plotless and meaningless play" (71-72). He finds himself "[b]etween two worlds," where the ordinary laws of time, space, and causality are suspended. May we consider this a revelation born of *hasard objectif*—"objective chance"—one of the favorite sources of inspiration for the Surrealists? And is such an event more likely to happen in Istanbul than in other places? Is this what Lale Müldür meant by her enigmatic utterance?

Let's turn to an early prose poem called "The Pathos of History." A dystopian meditation on time and reality, it was written in the 1920s under the full sway of Surrealism, perhaps before Roditi ever visited Istanbul physically, and first published in 1928 in *transition*. There are three sections. Section I opens with: "On the stereoscopic screen that's here and now, the beams of past and future meet and enjoy a transitory reality" (*New Hieroglyphic Tales* 27). Section II speaks of a letter dated "The Year of the Colorless Death," a year, however, that has not yet come to pass. Section III appears in quotation marks; it is perhaps the letter itself, though there is no way of knowing for sure. The passage describes a ruined metropolis of the future; but it is a metropolis that bears at least a passing resemblance to an Istanbul which can still be found today:

> ". . . Most poignant of all, an abandoned church on a hill above the sleepy harbor. A creaking wooden door hung loosely on a rusty, broken hinge. In the spacious dome from which the peeling plaster still fell like fine snow whenever a strong wind blew through the paneless windows, thousands of doves had nested. [. . .] The brittle bones of their dead lay buried in this accumulation of their own excrement and cast-off finery . . ."

". . . In an open space among rotting wooden shacks where cheese-pale hags watched the street fearfully from behind their cracked and filthy window-panes, a drunken invader from the truck-farming suburbs slowly dismounted from his donkey [. . .] and then solemnly pissed against the desecrated sarcophagus of a forgotten prince that stood on the sidewalk, tilted on its side, as if it had only just been tossed off a runaway hearse. . ."
[. . .]

". . . My day begins [the letter, if that's what it is, continues] "when a Muezzin's call summons me from my bed to watch the chilly grey dawn. Roused from a dream of gigantic cannibalistic women who cautiously conceal their quivering lips behind heavy veils, I leap to the window, stark naked. On his balcony across the street, the Muezzin is surprised to see me so unashamed; modestly, he looks the other way, down into the dark street. [. . .] . . ."

". . . Surreptitiously, an old Armenian bawd draws back the curtain of her window and watches me as I approach her door. In her tottering wooden tenement, the stairs creak beneath the stealthy tread of the whispering girls that wait there [. . .]. . . ."

". . . The wear and tear of a thousand years has left the city as fragmentary as any atom-bomb's crater. . ." (28-30)

This is a city that may or may not bear upon an historical, or apocryphal, Istanbul, described by an "I" that may or may not be contingent with the author Edouard Roditi. We are in a poetic landscape where it is not the rules of autobiography or of travel writing or even physics that apply, but those of the prose poem. We may remember that, as Jean-Pierre Cauvin remarks, "Surrealist imagery draws its meaning not from interpretation or explanation but from the immediacy of its illuminative power. Its success is measured by the degree of *dépaysement* it generates" (xxix). *Dépaysement* refers to the sense of being disoriented, out of one's element, or disconcerted by the unfamiliarity of a situation. In the service of Surrealist poetry it was meant to subvert repressive reason and to release the energy of the unconscious into spontaneous, unrehearsed images, thus leading us into a deeper knowledge, that of the surreal, which is a synonym for the marvelous (Cauvin xvii-xviii).

Finally we might briefly consider Roditi's collection of short narratives, *The Delights of Turkey: Twenty Tales*. These are not overtly Surrealist, but are rather anchored in the realism of the folk tale. Indeed, the author notes that many are based on "popular Turkish folklore of the same general nature as the anonymous tales about Karagöz or Nasreddin Hodja" (Acknowledgements). There are four sections. The first and fourth center on Istanbul ("A City Built on Seven Hills" and "The Eternal and Ubiquitous City," respectively); the second on the unlovely Bok Köy somewhere in Anatolia; the third ("Orient Express") ranges more widely across the Levant. The narratives document an extraordinary grasp of the minutiae of life in the Ottoman and Republican eras of Turkish history: the workings of the palace; the intricate social code of the Istanbul élite; the complicated interactions of the various *millets*, or peoples; the orientalist mindsets of foreigners; the geography of Beyoğlu night life; the contours of Jewish, Armenian, and Greek history in the capital city. This, however, is merely historical underpinning; what lends energy to the tales is the author's delight in hilarious juxtapositions, the extraordinary imaginations of his characters, and the deeply ironic and absurd situations in which they find themselves as they not only cope with but revel in a city where magic carpets, traveling hemorrhoids, and the whims of a vanishing aristocracy are the order of the day.

The wonderful "Vampires of Istanbul: A Study in Modern Communications Methods," for example, begins in the deadpan style of newspaper journalism but rises to a pitch of improbability that might happily be claimed by a Surrealist if not a Dadaist. The reader is left in stitches and the landscape strewn with hapless targets: neighborhood gossips, Turkish journalists, politicians, professors, the police, nationalists, and not to leave anyone out, Americans. It is as though Istanbul were the *locus classicus* of the *hasard objectif*. Here it is the labyrinthine byways not only of the city's history but its physical topography, laden with shards of its long and densely layered life as the capital of two empires, that supply the collisions so cherished by a Surrealist.

It would be idle, in a Surrealist poetics, to look for symbolic images of the kind favored by the Modernists. Still, it is possible, since the free-association and "automatic writing" techniques of the Surrealists resemble somewhat those of psychoanalysis, that the images of Istanbul found in Roditi's writing might offer, at least to a psychoanalyst, a glimpse of the construct we call the self, and in this respect could be considered autobiographical. But it is doubtful that Surrealists would be pleased with such an assertion, for it would imply the existence of a self whose existence they consider at best dubious. After all, "Which one of us is now the double of the other?", as the narrator of "Roditi's Metamorphoses" asks in *Choose Your Own World* (100).

Edouard Roditi's work thus reflects the Surrealist contention that the "normal" self—the one in which the bourgeoisie takes so much comfort—is an unreliable construct made up of time, space, causality, and other rational fictions. The Surrealist enterprise aimed to burst the confines of such an artificial self in order to see what might lie beyond it. Hence the fascination with the irrational—with dreams, nonlogical juxtapositions, arbitrary symbols, and other manifestations of preconceptual reality. According to Breton, the Surrealistic image should be arbitrary, contradictory, hallucinatory, untranslatable, and preferably laugh-provoking. It is in this context, perhaps, that the image of Istanbul may be regarded as a mirror of the self for Edouard Roditi.

Works Cited

Breton, André. *Young Cherry Trees Secured Against Hares. Jeunes cerisiers garantis contre les lièvres*. Trans. Edouard Roditi. New York: View, 1946.

Cauvin, Jean-Pierre. "The Poetics of André Breton." Introduction. *Poems of André Breton: A Bilingual Anthology*. Ed. and trans. Jean-Pierre Cauvin and Mary Ann Caws. Austin: University of Texas Press, 1982. xvii-xxxviii.

Caws, Mary Ann. Preface. *Poems of André Breton: A Bilingual Anthology*. Ed. and trans. Jean-Pierre Cauvin and Mary Ann Caws. Austin: University of Texas Press, 1982. ix-xv.

Emre, Yunus. *The Wandering Fool: Sufi Poems of a Thirteenth-Century Turkish Dervish*. Trans. Edouard Roditi and Güzin Dino. San Francisco: Cadmus, 1987.

Kemal, Yashar. *Memed, My Hawk*. Trans. Edouard Roditi. London: Collins and Harvill, 1961.

Nemet-Nejat, Murat, ed. *Eda: An Anthology of Contemporary Turkish Poetry*. Jersey City: Talisman House, 2004.

Roditi, Edouard. *Choose Your Own World*. Santa Maria: Asylum Arts, 1992.

___. *The Delights of Turkey: Twenty Tales*. New York: New Directions, 1972.

___. *The Disorderly Poet and Other Essays*. Santa Barbara: Capra, 1975.

___. *The Journal of an Apprentice Cabbalist: Prelude to a Vita Nuova*. Cloudforms 5. Newcastle upon Tyne: CLOUD, 1991.

___. Letter to Gregory Corso. No date. Gregory Corso Papers. Harry Ransom Center, University of Texas at Austin. 2 pages.

___. *New Hieroglyphic Tales*. San Francisco: Kayak, 1968.

___. *Poems 1928-1948*. New York: New Directions, 1949.

___. *Thrice Chosen*. Santa Barbara: Black Sparrow, 1981.

The Empirical Journey to the Self: Memory, Language and the Re-construction of Identity in Moris Farhi's *Young Turk*

Bronwyn Mills
Kadir Has University

Abstract: This paper focuses on Moris Farhi's *Young Turk* (2004), with occasional reference to his two prior novels, *Children of the Rainbow* (1999) and *Journey into the Wilderness* (1989). Recently translated into Turkish from its original English, *Young Turk* plus these other texts comprise a journey employing diasporic memory (in this case both of the Jewish experience and the Turkish one) to reconstruct the communal "self." Rather than advance the notion that a fiction writer literally draws from biography, I interrogate the novel directly as advancing biographical tropes. While one could focus on the truism that a fictional text may also function as a memoir—in this case, a virtual travel memoir—we might more profitably ask what is invoked when a diasporic fiction writer creates a work of fiction that retraces one's steps to one's former (and original) home, rather than to one's (newer) home abroad. Invoking some elements of postcolonial theory, the issue of language figures here. Subsequent to this paper, one might also interrogate the novel itself to reveal *its* autobiograph(ies)—indeed what guides such a novel in telling its own story?

Though I am most interested in Farhi's novel, *Young Turk* (2004), I will also make occasional reference to his two prior novels, *Children of the Rainbow* (1999) and *Journey into the Wilderness* (1989, rpt. 2002). I will speak a little about fiction and biography and *Young Turk*'s historical background, about subjectivities in the Imperium and in Farhi's novels, and about trauma and identity and the reconstruction of identity as interwoven with the idea of travel and the traveler. I will end with a brief discussion of memory and language vis-à-vis elements of postcolonial theory, with some reference to Benedict Anderson's idea of nineteenth-century colonial class solidarities as a form of community.[1]

Introduction

I want to put the notion of travel writing to rest. Patently obvious is the fact that travel writers do not write about home; rather they write *for* home. Just as obvious is the fact that none of the abovementioned novels are travel literature in the literal sense; although not unlike that genre, they contain the significant tropes of travel and the figure of the traveler. In other words, fictional characters and their authors travel and they, too, can tell us about real lives in motion. As this conference is about "life writing," I have some things to say about what constitutes Moris Farhi's "private geography," as Gerri Reaves might call it, after the title of a book she has written, *Mapping the Private Geography: Autobiography, Identity, and America*. In such a case the "map" Reaves refers to is what we assume to be a non-fictional way of documenting a life—a biography. Biography focuses on the individual, albeit *in situ*, as part of a culture, a collectivity, a city, a country, a region; and were I to follow such a map I would arrive at Moris Farhi himself, not necessarily his work. I would rather muck about in the terrain, the borderlands, between truth and fiction, between story and history or between the two meanings of Spanish *historia* whose co-existence in one word acknowledges that fact and fiction are more alike than they are different.

While I am foregoing the journey to the individual center—the author's subjectivity, his or her irreducible *self*—I am suggesting that a novel can map living geographies which are, or have been, traversed by *plural selves* as interesting as individual ones. Indeed, when I asked Farhi if his novel, *Young Turk*—set in Istanbul, with characters who, like him, had Roma (the preferred term for "Gypsy") playmates in Ankara, went to Robert College, or had family in Salonika, etc.—

---

[1] See his *Imagined Communities* (1983) and material quoted further along in the text.

when I asked him if the novel was biographical, he replied no, not exactly. Rather, he said, the novel was "the biography of a generation" (telephone interview, 18 Feb. 2006). Arguably a generation is an involuntary kind of association, and *Young Turk*, then, is the biography of a community. The process of writing about it, intimate as it is with such issues as language, the exhuming of memory, and the reexamination of identities, may constitute an empirical journey much like that of the late 30s Kenneth Patchen poem, "The Character of Love Seen as a Search for the Lost":

> You, the village; I, the stranger; this, the road:
> And each is the work of all.
>
> Then not that man do more, or stop pity; but that he be
> Wider in living; that all his cities fly a clean flag [. . .]. (73)

Subjectivity in the Imperium

Historically, this part of the world has flown a particularly "clean flag," of which it should be justly proud. Let me offer a quote from *The Collection of Turkish Jurisprudence on Asylum, Refugees and Migration,* a legal document prepared under United Nations auspices:

> [T]he Ottomans had developed a system of governance that granted considerable protection and autonomy to non-Muslims under its rule. This became an important motivation for particularly [sic] Jews to seek refuge in the Ottoman Empire. The most cited and remembered case was the one when in August 1492, Ottoman warships were sent to escort the last of Jewish refugees leaving the Spanish port of Cadiz. Just about the same time, Christopher Columbus was sailing out of the neighboring port of Palos to eventually discover a new

land that subsequently was to become a refuge for many millions. (United Nations 3-4)[2]

Take note, then, of 1) the phenomenon of a dispersion of persecuted peoples in the face of imperialist territorial ambition such as the dislocations brought about during the Nazi invasions of Europe and 2) the countervailing Turkish precedent: an honorable history of tolerating and welcoming peoples of other cultures and different faiths. More often than not, ethnic tolerance flies out of the window in the face of territorial ambitions—no matter whether those ambitions originate from the Spanish Crown, the British Empire, Nazi Germany, or the United States—and the stratagem, as any self-respecting postcolonial theorist will affirm, is to pejorate the value of a particular group, to assault their subjectivity in order to dominate them. While El Colón went West to find the East, and, collaterally, to wreak destruction upon the indigenous populations in the Americas ("collateral damage"), the fact that many of Spain's persecuted peoples also went East and were welcomed by people here in Istanbul is a testament to Turkey.

However, as Moris Farhi pointed out to me (18 Feb. 2006) and as shown in his novel, *Young Turk*, during World War II this legacy became a bit disheveled when the discriminatory *varlık* or "wealth tax" was imposed under Ismet Inönü upon Turkish Jews, some descendants of those very Sephardic[3] refugees welcomed long ago. Also affected,

---

[2] Among those leaving the troubled "Old World" for the "New," as I found in the early 90s in the *Archivos Nacionales de Costa Rica* (that country's national archives), were escapees from the Spanish Inquisition in the company of El Colón (Columbus). Some of these eventually settled in that tiny little country. Whether they were Jewish has not been addressed, but the presence of *conversos* is almost certain and the presence of non-converted persons, quite likely. Further, though outside the parameters of this discussion, it is notable that at the time that the Americas became a "refuge" for those from across the seas, it ceased to be a refuge for its indigenous peoples. To say otherwise would be to privilege a myth that both travel writers and imperialists buy into in one way or another—i.e., that the "native" was happy, carefree, and ever glad to see them.

[3] The Sephardim were Jews from the Iberian peninsula, primarily from the Muslim

as Dmetri Kakmi describes it, were "other ethnic minorities across the country. Those unable to pay were sent to labour camps, leaving behind families that would either starve or sink to some kind of ignominy."[4] Were it not for the outpouring of Muslim generosity— "[u]nable to remain unaffected by their plight Turkish friends and neighbours pooled their resources to look after them, until the law [was] eventually repealed"—many simply would not have survived. Indeed, it is with this history as backdrop—and with the author's gratitude—that Farhi's *Young Turk* appears, first written in English and now available in Turkish translation.

Trauma and Identity

Such times fracture not only one's community, but also one's sense of identity. Suddenly, it seemed, Jews and others were shut out of the very place they thought of as theirs as much as their neighbors'. Events resembled what Anderson says of colonial racism,

> [It] was [like] the typical "'solidarity among whites," which linked colonial rulers from different national metropoles, whatever their internal rivalries and conflicts.[5] This solidar-

---

Kingdom of Grenada, defeated in 1492 by Ferdinand and Isabella of the newly conjoined Kingdoms of Aragon and Castille. There followed a brutal period of religious repression culminating in the excesses of the Spanish Inquisition.

[4] The *Istanbul Literary Review*, where Kakmi's text is published, is a joint foreign and Turkish endeavor. Dmetri Kakmi is a Turkish-born essayist and critic, who works as senior editor at Penguin Books Australia, according to this online magazine's byline. The publication is an uneven mix of professional and amateur work. We wish it luck.

[5] Consider the suasion of Hitler's virulent policies linking with extreme rightist elements in Turkey, despite their disagreements over certain other issues. This happened early in the history of the Turkish Republic, according to E. Burak Arıkan, whose "The Programme of the Nationalist Action Party" chronicles the clothing of "a Fascist ideology in conservative language" (128).

Similarly, Ayşe Hür writes in the Turkish newspaper *Radikal* on 13 Mar. 2005: "[...] Sami Celik, the owner of Emre Publications, who recently printed 31,000 copies told Aksam newspaper on February 27, 2005: 'Following our research and

> ity, in its curious trans-state character, reminds one instantly of the class solidarity of Europe's nineteenth-century aristocracies, mediated through each other's hunting lodges, spas, and ballrooms; and that of the brotherhoods of "officers and gentlemen [. . .]. (152-153)

The paradigm is an interesting one. Indeed, it is not without irony that a similar expression of anti-semitism in my own country was described in an early (1947) exposé of the exclusionary and anti-semitic real estate practices in Darien, Connecticut, in a book titled, *A Gentleman's Agreement* by Laura Hobson (emphasis mine).[6]

How did the generation to which Farhi refers behave in, live through, this difficult time? *Young Turk* is that story, written in a series of thirteen first-person narrative sketches about Farhi's generation and their experiences from 1939 till the early 50s. The format is, if I can put it this way, pseudo-autobiographical, simply from the fact that each chapter is told in the first person by a fictional observer resonant with the times and sensibilities of the generation of young Turks that the author, himself, knew and was part of. They are Turkish, Sephardim, Roma, Dönme (Sabbatean)—a dizzying array of differences. That is, difference in the sense that a beloved teacher uses in addressing Zeki, a character much like Farhi himself: "One thing, Young Turk, don't forget the young Jew" (315). Identity is, Farhi believes, inescapable and worthy; however, he enjoins through this character,

---

observations, we thought that *Mein Kampf* would be a book that would be sought after and read by the public. [...] *Mein Kampf* was [indeed] affected by [recent] developments and its sale figures peaked.' [. . .] As a matter of fact it has become a sort of handbook for the [electorate] base of MHP [the ultra-nationalist 'National Movement Party'] and 'Genc Parti' [the Youth Party]" (qtd. in MEMRI; additions in square brackets to the quotation are by MEMRI). There is further corroboration in Hugh Poulton's recent *Top Hat, Grey Wolf and Crescent* (esp. 134-135, 152-153).

[6] It was made into a movie in 1947, directed by Elia Kazan, starring Gregory Peck and Dorothy MacGuire. The movie can be purchased from Amazon.com.

"[c]herish everybody's difference. If we all become the same, we're bound to perish."

The Traveling Trope

I would like to return to the tropes of travel and travelers.[7] In *Rainbow*, we have Benedict/Branko as a heroic archetype, a "Roma Moses" wandering in exile as his people have, finally leading them to a fictionalized Romanestan; in *Journey,* we have Daniel, the Christianized Balkan Jew, as a Nazi tracker journeying to South America in reluctant, failed pursuit. In *Young Turk*, we have several protagonists whose journeys are constrained or failed: for example, take that of the young Bilal who, at the time of the Nazi threat, goes off to rescue Jewish relatives in Salonika and is never seen again. Indeed, while in this last novel the journeys are often chosen, the historical, known forced exiles and forced marches into death shadow these narratives and intertwine with what is already known as World War II.

On the other hand, much of *Young Turk* is not about traveling, but about who stays home. Which brings us as close to the question of *authorial* identity as we are going to get. Farhi has apparently made a one-way trip from Turkey to Britain. Is Farhi an exile? He has been in Britain for 50 years—since 1956, when he left to study at RADA (the Royal Academy of Dramatic Arts)—and he holds a British passport. In my Kadir Has colleague, Dr. Mary Lou O'Neill's, words, he is not an exile but "a migrant"—"he has a permanent home in [his new country] Britain"—but he also fits her definition of a transnational, whose life "is a movement between the two points, two cultures …

---

[7] One archaic version of the dislocated, journeying figure I would like to dispense with immediately, however, is that of the Wandering Jew, the Jewish shoemaker who, for mocking Jesus as he was laboring to carry his cross, must wander deathless till Christ comes again. This is a Gentile invention whose earliest mention was in a pamphlet issuing from the town of Leiden in 1602. It is an othering of Jews and a perpetuation of the "Christ-killer" myth—i.e., merely another shopworn caricature born of anti-semitism ("Wandering Jew").

drawing from both" (personal communication 13 Apr. 2006). Farhi's words, "the older I get, the more I feel like a Turk," would suggest this analysis (18 Feb. 2006). And there we have yet another journey— a worn path back and forth, from old home to new; first culture to second, first language to second, and back again. While raised in one language, moved to the land of another's mother tongue, he has chosen to write in his second language, his "step-mother tongue."[8]

Clearly, travel interlocks with traveler and traveler subjectivity. As Farhi's treatment of identity unfolds and his characters become locked out of the "club" of the dominant community, we begin to see something that resembles a postcolonial paradigm, an experience not unlike that of a colonized subject, as I have alluded to much earlier. The subject may implement several strategies to affirm his or her subjectivity, to slough off their identity, to assimilate into the dominating culture or failing all that, to confront the damage done to them as an identified "other" in order to reconstruct one's identity or self. In the Salonika branch of Farhi's maternal family, nineteen family members died in the Nazi camps; and he has said that because he could not write about it directly, in *Rainbow* he wrote about the Roma genocide. In other words, his confrontation with these issues on a personal level has been through the exercise of his imagination rather than in the performance of biography. As his *Children of the Rainbow* suggests, one may need to negotiate a (postcolonial) space where one's agency is affirmed, where one's "otherance" is shed, where one can reconstruct an identity, even though in the novel this space is intriguingly placed in the imagination, not on the map.

Language and Memory

Farhi's text is littered with memories which, while we can avoid the personal biography of the author, we know belong to him in some ir-

---

[8] See the volume *Step-Mother Tongue: From Nationalism to Multiculturalism*, edited by Mehmet Yashin.

revocable way. Let us look at what part language plays here. With some justification, one might consider English as a neocolonial language, not simply the lingual vestiges of an Empire whose sun has set, or a convenience imposed by U.S. technological hegemony. The use of language is one which I and my fellow Caribbeanists and Africanists discuss all the time, and I believe there are some relevant points here. One is that language "purity" is nonsense. Martiniquan Prix Goncourt winner, Patrick Chamoiseau, says it loud and clear: without his "creole" French, he could not write; but, at the same time, he also says, "I use the entire French language. [T]here are no out of date, unused, or vulgar words" (vii). The other point is that our choice of language eliminates or introduces certain creative moves. Ngũgĩ wa Thiong'o, the Kenyan writer, deliberately abandoned his missionary-schooled, British colonial English to use his native tongue (Gikuyu) when he began writing *Devil on the Cross* (1982) as a political prisoner; with it, he found an entirely new voice. He refers to the process as "decolonizing the mind" in his classic work of the same name; for in colonized places like Kenya, "[l]anguage was the means of spiritual subjugation" (9). The issue here regarding Farhi that I would interrogate is his use of English as his preferred literary tongue. Farhi's Turkish is silent. So, if it existed in his household, it is the Ladino of his Salonika mother's tongue, the Romany of his Roma playmates, the Anatolian Greek, and so on.

We have all heard anecdotes about traumatized children going mute.[9] Certainly traumatized people experience memory loss, but I don't think we can argue that Farhi deliberately uses a "pastiche" method to relay the story of *Young Turk* in order to recreate that trauma. Nor do I think he uses English because Turkish stirs up too much in his psyche. I do wonder, though, if abandoning your mother's tongue in creative endeavors also fractures memory *and* language.[10]

---

[9] The best-selling "airport book," Khaled Hosseini's *The Kite Runner*, has such a fictionalized child.

[10] I have no answer for this, but am simply exploring the idea.

Was it not your mother and, by extension, the language she used to sooth you to sleep and inform you of the world—and, OH! what a wonderful boy, or girl, you are!—was it not the combination of mother and mother's tongue that gave you your first experience of love? Leaving one's mother tongue behind, failing to retrieve the words that name a memory or finding the memory absent because you cannot remember the word for it, or having the memory's picture imprinted in your brain, but suddenly being unable to articulate it, finding the words rusty from disuse—all I would surmise, must only compound the sense of dislocation got from leaving the family and the home, where that language was spoken, behind.

Perhaps an adopted tongue disturbs the writer's voice; for, in a more critical review of *Young Turk*, in the journal, *Forward*, Jay Michaelson says, "Its characters increasingly sound like [. . .] Farhi himself" and Michaelson goes on to quote a letter from Gül in *Young Turk* that, as he asserts, is far too didactic and developed for "any 16-year-old I know." I must agree. In places Farhi's language appears as the logical gesture of the biographer assembling the facts of a life or a period, rather than the more fluid and intimate language of the *auto*-biographer.

Five years ago, I published an interview with Ngũgĩ wa Thiong'o on the matter of his own exile. At that time, he calculated that to his astonishment he had been out of Kenya for 18 years. I wonder, rereading the present paper now, if we can say that Farhi has completely shed his identity as an exile, for though it is not life writing in the biographical sense, Farhi's *Young Turk* reveals a sense of connection that is remarkably strong. What wa Thiong'o says might well apply to Farhi here: "I try to reach home by writing, by having a dialogue with home.... Home is still part of the imagination and writing helps to make it more real."

Works Cited

Anderson, Benedict. *Imagined Communities: Reflections on the Origin and Spread of Nationalism.* New York: Verso, 1983.

Arıkan, E. Burak. "The Programme of the Nationalist Action Party; An Iron Hand in a Velvet Glove?" *Turkey before and after Ataturk: Internal and External Affairs.* Ed. Sylvia Kedourie. London: Frank Cass, 1999, 120-134.

Chamoiseau, Patrick. *Childhood.* Trans. Carol Volk. Translator's Note. Lincoln: University of Nebraska Press, 1999. vii-viii.

"Exodus and the Children of the Exodus 1 June-29 July, Botanique, Brussels, Belgium, show of refugee photographs by Sebastião Salgado. *Courier ACP-E,* July-August 2001. 12 Apr. 2006 <www.eu.int/comm/development/body/publications/courier/courier187/en/en_053.pdf>.

Farhi, Moris. *Children of the Rainbow.* London: Saqi Books, 1999.

___. *Journey through the Wilderness.* 1989. London: Saqi, 2002.

___. *Young Turk.* London: Saqi, 2004.

Hobson, Laura Z. *A Gentleman's Agreement.* New York: Simon and Schuster, 1947.

Hosseini, Khaled. *The Kite Runner.* New York: Penguin, 2003.

Kakmi, Dmetri. Rev. of *Young Turk*, by Moris Farhi. *Istanbul Literature Review* Winter 2006. 15 Apr. 2006 <http://www.ilrmagazine.net/arcritical3.htm>.

MEMRI The Middle East Media Research Institute. "Antisemitism in the Turkish Media: Part 1." Special Dispatch Series No. 900, 28 Apr. 2005. 13 Apr. 2006 <http://memri.org/>.

Michaelson, Jay. "Fragment of a Lost Jewish World." Rev. of *Young Turk*, by Moris Farhi. *FORWARD* 28 Oct. 2005. 10 Apr. 2006 <http://www.forward.com/articles/fragments-of-a-lost-jewish-world/>.

Mills, Bronwyn. "Ngugi Wa Thiong'o: Exile and Resistance." *Frigate.* Issue No. 2 November 2000-January 2001. 17 Apr. 2006 <http://www.frigatezine.com/essay/lives/eli02mil.html>.

Poulton, Hugh. *Top Hat, Grey Wolf and Crescent: Turkish Nationalism and the Turkish Republic*. London: Hurst, 1997.
Patchen, Kenneth. *The Collected Poems of Kenneth Patchen*. New York: New Directions, 1970.
Reaves, Gerri. *Mapping the Private Geography: Autobiography, Identity, and America*. Jefferson & London: MacFarland, 2000.
United Nations High Commission for Refugees. *The Collection of Turkish Jurisprudence on Asylum, Refugees and Migration*. 2nd edition. Istanbul: UNHCR, 2000.
"Wandering Jew." *Wikipedia*. 15 Dec. 2006. 23. Dec. 2006 <http://en.wikipedia.org/wiki/Wandering_Jew>.
wa Thiong'o, Ngũgĩ. *Decolonizing the Mind*. London and Nairobi: James Currey/Heinemann, 1986.
___. *Devil on the Cross*. Trans. by the author. London: Heinemann, 1982.
Yashin, Mehmet, ed. *Step-Mother Tongue: From Nationalism to Multiculturalism*. London: Middlesex University Press, 2000.

Quest for the Lost Mother: Autobiographical Elements in Jean Genet's *Un captif amoureux* (*Prisoner of Love*)

Clare Brandabur
Doğuş University

Abstract: Many admirers of Jean Genet's *avant garde* drama have until lately been unaware that, years after his last play and dying of throat cancer, he wrote *Un captif amoureux* (1986; *Prisoner of Love*). An account of his sojourn in Jordan with groups of young Palestinian *fedayeen* who were training to wrest their homeland back from the Israelis in the months leading up to Black September, Genet himself called it "my Palestinian revolution, told in my own chosen order" (355).

Looked at from the point of view of its autobiographical qualities, *Un captif amoureux* at its heart is Genet's discovery of what must have been a life-long quest. He was given up to an orphanage shortly after birth and never experienced a real maternal love. The central autobiographical experience revealed in this book is Genet's discovery of a mother for himself. In a most unlikely setting, a poor Palestinian shelter in a refugee camp in Irbid, Genet sleeps in the bed of a young fedayee, is served Turkish coffee by the boy's mother, and feels himself to have been for that moment her son.

What concept of his own special vocation drove him to write this amazing document in the weeks before his death, cutting back on pain medication to maintain his lucidity so determined was he to complete the writing before he died?

> Put all the images [. . .] in a place of safety
> and make use of them for they are in the desert, and
> it's in the desert that we must go and look for them.
>
> —Epigraph of Jean Genet's *Un captif amoureux*

Little serious criticism in English has been devoted to Jean Genet's *Prisoner of Love* (*Un captif amoureux* [1986]), a book which is highly personal—part journal, part travel narrative, part political commentary. Leila Shahid[1] speaks of the initial response at Gallimard Press when Genet delivered the manuscript: "What is this? An essay? An autobiography? Reporting? A poem?" As we shall see, the answer to this question might have been "all of the above." Whatever its genre, this has turned out to be an important book: in a paper entitled "The Princes of Exile: Choukri and Genet in Tangier," presented at a recent conference in Morocco, Andrew Hussey remarked that *Prisoner of Love* "by general consensus, remains Genet's most puzzling and politically challenging work" (152). A review of the book in *Le Matin* when *Un captif amoureux* was first published in France pronounced that it has "all the sacred fire and poetry of his earlier work" (qtd. in Soueif, introduction ix).

Now there are several sources in addition to the self-revelatory aspects of the book itself: Ahdaf Soueif's introduction to the new English edition (2003), Leila Shahid's essay "Jean Genet and the Position of Sudden Departure" (2001), and a small book by Mohamed Choukri, *Genet in Tangier*, which was written in French in Morocco and translated to English by Paul Bowles (1973). This rather modest book records a brief and apparently casual acquaintance between Choukri and Jean Genet over a period of several months in 1969 before Genet would have traveled to Jordan in 1970 and documents a number of important features of Genet as he then was. For one thing, when Choukri knew him in Algiers, Genet had no more plans to write.

In *Genet in Tangiers*, in a passage dated October 3, 1969, Choukri (38-39) asks Genet about his writing, observing that he hadn't written anything for several years: "Do you consider your literary silence and your assumption of a political position another kind of creation, part

---

[1] Leila Shahid's essay, "Jean Genet and the Position of Sudden Departure," is documented with the following editor's note: "This text is an excerpt from a long interview conducted by Jérôme Hankins published in *Genet à Chatila* (Actes Sud, Babel), an adaptation from the production of *Quatre heures à Chatila* directed by Alain Milianti in 1991 at the Volcan du Havre."

of your writing?" Genet answers, "Literally, I've said what I had to say. Even if there were anything more to add, I'd keep it to myself." Indeed, all the plays and most of the poems were behind him. The Genet sketched out in Choukri's (12) book already has a predilection for the Quran as opposed to Judeo-Christian culture; he is already eating little and taking Nembutal to kill the pain from kidney problems; and he had read little or nothing of Arabic literature. In fact, though the author at this period was willing to talk about *Our Lady of the Flowers* and to ask Choukri and others what they were reading, he himself was "reading nothing" (Choukri 44). However, when he praised Mallarmé, one of the group went to a book store to bring back Mallarmé's poems and Genet read "Brise marine" ("Wind from the Sea"), remarking, "Isn't it a miracle, that poem?" and singled out for special comment a line that particularly pleased him: "Et la jeune femme allaitant son enfant" (Choukri 59). Choukri omitted one word from the line: It actually reads, "Et ni la jeune femme allaitant son enfant." So in context it reads literally, "Nor the young mother breast-feeding her baby," one in a list of the beautiful things like the "ancient gardens pictured in his eyes," which, in spite of their attraction, will not keep the poet from leaving on a sea-journey, even though the ship's masts may be struck by lightning, the ship drowned and unmasted, lost forever.

That he should single out this line with its image of the mother nursing a baby for special remark suggests that, at the root of Genet's rage and iconoclasm, there remained a wound of having been abandoned by his mother, and therefore he went about the rest of his life perhaps unconsciously searching for a lost maternal love. After reading *Prisoner of Love*, one cannot help being struck that Genet should have singled out a maternal image for attention, because the most important personal revelation in the entire book is Genet's adoption of a Palestinian fighter and his mother (who also carried a Kalashnikov) as a kind of surrogate family. He places himself in the role of the son for a single night in the refugee camp in Irbid, a touching ritual which he later associates with the *Pietà*, a theme to which we shall return. His friend Leila Shahid, a leader of the Palestinian resistance and now PLO ambassador to France, says that what first drew Genet into the Palestinian struggle was his fascination with Palestinian women. Genet was attracted, Shahid records, especially to their traditional embroidery. Having first met Genet in the 1970s, Shahid later traveled with him to Beirut, arriving just in time to see the ghastly effects of the massacres in the refugee camps of Sabra and Chatila in 1982. Shahid stresses Genet's rapport with women:

> Besides, nobody has ever spoken of women like Genet—women in general but especially women of the third world, poor women. For he understood them wordlessly, there was a complicity between them. He did not speak Arabic, it is true, and they did not speak French. All communication between him and the Palestinian women in the Jordan camps took place via winks. (2)

Genet was fascinated, Shahid says, with the embroidery worn by the women the creation of which occupied them by the hour. Traditionally, of course, Palestinian women from different villages and towns wore dresses of distinctive colors which they made from the age of twelve, collecting Syrian silk thread, to adorn the bodices of the dresses they would wear at their weddings. Like many other Palestinian women, Leila Shahid's mother encouraged and practiced the preservation of this tradition of their culture in exile.

Shahid describes a rather strange episode in Beirut just after she and Genet had arrived in 1982. Her mother had gathered a large collection of Palestinian embroidered dresses and kept them in a trunk in her flat. As Leila and Genet approach the apartment building, they look up and see dozens of these dresses hanging on the balcony of her mother's flat where a visitor had hung them out to air:

> And Jean says, "Leila, look!" And we see all those dresses hanging on the balcony. We go tearing down the avenue and climb nine floors shouting, "Get the dresses in! Get the dresses in!" The Israeli army was in town and Palestinian dresses were hanging on the balcony. [. . .] these dresses were like flags, and were the Israeli intelligence agents in their cars to see all those dresses hanging there, it would be as if we were flying Palestinian flags.

This episode, Shahid says, quite amused Jean, and he saw in these works of art a form of expression more subtle than the verbal political discourse: "embroidery was a discourse too—everything that can be said about our relation to the land, identity, memory, but it was not channeled through the obvious words but through subtle signs, colors, an aesthetic symbolism." She continues,

> It was in fact the gesture in embroidering that most fascinated Jean. When one puts the needle through the fabric, one traces a circle. As for me, I was always saying apropos of his life: it's come full circle. Jean's life [. . .] begins somewhere with public assistance, passes through rebellion and prison, goes toward the East when he is a soldier [Genet served in Syria in the French Foreign Legion as a very young man], returns towards the East with the Palestinians, and ends in front of the corpses he finds at his feet in Chatila. (3)

Shahid (3) goes so far as to suggest that the patterns of the embroidery and the process of its creation served as a model for the shape of Genet's last book:

> It's also what *Un captif amoureux* is all about. The weaving of his life. [. . .]

> This idea that embroidery inspired the structure of this text is very beautiful, and I do believe the book was poorly received because people did not understand it.

It is at this point in her story that Shahid remarks, as we have already quoted above, what happened when Genet delivered the manuscript to Gallimard: the editors did not know what to make of this multi-genred or "hybrid" text. And his reply indicates that he was fully aware of the formal dissonance of the book: "Jean called it 'the bit of disorder in the order.'"

Shahid continues,

> And since they could not find a definition to paste on this text, they said, 'It's not important. It's not interesting, He's getting senile. This is a text where Genet is pimping everybody.' They did not understand that it was exactly the contrary. Facing death, Genet does what he refused to do for seventy years: he lays himself bare, completely, and with a limpidity, a transparency, that I can only regard as mystical. (4)

Comparing the nomadism of Genet's life to that of the Palestinians, Shahid speaks of the same "itinerary of perpetual displacement" which they had in common. Genet spoke (in his report on the Chatila massacre entitled "Four hours in Chatila") of his always staying ready to move—his "position of sudden departure," which is also the position of the refugee, the displaced person. Genet is, says Shahid, weaving his life, as he has woven the book, stitching together "[t]he images of weaving, net, and spider web that recur so frequently in *Un Captif amoureux* disclose the unique way Genet had of inhabiting the world" (Shahid 4).

Autobiographical elements, then, weave in and out of this mesmerizing account of Genet's perspective on the Palestinian revolution like a delicate motif in a Palestinian embroidery or a traditional Turkish kilim.

Ahdaf Soueif recounts from that 1982 experience in Beirut his reaction when, still in shock from what he had seen, he was dragged by Lebanese Phalangist soldiers before their officer: "'Have you just been there?' (pointing to Chatila) 'Yes.'—'And did you see?'—'Yes.'—*'Are you going to write about it?'*—*'Yes'*" (x; emphasis added). And that "yes" is a crucial element of autobiography: the poet remembering the commitment made in the face of great danger, his commitment to write the Palestinian story.

Some history will be indispensable for readers unfamiliar with the Palestinian tragedy. In 1948 Israel was formed by driving out the Palestinians from the coastal plane by means of terrorist attacks by three different Jewish groups—the Stern Gang, the Irgun and Lehi, a disaster known as the Nakbah. Many villages were totally emptied by massacres, some now well documented like Deir Yassein, others have come to light only recently. In June 1967, in the second major stage of ethnic cleansing, the rest of Palestine to the Jordan River was conquered by Israel with the collusion of the US whose cryptographers helped to destroy the Egyptian Air Force. Napalm was used against civilian families fleeing Jerusalem on foot or by bus, and napalm was used to drive 25,000 refugees from 1948 out of the huge refugee camp at Jericho and across the Jordan River into Transjordan. This is documented by Arthur C. Forrest in his book *The Unholy Land* (15-17). At the time of Black September, 1971, the Palestinians were only four years away from the Catastrophe of 1967, and only a single generation—a mere 23 years—away from the original Nakbah of 1948. Many of the young fedayeen encountered by Jean Genet in Jordan would have been children carried across the Jordan River by frantic parents. When the Palestinian organizations armed themselves hoping to re-take their homeland, King Hussein began to feel threatened, and he received a green light (as well as money and weapons from the US) to crush their movement (Genet 43).

The story Genet tells is so fascinating that one forgets to read critically. Yet, to look for the elements of autobiography in *Prisoner of*

Love, it is necessary to look beyond his keen insights into the Palestinian revolution—that ephemeral and in his eyes foredoomed though brilliant performance—and in particular to notice the stress Genet lays on his experience of finding a mother. To place this theme in its proper perspective, let us first turn to the conclusion of the book where Genet is "taking stock." He reflects on the massacres at Sabra and Chatila, asking himself whether they had been a turning point. "But while the act of writing came later, after a period of incubation, nevertheless in a moment like that or those when a single cell departs from its usual metabolism and the original link is created of a future, unsuspected cancer, or of a piece of lace, so I decided to write this book" (429).

Earlier in the book he describes the process of remembering that writing the book required:

> I remember like an owl. Memories come back in "bursts of images." Writing this book, I see my own image far, far away, dwarf size, and more and more difficult to recognize with age. This isn't a complaint. I'm just trying to convey the idea of age and of the form poetry takes when one is old: I grow smaller and smaller in my own eyes and see the horizon speeding towards me, the line into which I shall merge, behind which I shall vanish, from which I shall never return.
>
> (134)

At times in *Prisoner of Love,* Genet imagines his life as having become fused with that of his subjects:

> But I must stress that it's my eyes that saw what I thought I was describing, and my ears that heard it. The form I adopted from the beginning for this account was never designed to tell the reader what the Palestinian revolution was really like. [. . .] What I recount may well be what I experienced but it was different in that the disparateness of my own existence had

merged into the continuity of Palestinian life, though still leaving me with traces, glimpses of, sometimes severances from, my former life. [. . .] Sometimes I wonder whether I didn't live that life especially so that I might arrange its episodes in the same *seeming disorder* as the images in a dream.

(354-355; emphasis added)

Writing the book seemed to Genet to involve a sorting process during which Europe had "become terra incognita" (428). He records having felt as though anything not to do with the book came to seem so far away as to be invisible. There was the Palestinian people, my search for Hamza and his mother, my trips to the East especially to Jordan, and my book. But France, Europe, all the West, no longer existed. [. . .] By the middle of 1983 I was free enough to start writing my *souvenirs,* which were meant to be read as reporting" (429).

I now quote the rest of the final page of the book—the retrospective page in which he sums up for himself what the book has been about:

> Any reality is bound to be outside me, existing in and for itself. The Palestinian revolution lives and will live only of itself. A Palestinian family, made up essentially of mother and son, were among the first people I met in Irbid. *But it was somewhere else that I really found them.*
>
> *Perhaps inside myself.* The pair made up by mother and son is to be found in France and everywhere else. Was it a light of my own that I threw on them, so that instead of being strangers, whom I was observing they became a couple of my own creation? An image of my own that my penchant for day-dreaming had projected on to two Palestinians, mother and son, adrift in the midst of a battle in Jordan?
>
> All I've said and written happened. But why is it that this couple is the only really profound memory I have of the Palestinian revolution?

> I did the best I could to understand how different this revolution was from others, and in a way I did understand it. But what will remain with me is the little house in Irbid where I slept for one night, and fourteen years during which I tried to find out if that night ever happened.
>
> This last page of my book is transparent. (430; emphasis added)

In a curious way, after all his emphasis on the importance of the "image," the Palestinian revolution came to be epitomized for Genet in this frieze, this archetype, so deeply personal that he felt he might have found it in himself and then projected it out into the world. Having looked at the importance Genet gives to this connection with a Palestinian mother and son in his final summing up, I will now try to trace it through the book.

The finding of the lost mother is foreshadowed early in the book when he describes an event that took place when he was in Lebanon, where, like Michael Ondaatje's Kim in *The English Patient,* Genet witnessed a procession of fishermen carrying a picture of Our Lady of the Sea. This image he at first identifies as the Virgin Mary but learns that it actually belongs to an older pagan tradition, a woman on a sea-blue background whose head was surrounded by the stars in Ursa Minor standing on a crescent which represented Islam. But a Benedictine priest tells him, "the lady in the picture was neither virginal nor Christian but belonged to the pre-Islamic 'Peoples of the Sea.' Her origins were pagan, and she'd been worshiped by sailors for thousands of years. In the dimmest of nights she infallibly showed them the North, and because of her the worst-rigged ship was sure to reach harbour safe and sound" (11).

Sleeping under the stars that night at Ajloun, Genet falls asleep watching the constellations and marveling that in a Muslim country "where, as I still believed, woman was something remote" (12), he was able to conjure up a procession of men who had captured the image of a beautiful lady, a lady who represented the Pole Star, eternally fixed immeasurable distances away and who belonged "like every woman" to a different constellation. That night he has an almost mystical experience of feeling soothed by maternal arms: "Though I was lying still in my blankets as I looked up into the sky, following the light, I felt myself swept into a maelstrom, swirled around *and yet soothed by strong but gentle arms.* A little way off, through the darkness, I could hear the Jordan flowing. I was freezing cold" (12; emphasis added),

Several times throughout the story, it is clear that Genet is aware of the Jordan as the locus of the baptism of Christ by John the Baptist. Yet for Genet, the encounter with the Palestinians is prefaced by a sloughing off of the Judeo-Christian morality which he feels has killed him. This experience is dramatized by an account of flying over the North Pole, hearing the word 'Sayonara' from a Japanese airlines hostess, an experience intimately connected with his decision to write this book: "The image I want to record here came to me in a crowd of others which gradually yielded to it in vividness, force and persuasiveness as my decision to write became clear and concentrated on that *image* alone—the *image* of the night at the Pole" (51; emphasis added).

Genet uses "image" here in much the same way Ezra Pound used it to indicate an intense insight, a kind of epiphany, the name it took in James Joyce's modernist style. Genet describes an experience on a flight over the North Pole in 1967 of being cleansed of a "thick black layer of Judeo-Christian morality" against which he had fought so long that his "struggle had become grotesque" (52). The vivid sensation of "clean-up" seems to have been precipitated by hearing a feminine voice pronouncing the Japanese word 'Sayonara' (pronounced like 'Sayonala').The author describes feeling cleansed, at peace, and celebrates by going to the toilet to get rid of a tape-worm "three thousand years long" (53). His "wretched body" (wretched because of the "long degrading siege it had had to withstand from Judeo-Christian ethics") is being cleansed (52). Perhaps this represents the feeling of someone gay suddenly finding himself in an ambience in which his sexuality is no longer regarded as deviant, dirty, and perverse. A comparable feeling of joyful relief is described later when Genet discusses the assumption of feminine costume by a transvestite male as a liberating experience, an event that is discussed several times in this book (see for example 62 and 173-174).

The archetypal family of which Genet speaks in the final page of his book is composed of a young fedayee called Hamza and his mother. Though Genet searches for a way to transpose the Christian iconography into something more Islamic, oddly he never transposes the *Pietà*, the image of the mother Mary holding her dead son Jesus on her lap after he is taken down from the cross, into the image of Hagar and Ishmael, as they are sometimes pictured under the palm tree in the desert. Perhaps Genet was unaware of any corresponding graphic representation of Hagar holding a dead Ishmael. Some such Islamic image seems to be a cultural icon for which he is searching. Before he has even recounted meeting Hamza, Genet mentions Hamza's mother as though in passing: "The various scenes in which Hamza's mother appears are in a way flat. They ooze love and friendship and pity, but how can one simultaneously express all the contradictory emanations issuing from the witnesses?" (32-33). Thus he alludes to the centrality of this meeting several times in the earlier pages, though he reserves its complete exposition for the almost exact center of the text which is also the dramatic climax, since it is both the moment just before his departure from Jordan and the moment immediately before the crushing of the Palestinians in what became known as Black September.

Looking back, Genet realizes that he is interpreting his encounter with Hamza and his mother within the iconography of acts of Christian liturgy. For example, out of the blue, after describing the Phalange and their almost obscene kissing of the gold cross on a young woman's breast, Genet moves to Franco's Spain at Pentecost where he attends a Mass part of which involves a procession of all the celebrants and the faithful out into the wheat fields, the singing of *Veni Creator Spiritus* (Come Creator Spirit) and the blessing of the fields. Genet records a kind of epiphany in which the old pagan animism seems to emerge from the midst of this Catholic ceremony. But he introduces this scene (in which "for me alone, a wonderful thing happened") by saying: "After having looked on with some emotion—*the significance of which, before my meeting with Hamza and his mother, will appear later*—as the black Virgin proffered her child (as it might have been some hoodlum showing a black phallus), I sat down on a bench" (40; emphasis added).

The definitive moment when he actually meets Hamza and his mother occurs just before the culmination of Black September. Because one of the Palestinian leaders decides it is too dangerous for him to stay with the fedayeen, they arrange to get Genet to the Syrian border at Deraa. This plan requires that he stay in the Irbid refugee camp that night to take a taxi in the morning. One of the fedayeen is asked if Genet can stay in his house—this turns out to be Hamza.

> He was twenty, with black hair, a keffiyeh, and just a nascent moustache. He was pale—sallow, rather—despite his tan and the dust.
> "Has your mother got a room free?"
> "Mine."
> "Tonight?"
> "Tonight I'm fighting. He can have my bed."
> "Take him there, then. And God protect him—he's a friend." (179)

It is about noon, in Ramadan in October 1971, with the noise of artillery coming closer, and as they enter the refugee camp, people greet them, some looking curiously at this white-haired foreigner.

In a move typical of the discontinuity of this narration, Genet interrupts his visit to Hamza's house to narrate the murder of three important Palestinian leaders in Beirut on April 9-10, 1973: Kamal Nasir, Kamal Udwan, and Muhammad Yusif al-Najjar were gunned down in their apartments in Beirut by an Israeli death squad posing as drunken gay Arab men. This leads Genet to speculate about whether, had his mother been Jewish, he might have been among those "special forces." "Instead of having me baptized, the orphanage, even though it didn't know whether my mother was Jewish, might have had my body marked with the 'shallow slandered stream'" (184), i.e. circumcised. Once again we are reminded that Genet had been abandoned shortly after birth, leaving him searching, perhaps unconsciously, for a mother.

When they enter the small courtyard of Hamza's home, they find his mother wearing a Kalashnikov like her son's slung over her shoulder. Her smile suggests to Genet "the faint echo and only visible sign of a great peal of laughter filling her whole being" (187). When Hamza tells her that Genet doesn't believe in God, she says, "Well, if he doesn't believe in God I'd better give him something to eat." The family had fled from Haifa after it was bombed in 1948. She prepares a tray of food the sharing of which takes on retrospectively an almost sacramental quality:

> Two plates heaped with pancakes, together with a few lettuce leaves, some quartered tomatoes, four sardines and, I think, three hardboiled eggs.
>
> They ate them, Hamza and the godless Christian, at about three in the afternoon in the month of Ramadan, when the sun had scarcely started to sink in the sky.
>
> I can still see the sky-blue of the little table and its black and yellow flowers, just as I can the details of everything else my eyes and those of the fedayeen once rested on: rocks, trees, fields, the fabric of tents from close to or far away, fir trees, still water, running water, water dark and stagnant. From the twinge of melancholy I feel if it ever leaves me, I

> know that this emotion will never cease to exist. Even if I myself am shot dead it will still go on, felt by someone there, and after him by another, and so on. [. . .]
>
> Hamza and his mother would never see Haifa again. (189)

Here Genet writes without irony or sarcasm: this experience, as I have pointed out, seems to have taken on an iconic reality for him as through it, he gains a kind of immortality:

> Hamza and I were in his mother's house. That seems to suggest that his mother was the head of the family. But having seen her with her son, and remembering the looks they constantly exchanged, I can guess now what their then imperceptible communications really meant. She was a widow, but very strong; a mother armed exactly like her son, and in fact the head of the family. But every microsecond she smilingly delegated her powers to Hamza. And he, while taking orders from Fatah, left her in command and was secretly guided by her. (191)

For Genet, this acceptance into the family is like the initiation into a mystery. He continues: "Remember the Black Virgin of Montserrat, showing her son as greater than herself, as taking precedence of her so that she might exist, and of the child so that he might live forever" (191). Immediately after this reference to the Black Virgin of Montserrat, Genet tells of helping to load the guns of Hamza and his brother-in-law: he speaks of taking part in "the mysteries of the Resistance." His meditation on these "mysteries" shows clearly his Catholic theological training: "The fact that the Virgin Mary is called the Mother of God makes you wonder, since the chronological order is the same for parent-hood human and divine, by what prodigy or by what mathematics the mother came after her Son but preceded her own Father. The order becomes less mysterious when you think of Hamza" (192).

Genet tells of lying fully dressed on Hamza's bed, the shelling deafening and coming closer, when two little raps at the door signal Hamza's mother.

> I could see everything. The mother had just come in. Was she taken in by my pretense? Had she come out of the now ear-splitting darkness, or out of the icy night I carry about with me everywhere? [. . .] Without making a sound she went out and shut the door. The starry sky was gone, I could open my eyes. On the tray were a cup of Turkish coffee and a glass of water. I drank them, shut my eyes and waited [. . .] Another two little taps at the door [. . .] In the light of the stars and the waning moon the same long shadow appeared, as familiar now as if it had come into my room at the same time every night of my life before I went to sleep. Or rather so familiar now that it was inside rather than outside me, coming into me with a cup of Turkish coffee every night since I was born. Through my lashes I saw her move the little table silently back to its place and, still with the assurance of someone born blind, pick up the tray and go out, closing the door.
>
> I realized that the mother came every night with a cup of coffee and a glass of water for Hamza. Without a sound, except for the four little taps at the door, and in the distance, as in a picture by Detaille, gunfire against a background of stars.
>
> Because he was fighting that night, I'd taken the son's place and perhaps played his part in his room and his bed. For one night and for the duration of one simple but oft-repeated act, a man older than she was herself became the mother's son. For "before she was made, I was." *Though younger than I, during that familiar act, she was my mother as well as Hamza's.* It was in my own personal and portable darkness that the door of my room opened and closed. I fell asleep.
>
> (193; emphasis added)

Jean Genet's Un captif amoureux   227

Hamza returns at dawn covered in dust and, pleased with his night's work, falls almost immediately to sleep. When Genet goes into the mother's room to say goodbye, she interrupts her bread baking to make him tea. He learns that the Syrian frontier is open, and around eleven Hamza puts him in a taxi and they say goodbye. He counts up the time they were together and figures it is just eleven hours (196). As the taxi takes him from Jordan through the Deraa crossing into Syria, though he is surrounded by the chaos of the war-torn country he is leaving behind and the dangers of the country destabilized by a military coup, he is preoccupied by thoughts of Hamza:

Reflecting on the images of the Mother and Son in world art, the *Pietás, the mater dolorosa,* the Black Virgin of Montserrat, etc., Genet realizes that the theme is archetypal, "some other image farther back in time and in some place other than Europe, Judea or Palestine [. . .] India [. . .] or perhaps in every man" (202-203). And the reason why he meditates in such depth, the reason why he is compelled to return in 1984, is surely summed up in those words describing the night he slept in Hamza's bed and Hamza's mother served to him the coffee and water she habitually served to Hamza: "Though younger than I, during that familiar act, she was my mother as well as Hamza's" (193).

By some strange alchemy, in that Palestinian refugee camp, just as the horrors of Black September were coming to their tragic end, the quest of Jean Genet for his own lost mother finds a paradoxical resolution. For some mysterious reason, he has come to feel that "an invisible scarf" binds him together with Hamza and his mother (68). And this discovery forms the heart of our investigation into the autobiographical elements in Genet's last book. It was a book which, after witnessing the horrors of the massacre in Chatila Camp in Beirut in 1982, he felt compelled to write. So determined was he to finish it that he cut back on pain-killers in order to retain the lucidity of mind necessary for the task. He had seen the mutilated bodies of women in Chatila, women who had been tortured and then crucified, women whose fingers had been cut off for their rings. And he knew that these atrocities had been arranged and supervised by what he calls, more in sorrow than in anger, "the darkest of all people" (166).

Resistance had to be fought, as he learned from the Palestinian poet, Khaled Abu Khaled, even if there was no hope of winning against "the darkest of all people" because they had the backing of the United States (179). The Palestinian people, Genet says, found their reality suddenly threatened because they had been, without knowing it, characters in someone else's dream "though they still didn't foresee the rude awakening that would take away both their lives and their living" (321). In spite of—or perhaps because of—his premonition that the Palestinian struggle was doomed, Genet found a great peace and serenity, "a precious harvest of time" (118) under the trees in their camps at Ajloun when they played and sang (drumming on empty coffins) music that "let me hear a song that has always been shut up silent within me" (42). Like the music that he found already shut up inside himself, Genet also found the answer to his own quest: on the final page of the book in the passage already quoted above, he says: "A Palestinian family, made up essentially of mother and son, were among the first people I met in Irbid. *But it was somewhere else that I really found them. Perhaps inside myself*" (430; emphasis added).

A great poet, a slum child who never knew his own mother, Jean Genet felt himself included in the loving embrace of a mother and son engaged stoically in what appeared to him a losing battle one violent night at the end of Black September. This embrace inspired in the form of *Prisoner of Love* the most eloquent of elegies.

I think that this book verifies Kate Millett's glowing appraisal of Genet's contribution to the analysis of sexual malaise. In *Sexual Politics*, Millett says: "[Genet] appears to be the only living male writer of first-class literary gifts to have transcended the sexual myths of our era. His critique of the hetero-sexual politic points the way toward a true sexual revolution, a path which must be explored if any radical social change is to come about" (22). Perhaps what impressed Genet so much was the absolute equality between mother and son which allowed them to change roles without missing a beat. The woman silently serving coffee to her guest/son is the same woman who carries the Kalashnikov just like her son's. Perhaps it is this egalitarianism which accounts for his later fantasies of the two in which Genet saw them switch roles, each guarding the other turn about, their nurturing and military roles perfectly shared between them, without any sense of subordination or dominance. In Hamza and his mother, Genet found not only his own mother but an affirmation that the true sexual revolution was at least possible, whatever would happen to the Palestinian revolution, one phase of which ended with Black September.

Works Cited

Choukri, Mohamed. *Jean Genet in Tangier*. Trans. Paul Bowles. New York: Ecco, 1974.

Darraj, Faisal. "The Current State of Arab Culture." *Democratic Palestine*. June 1989. 25-29.

Forrest, Arthur. *The Unholy Land*, Toronto: McClelland and Stewart, 1972.

Genet, Jean. *Un captif amoureux*. Paris: Gallimard, 1986.

___. "Four Hours in Shatila." *Journal of Palestine Studies* 12.3 (Spring 1983): 4-5.

___. *Our Lady of the Flowers*. New York: Grove Atlantic, 1963. Orig. French edition *Notre-Dame-des-Fleurs*. Lyons, France: *L'Arbaléte*, 1943. Revised edition published by *Libraire Gallimard*, introd. J. P. Sartre, 1952.

___. *Prisoner of Love*. Trans. Barbara Bray. Introd. Ahdaf Soueif. New York: New York Review of Books, 2003.

Hussey, Andrew. "The Princes of Exile: Choukri and Genet in Tangier." *Voices of Tangier: Conference Proceedings*. Ed. Khalid Amine, Andrew Hussey and Barry Tharaud. Tangier: Center for Mediterranean and Maghreb Studies 26-28 January 2006. 151-156.

Mallarmé, Stéphane. *Brise marine. Du Parnasse contemporain,* Paris 1865. *Brise marine* annotated by Maureen Jameson. 27 Dec. 2006 <http://www.wings.buffalo.edu/litgloss/mallarme/text.shtml >.

Millett, Kate. *Sexual Politics.* 1969. London: Virago, 1999.

Shahid, Leila. "Jean Genet and the Position of Sudden Departure." *Autodafe* 2, Autumn 2001. 4 Sept. 2006 <http://www.mafhoum.com/press3/92C41.htm>.

Soueif, Ahdaf. "Genet in Palestine." *Al-Ahram Weekly,* Cairo. *Monthly supplement* Issue no. 51, July 2003. Books 2.

Soueif, Ahdaf. Introduction. *Prisoner of Love.* By Jean Genet. New York: New York Review of Books, 2003. ix-xx.

The Brother, the Friend, the Stranger and I: Uwe Timm's Biography of a Post-War German Generation

Jutta Birmele
California State University, Long Beach

Abstract: Uwe Timm's latest books, *In My Brother's Shadow* (*Am Beispiel meines Bruders*), and *Der Freund und der Fremde* (The Friend and the Stranger; not yet translated) are testimonies to the trauma suffered and the obsession with (or absorbedness by) societal changes that have affected Timm's generation: Born in 1940, his life's experience is rooted in the most devastating period of recent German history, but also heavily influenced by the singularly fast-paced reconstruction phase of post-war society, its seeming setbacks during the 1960s and 70s, by explosive "extra-parliamentary" unrest and challenges to the democratic order, and is currently confronted by the repositioning of German national identification after reunification in 1990 and the reopening of debates on how to interpret German history.

The paper will focus on Timm's method of interweaving his own biography with the purported object of his writing, the biography of his unknown brother who died in the Second World War, and the biography of Benno Ohnesorg, who was shot to death by police during a demonstration against Reza Shah Pahlavi of Iran in 1967 in Berlin. To be sure, Timm's probe into the biography of his protagonists is bringing to the fore also the circumstances and predicaments of the lives of an entire generation of young men, but the narration is even more revealing about the author's maturation process and its pain, shortcomings and contradictions. Retrospectively, Timm explores with seriousness and honesty what options existed, what roads were taken, what self-delusions governed and are now in the process of being dismissed or at least questioned. As such, the author captures a strand of a nation's biography and presents it powerfully enough to evoke empathy, and possibly tolerance and understanding in the attentive reader.

Uwe Timm is currently one of the most successful writers in Germany. Born in 1940, he belongs to a generation whose outlook on German society and history was profoundly shaped by the living memory of the German catastrophes of the twentieth century. His life's experience roots in the most devastating period of recent German history, but also is heavily influenced by the singularly productive reconstruction phase of post-war society, the seeming setbacks or at least slow-downs during the 1960s and 70s, and by the "extra-parliamentary" unrest and challenges to the democratic order. In addition, this generation is currently confronted by the repositioning of German national identification and purpose after reunification in 1990 and the reopening of debates on how to interpret German history in retrospect. Timm's latest books, *In My Brother's Shadow*, and *Der Freund und der Fremde* (The Friend and the Stranger; not yet translated) are testimonies to the traumata suffered and the obsession with (or absorbedness by) societal changes that have affected Timm's generation.

The paper will focus on Timm's method of interweaving the purported object of his writing with his own biography, the biography of his brother who died in the Second World War, and the biography of Benno Ohnesorg, who was shot to death by police during a demonstration against Reza Shah Pahlavi of Iran on the occasion of his state visit in 1967 in Berlin. In that sense, Timm is conducting "a dialogue with ghosts," to use a phrase in Claire Martin's essay in this volume on "Theorizing Life: Argentinean History Recovered" (255). Timm's probe into the biography of his protagonists is bringing to the fore also the circumstances and predicaments of the lives of an entire generation of young men and women in West Germany, but the narration is equally revealing about the author's own maturing process and its pain, shortcomings and contradictions. Retrospectively, Timm explores in great honesty what options existed, what roads were taken, what self-delusions governed and are now in the process of being dismissed or at least questioned. As such, the author captures a strand of a nation's biography and presents it powerfully enough to evoke empathy, and possibly tolerance and understanding in the attentive reader.

Timm's exploration of his brother's short diary written during 1943 while serving as a 19-year-old soldier in the SS at the Eastern front, was published in 2003 under the German title *Am Beispiel meines Bruders* (On the Example of my Brother) and in English as *In My Brother's Shadow: A Life and Death in the SS* (2005). Both titles announce the intended exemplary nature of this biographical study that follows on the coattails of several events which succeeded in putting into question some ingrained taboos and ignited public debate about aspects of the unquestioning orthodox reading of German history.

There was, for one, the *Wehrmachtausstellung* of 1999, a photo exhibition depicting German military units engaged in atrocities flying in the face of public perception that only special units had committed war crimes and that the regular troops were "clean." In the same year, the German author and literary professor, W. G. Sebald, had given a series of lectures on *Luftkrieg und Literatur* (later published under the title *On the Natural History of Destruction*) in Zurich, which opened for discussion the topic of German suffering (Allied bombing had resulted in 900,000 civilian casualties). Sebald, as an author had made it his literary mission in his novels and his academic essays to serve the cause of those "to whom the greatest injustice was done," the most horrific case being the Holocaust. Pointing to the immense suffering by German civilians on account of the vast carpet bombings of German cities did therefore not make him vulnerable to having his motive questioned (i.e. offsetting German guilt with German victimhood).

Sebald, who had lived and worked for most of his adult life in England, set in motion a series of new documentary and fictional accounts in which Germans were portrayed as victims, e.g. historian Jörg Friedrich's book *Der Brand* (2002) detailed the fire-bombing of Dresden, and Noble Prize author Günter Grass' novella, *Im Krebsgang* (Crabwalk), appeared in the same year, centering on the sinking of the Wilhelm Gustloff in 1945 in the Baltic Sea. The ship was crammed with refugees fleeing from the advancing Soviet forces. It is estimated that as many as 9000 German refugees drowned, making it the largest sea disaster in history. This horrific event was largely ignored by German and non-German historians and fiction writers, as well as the German public since German suffering was turned into a taboo by the mainstream press and German scholarship. Clearly, at the turn of the millennium, a paradigm change in the interpretation of history is noticeable among writers and scholars in Germany. Perpetrators and victims are in some instances no longer neatly separable.

It was therefore timely in 2003 that Timm turned to a literary rendition of the brief life of his brother Karl-Heinz and to questioning his role as perpetrator and victim (Timm's brother died at age 19, after enduring the amputation of both legs), a painful subject in his family which Timm did not have the courage to address until after his parents and older sister had died. 16 years his senior, the ghost of the unknown brother, kept alive by the parents' grief and idolization, obviously and understandably burdened the author's childhood with feelings of guilt and nagging questions. Timm's is a family like numerous others who tried to find ways to cope with losses, displacement (they lost their home during the air raids on Hamburg in July 1943) and economic uncertainty at best, if not outright chaos.[1] As Timm states, "writing about my brother means writing about my father too." And at another occasion, he refers to his "decision to write about my brother, and thus about myself too" (10), turning the book into an exemplary study of a lower middle-class German family which had undergone loss of life and home. This universal biographical character is underlined by the fact that Timm rarely uses names but rather appellations like "my brother" or even "the boy" and "my mother" and "my father" and "my sister." After all, they could be the family members of millions of other Germans.

The central and for Timm most painful question that has cast a shadow over his entire life, is the nagging fear that his brother, like thousands of other SS soldiers, was perhaps involved in war crimes

---

[1] The novel *Der Verlorene* (*Lost*) by Hans-Ulrich Treichel has a similar theme.

and other atrocities, particularly as they have been recorded on the Eastern front, e.g. in Christopher R. Browning's book *Ordinary Men: Reserve Police Battalion 101 and the Final Solution in Poland* which had uncovered and brought this sordid history into the public's awareness.[2] Like most of Browning's subjects, Timm's brother was "ordinary" and actually a rather sensitive, quiet youngster praised for his honesty and love of animals. How are we to interpret, asks Timm, the diary notes which Karl-Heinz wrote between February and August 1943 in which the sentence "75 m away Ivan smoking cigarettes, fodder for my MG" stands out (10, 27)? Did Timm's brother, the blond, tall, good-looking and dreamy youngster, turn into an unfeeling brute, a killing machine? All that is left of him is a small box that contains his toothbrush, a comb, a few letters and a brief diary. But even the most careful scrutiny of the cryptic diary entries and additional archival research in Ukraine on his brother's SS unit do not reveal any incidents of atrocities in which the brother could have been implicated. Yet, this is not exculpating his brother in Uwe Timm's eyes who has been shaped by the extreme and often violent, very self-righteous student unrest of the so called 1968 generation. They had denounced the silence of the father generation and their complicity in the fascist regime. Rather than subscribing to the maxim when in doubt, when no evidence is brought to light, the accused is to be considered innocent, Timm blames his brother (and his father) for having gone along with rather than resisted the Nazi regime, that they used the excuse "we only carried out our duty, we only followed orders." He condemns his father for keeping silent after the war, and will not consider this silence as an excusable coping mechanism for loss and grief incurred.

Timm is most of all appalled, and even horrified, by his brother's *voluntary* entry into the SS, and his father's lifelong unwavering support of him, yet at the same time he confesses: "sometimes, very occa-

---

[2] In view of his long history of judgementalism, the recent revelation of his own membership in the SS by 78-year-old Günter Grass in his autobiography *Beim Häuten der Zwiebel* (Peeling the Onion) is ironic.

sionally, I feel him close to me" (143). He recognizes a "curious likeness to my son and me" (144). This acknowledgement signals a more nuanced stance towards those who wore the uniform and indicates a new distancing from the single-minded self-righteousness and judgemental attitude of past times which characterized the 1968 generation. It recognizes the magnitude of complexity, ambiguity of motives and mentality of the father generation. Whether this signals a new understanding, rather than just emotional attachment, is, however, somewhat questionable since Timm ignores the psychological, political and economic circumstances under which the father generation and his brother's cohorts acted. Viewed with hindsight, Timm still sits in judgement (as in 1968) but at the same time, and that is new, he attempts to generate a level of empathy. Very visibly, Timm takes great pains to be clear that in no way is he suggesting to "make the guilt relative, to shift the guilt to the victors, to make them participants in our guilt" (121). His brother's suffering does not exculpate him. German suffering is not offset against German guilt (Gerstenberg). The story of Timm's family "serves as a microcosm of the German catastrophe" (Johnson), the biography of Timm's family is the biography of countless families in Germany.

In his latest book, *Der Freund und der Fremde* (The Friend and the Stranger), Timm takes again a critical view of the 68 generation, not unlike what he did in his novel *Rot* (Red) of 2001, and in a much earlier novel, *Kerbels Flucht* (Kerbel's Flight), of 1980. His own autobiographical description is in many respects exemplary for many of his contemporaries. Thus the following elements are all prominent in Timm's biography: issues of social advancement (Timm, coming from a lower-middle-class background, was given the opportunity to qualify for university entrance), life-style liberties as the result of West Germany's Americanization (frequenting the *Amerikahaus*, thinking of emigration to the USA, seeking his own destiny outside the confines of the family), the decidedly radical turn to the left political spectrum (Timm becomes a member of the Communist Party), the rejection of authority, the search for a new intellectual home (his place of choice was Paris), fascination with existentialism, especially Albert Camus' *L'étranger* as a decisive influence on his generation. Timm is indeed to live in Paris and write a doctoral dissertation on Camus with the title "Das Problem der Absurdität bei Camus" (The Problem of Absurdity in Camus), and he is to exhibit a reluctance to make commitments in friendships and partnerships (cohabitation rather than marriage), a typical aspect of Timm's generation.

The book is exemplary for Timm's self-reflective writing style as it attains almost the character of a private notebook. He recalls in non-chronological fashion a series of incidents, dialogues, and situations that bring to life his relationship with Benno Ohnesorg. Like Timm, Ohnesorg was born in 1940 and like the author he grew up in a lower middle-class milieu, became a shop window decorator, and like Timm, qualified himself for higher education at a state-sponsored special prep-school at a time when less than 10% of their cohorts attended a university. Having left their family's social standing behind, they subscribed to French existentialism, attempting to find their destiny on their own, and dreamed of a just society. They became each other's first literary critics, but then parted ways. Years later, Timm sees the infamous photo in the newspapers that depicts Ohnesorg dying in the streets of Berlin, shot by a policeman during a demonstration on June 2, 1967.

Although Ohnesorg was hardly a student rebel and was more by accident than by design at the periphery of the fateful demonstration against the Shah of Iran, the 26-year-old who did not belong to any political group would become after his senseless death the icon of German radical student activism. In his book, Timm wants to explore what was typical and what was singular in Ohnesorg's biography. His retrospective book looks at the hollow and conceited as well as the justified goals and tactics of the student movement. He uses Camus' *The Stranger* and the senseless, even absurd murder that it describes, as a foil for Ohnesorg's death.

The title of the book is ambiguous, the friend is at the same time *the stranger*, since Timm has only limited insight into Ohnesorg's thoughts and motivations (after all, they had contact only for about two years), and although Ohnesorg, like Timm, wanted to become a writer, there is only one poem that Timm can locate of his friend. The entire idea of friendship is put into question, and in the relationship between Ohnesorg and Timm resonates their fascination with Camus' *The Stranger*, which became a pivotal text for Timm's and Ohnesorg's generation in West Germany. Timm clearly sees a parallel between the senselessness of Mersault's killing of an unknown Algerian Arab in *The Stranger*, and policeman Kurras' shooting of Ohnesorg in Berlin. Ohnesorg had spent a year in France, and Timm had stayed there for several years. They emulated the detachment of the individual described in Camus, the rejection of ideology which for them does not, however, lead to a rejection of commitment to social causes, and even equated their own "resistance" against state authority, which they felt compromised by surviving, unrepentant Nazism, with Camus' activism in the Resistance during the Second World War.

In 1968, student activists made use of Ohnesorg's death for the purpose of justifying violence against the state that, to their minds, had evolved into a force of occupation. This brought them into line with Camus' role in the resistance against the German occupiers during the war and made them, in their own eyes, descendants of Camus, the father figure. The Vietnam War, the oppression of the Third World, the stifling hierarchical structure at the German universities, the confining bourgeois culture in Germany, gender discrimination, environmental depletion, and a host of other issues subsequently became additional causes for radical activism which did not shy away from the use of violence in an effort to radicalize and polarize public opinion. In focusing on "The Friend," limited though as Timm's personal knowledge of him is, and on his own biography, Timm recreates a mosaic of features that recalls for us the biography of a whole generation. To be sure, in retrospect, the author recognizes the simplistic and distorted understanding of the state that carried left-wing radical activism to a boiling point and that was, to some extent, self-defeating.

In conclusion, by seemingly focusing on episodes in the biography of one person (his brother, his "friend" Ohnesorg), Timm injects his own biography into the narrative and the characteristics of his contemporaries who underwent similar intellectual and emotional developments. His persistent use of definite articles and pronouns instead of names indicates the author's intention to draw generational rather than singular life stories. He succeeds in uncovering buried taboos, questions assumptions, and steers towards new approaches to a fuller understanding of the mentalities and events that shaped his generation of Germans, who inherited the fall-out from the fathers' bad deeds. Joschka Fischer's (the former German foreign minister) cohorts, to whom Timm belongs, have noticeably mellowed and made compromises. While politically remaining situated on the left, they are less certain of the clear division of the German population into black and white, good and bad, and do not automatically view Germans collectively as perpetrators. Though they also seem to question or rethink now the legitimacy of violent confrontations that recklessly endangered the democratic process in the 1960s and 1970s, this is an ongoing process that has not yet reached a satisfying consensus.

Works Cited

Friedrich, Jörg. *Der Brand: Deutschland im Bombenkrieg 1940-1945*. München: Propyläen, 2002. English trans.: *The Fire: The Bombing of Germany, 1940-1945*. Trans. Allison Brown. New York: Columbia University Press, 2006.

Gerstenberg, Katharina. German Guilt, German Victims: The Return of the Past in Recent Literature. H-Net List on German History. H-German@h-net.org (Feb. 2, 2005).

Grass, Günter. *Im Krebsgang*. Göttingen: Steidl, 2002. English trans.: *Crabwalk*. Trans. Krishna Winston. London : Faber, 2003.

———. *Beim Häuten der Zwiebel.* Göttingen: Steidl, 2006.

Johnson, Daniel. "In My Brother's Shadow, by Uwe Timm." *The Daily Telegraph* 20 Aug. 2005.

Martin, Claire Emilie. "Theorizing Life: Argentinean History Recovered." This vol. 253-262.

Sebald, W. G. *Luftkrieg und Literatur.* München, Wien: Carl Hanser, 1999. English trans.: *On the Natural History of Destruction.* Trans. Anthea Bell. New York: Random House, 2003.

Timm, Uwe. *Am Beispiel meines Bruders.* Köln: Kiepenheuer & Witsch, 2003. English trans.: *In My Brother's Shadow: A Life and Death in the SS.* Trans. Anthea Bell. New York: Farrar, Straus & Giroux, 2005.

———. *Der Freund und der Fremde.* Köln: Kiepenheuer & Witsch, 2005.

———. *Kerbels Flucht.* Köln: Kiepenheuer & Witsch, 1991.

———. *Rot.* Köln: Kiepenheuer & Witsch, 2005.

Treichel, Hans-Ulrich. *Der Verlorene.* Frankfurt am Main: Suhrkamp, 1998. English trans.: *Lost.* Trans. Carol Brown Janeway. New York: Vintage, 2000.

Being in Time: Reading the Written Self in Alev Tekinay's *Nur der Hauch vom Paradies* (Only the Breeze from Paradise)

Özlem Öğüt
Boğaziçi University

Abstract: Izmir-born Alev Tekinay teaches at Augsburg University and is an award-winning poet and novelist, who lives in Germany and publishes her literary and scholarly works in German. Engin Ertürk, the narrator-protagonist of her novel *Nur der Hauch vom Paradies*, is an acclaimed "Turkish" or "immigrant" author, who is working on his degree in German Linguistics under the supervision of Turkish-German professor Faika Sander ("Fa") in Augsburg, where Tekinay herself is a professor.

The novel revolves around Engin's "intercity life," as he calls his travels between cities in Germany to read from his famous autobiographical novel *Nur der Hauch vom Paradies*, and it is from the passages he selects from his novel before, during or after his presentations, as well as his reminiscences in trains and hotel rooms that the reader derives information about his life, particularly the difficulties and dilemmas he and his sister have had to experience as children of first-generation Turkish immigrant parents who had a hard time accommodating themselves to German culture.

Although Engin constantly alerts the reader to the fictional elements in his autobiography, which either compensate for fading memories or merely satisfy the author's need for fantasy, the reader cannot help but associate Engin's life with Tekinay's, especially because Engin, Fa, and Emel (Engin's sister) each reflect different elements from Tekinay's life and identity.

> If the autobiographical moment prepares for a meeting of 'writing' and 'selfhood,' a coming together of method and subject matter, this destiny—like the retrospective glance that presumably initiates autobiography—is always deferred. Autobiography reveals gaps, and not only gaps in time and space or between the individual and the social, but also a widening divergence between the manner and matter of its discourse. That is, autobiography reveals the impossibility of its own dream: what begins on the presumption

> of self-knowledge ends in the creation of a fiction that covers over the premises of its construction.
>
> —Shari Benstock, *The Private Self: Theory and Practice of Women's Autobiographical Writing* 11

Contemporary autobiographical studies tend to undermine the humanist, essentialist agenda of traditional autobiography, based on the representability of a central, stabile self. They shift attention to "pluralist, multidimensional, multifaceted" subjectivity (Bergland 133), a shift which undoubtedly was propelled by postmodernist/poststructuralist approaches to subjectivity as well as to history as constantly being (re)constructed, and therefore processual.

Betty Bergland reads at the center of the autobiography a postmodern "dynamic subject that changes over time, is situated historically in the world and positioned in multiple discourses" rather than "an *essentialist individual*, imagined to be coherent and unified, the originator of her own meaning" (134). In her *Subjectivity, Identity, and the Body*, Sidonie Smith writes that "self signals an understanding of the human being as metaphysical, essential, and universal," whereas the term "subject" implies "the culturally constructed nature of any notion of 'selfhood'" (189 n; qtd. in Henke xiv).

Most scholars who take a critical stance towards essentialist notions of selfhood as well as towards autobiography as a reflection of it also underscore the "androcentricity"[1] of such notions. Leigh Gilmore writes that "traditional studies of autobiography naturalized the self-representation of (mainly) white, presumably heterosexual, élite men," thus "participating in the cultural production of a politics of identity, a politics that maintains hierarchies through its reproduction of class, sexuality, race, and gender as terms of 'difference' in a social field of power" (5). As Gilmore further remarks, one of the ways in which such fixed categories can be undermined is by accentuating the disso-

---

[1] See, for example, Sidonie Smith's *A Poetics of Woman's Autobiography* and Shari Benstock's *The Private Self*.

nance between the person who says 'I' and the 'I' as a function of language (6-7). Shari Benstock points to how that dissonance is carefully disguised in traditional autobiographies which seek to foreground the autobiographical self:

> In definitions of autobiography that stress self-disclosure and narrative account, that posit a self called to witness (as an authority) to 'his' own being, that propose a double referent for the first-person narrative (the present 'I' and the past 'I'), or that conceive of autobiography as 'recapitulation and recall',[2] the Subject is made an Object of investigation (the first-person actually masks the third-person) and is further divided between the present moment of the narration and the past on which the narration is focused. These gaps in the temporal and spatial dimensions of the text itself are often successfully hidden from reader and writer, so that the fabric of the narrative appears seamless, spun of whole cloth. The effect is magical—the self appears organic, the present the sum total of the past, the past an accurate predictor of the future. (19)

According to Benstock, "this conception of the autobiographical rests on a firm belief in the *conscious* control of artist over subject matter" and "this view of the life history is grounded in authority" (19). She argues that, contrary to this definition of autobiography, the most interesting aspect of the autobiographical is

> the measure to which 'self' and 'self-image' might not coincide, can never coincide in language—not because certain forms of self writing are not self-conscious enough but because they have no investment in creating a cohesive self over time. Indeed, they seem to exploit difference and change over sameness and identity. (15)

---

[2] Benstock specifically refers to James Olney's view of autobiography. She also takes a critical stance against Georges Gusdorf in this respect.

Alev Tekinay's *Nur der Hauch vom Paradies* (Only the Breeze from Paradise) is a novel which defies essentialist or universalizing conceptions of (autobiographical) self. Not only are the unity of the author/narrator/character interrogated and problematized in it but also the hegemonic conceptions of gender and nation. The narrator splits himself into the subject of self-writing, self-reading, and self-reminiscing, constantly emphasizing the part imagination and intertextuality play in his narrative, especially when he cannot fully retrieve his past through memory, thereby undermining the mimetic notion of autobiographical writing, which presumes an unproblematic representation of reality as well as a unified subject. Tekinay's writing successfully exposes "the gaps in the temporal and spatial dimensions of the text," thus transgressing the limits of genre and identity (Benstock 5).

Tekinay aptly merges autobiographical elements with fiction since she divides her life experiences between at least three personae in her novel: the narrator-protagonist Engin Ertürk, a male doctoral student of German Linguistics and a famous Turkish-German writer like herself, Engin's professor and dissertation supervisor Faika Sander. "Die Fa," as her students call her, is, again like Tekinay herself, a professor of German at Augsburg University. Engin's twin sister Emel is a young Turkish college student in Germany just as Tekinay herself was. It is through lengthy excerpts that Engin reads from his "autobiographical novel," which bears the same title as Tekinay's, and through his comments and reminiscences in the fictional present about its content as well as the conditions of its writing, that the novel unfolds. In fact, the novel centers around Engin's "intercity life" as he describes his frequent trips between different cities in Germany which he undertakes to read from or give presentations on his famous autobiographical novel. He selects and reads passages from it before, during or after his presentations, and reflects on them in trains and hotel rooms, tries to revive and revise memories, talks to his readers and strangers on the way who respond differently to his authorship and/or foreignness.

Sometimes it is his remembrance of a certain time or experience in his life that compels him to find pages in the book which focus on it, to compare his present sentiments about it with those in the past, only to find that they often are different. He ponders to what extent he inflated the effect of certain incidences in his life or the intensity of certain emotions. Engin also often underscores the discrepancy between his memories and those of other characters concerning the same events. Thus, he constantly alerts the reader to the fictional elements in his autobiography, which either substitute for faded memories or merely satisfy the author's urge to fantasize.

Intertextual references in the novel also point to the crossings between fact and fiction. At the same time, they underscore multifaceted identities in Engin's narrative. He associates his dark curly hair as well as his spontaneity with the same characteristics of the German author Clemens Brentano, whose "half Italian" (52) temper he admires. He also compares his relationship to his sister Emel as well as her relationship to his best friend Martin to Brentano's relationship to his sister Bettina and hers to Brentano's best friend Achim von Arnim. Moreover, his awareness of multiple selves makes him think of the magic theater in Herman Hesse's *Steppenwolf.*

Tekinay's choice of a male narrator/protagonist can be considered as a move to unsettle the boundaries of genre along with those of gender. This parallels her problematization of other hegemonic systems in the novel, for instance nation. Neither Turkishness nor Germanness appears as unified, stable concepts in *Nur der Hauch vom Paradies*, which especially becomes evident in the variety of reactions to his novel from German and Turkish readers, both from Germany and Turkey. While some pay tribute to Engin's work since they think that Engin serves as a role model for young Turks in Germany, or that his novel will challenge the stereotyping and prejudiced attitudes of Germans towards the Turkish minority, others condemn his novel for portraying his family, especially his father, in a negative light and for not paying due respect to Turkish and Muslim culture. The novel presents gender and national identity as pluralistic rather than authentic, which is precisely what Steven V. Hunsacker expects to find in autobiography:

> Autobiographers [. . .] imagine new versions of the community against dominant forms of national identity in an attempt to clear space for themselves within otherwise restrictive national situations [. . .] to establish new, more liberating, and more convenient models of nationality [. . .] to imagine the nation anew and to thereby choose and fashion identity through the combination of disparate and often contradictory elements [. . .]. (5)

Drawing on Julia Kristeva's *Nations without Nationalism*, Hunsaker emphasizes "the right and the power to identify oneself by selecting, discarding, altering, and preserving models of religious, gender, political, ethnic and national identity" (5), which has direct bearing on Tekinay's protagonist Engin, who moves from exclusive to inclusive conceptions of self-identity.

Engin Ertürk was born in Germany to first-generation Turkish immigrant parents and distinguished himself as an award-winning writer of "immigrant literature." Engin detests this label attached to his work and identity. He does not consider himself as a foreigner or a migrant. On the contrary, he regards Germany as his native country since he was born and raised there, and German as his native language since it is the language in which he expresses himself most comfortably; he even writes his poetry and fiction in German. Furthermore, he feels like a foreigner in Turkey because his Turkish is not as good as his German and he cannot relate to the customs and habits of the people there. He does not yet realize that it is also a lack of interest and effort on his part to understand and embrace that component of his identity, which, in fact, implies his submission to the totalizing and "otherizing" discourses of patriarchy and nationalism.

Being the son of a "simple fruit and vegetable salesman," which finds special emphasis both in the media and his conversations with his readers, he is admired as a striking symbol of second-generation Turkish assimilation to German language and culture. Engin's image appears in newspapers, magazines, and on TV, together with his family in their modest home, his father with his typical Turkish moustache and his mother with her headscarf; her "modern-looking" sister Emel, who studies medicine, is another example of immigrant integration into the host culture although she was also born and raised in Germany.

Engin's tension-laden relationship with his parents, especially with his father, whom he often describes as a "tyrant" due to his obsessive insistence on his children's adherence to Turkish customs and lifestyle to avoid the "corrupting" habits of German youth, constitute a significant part of the novel. Engin's circle of friends, however, consists of young people from various ethnic, national, religious backgrounds. *Nur der Hauch vom Paradies* is set in highly multicultural environments in Germany. The novel displays the multifarious dynamics of relationships in such multinational and multiethnic societies, in which minority groups either stick together to resist being absorbed by the dominant culture, or reject their minority position, sometimes with the purpose to assimilate fully to the host culture, but often as a refusal to belong to any particular community. The levels of allegiance and alienation vary to such a great extent, even in the case of individuals who are allegedly members of the same national, cultural or religious community, and the intersections between supposedly distinct communities are so multifaceted that closure of identity becomes illusory. Rather, all of those supposedly distinct communities, from the smallest minority to the majority, inevitably undergo constant transformation though their interaction. Therefore, they can only be conceived of as communities or identities in process or in transition. Pierre Bourdieu underlines the significance of "cultural contact" in engendering different "fields of opinion," "the loci of the confrontation of competing discourses, orthodox and heterodox beliefs, to challenge 'doxa'" which he defines as "the naturalization of the arbitrariness of established orders or systems of classification, which reproduce the objective classes, such as the divisions by sex, age, or position" (160), or as "what *goes without saying because it comes without saying*," silent, unformulated, because unquestioned (163). Bourdieu further contends that "[t]he dominated classes have an interest in pushing back the limits of *doxa* and exposing the arbitrariness of the taken for granted," whereas "the dominant classes have an interest in defending the integrity of *doxa*, or, short of this, of establishing in its place the necessarily imperfect substitute, *orthodoxy*" (164).

The significance attached to religious and national conventions on the part of both the Turkish-Muslim community and German-Christian majority in *Nur der Hauch vom Paradies* illustrates Bourdieu's discussion of tensions between *doxa* and the field of opinions. As Bourdieu argues, "The taxonomies of the mythico-ritual system at once divide and unify, legitimating unity in division, that is to say, hierarchy" (160). He further comments that "one function of symbolic exchanges such as feasts and ceremonies" is "to favor the circular reinforcement which is the foundation of collective belief" whose "self-evidence needs to be reduplicated and thus affirmed by the instituted discourses" (162). *Nur der Hauch vom Pradies* exhibits different dynamics of hierarchies at play in multicultural Germany, which empower Engin's father in a system of patriarchy, who, however, is disempowered as an immigrant. Therefore, he feels all the more the need to hold on to and assert his national and religious identity, which also secures his privileged position as a father/man granted him by patriarchy. Engin, however, refuses to take advantage of his patriarchal power position. He realizes that patriarchy and nationalism impose limitations on his identity. Therefore, he constantly tries to refute and transcend them. For example, he encourages his sister to elope with her German boyfriend Martin, who, as mentioned earlier, is Engin's best friend, instead of continuing the patriarchal tradition, which entitles him to protect the so-called honor of his sister. He chooses German as his field of study instead of medicine, law or engineering, thus disappointing his father. It is important to note here that his father, by encouraging Engin to study one of those "decent" subjects, motivates him to become different from his parents, which contradicts his attempts to keep him within familial, national and religious boundaries. Although Engin's defiant attitude and his indifference to traditional Turkish or Muslim lifestyles are a constant source of grief and anger for him, Halil Ertürk encourages Engin from his early childhood on to gain full command of German, and is proud of his son who becomes a famous writer after all his objections to his literary endeavors. Now he is the father of the author who is acclaimed as the "exceptional immigrant," a label whose meaning, as mentioned earlier, is highly contested. Halil Ertürk is also proud of his daughter who studies medicine although he initially objects to her leaving home to go to university and is rather concerned about the possibility that she may lead an independent life, which is not becoming for a Turkish-Muslim girl.

It is not only Halil Ertürk but also Engin himself, who constantly has to revise his pre-formed ideas and accordingly transform his identity. Instead of replacing one nationalism with another he opens himself more and more to the effects of different cultures he has access to, realizing the shortcomings of an exclusionary attitude. He starts dreaming about a Turkish wedding in Izmir with his German girlfriend Sabine. His habit of adopting new names for himself when he talks to strangers now also includes names from Muslim countries. He decides to let a Turkish film director produce a film version of his novel. He feels like "moonlight dancing" (page) as his father. In addition to all, he decides to improve his Turkish language skills.

The role that "Fa," Engin's Turkish-German professor and dissertation advisor at Augsburg University, plays in Engin's readiness to embrace different components of his identity is undeniable. She gradually becomes a role model for Engin because she has made it to the top accepting rather than denying her Turkishness as an indispensable and enriching part of her identity. Engin implies that his *Nur der Hauch vom Paradies* is in fact Fa's life story, by referring, in a flashback, to his thoughts about her after his previous novel and his decision to make her the heroine of his next, also underlining that the novel will not completely leave out reality although it will leave much room for imagination (123). He describes the central idea of the novel as "the awakening of a young woman without identity in a foreign room," also alluding to Kafka's *Metamorphosis* except that Gregor Samsa already has an identity as a giant insect when he wakes up (123; my translation).

In her *Shattered Subjects*, Suzette A. Henke emphasizes how simultaneous historicity and narrativity of autobiography can challenge hegemonic structures of power:

> Autobiography has always offered the tantalizing possibility of reinventing the self and reconstructing the subject ideologically inflected by language, history, and social imbrication. As a genre, life-writing encourages the author/narrator to reassess the past and to reinterpret the intertextual codes inscribed on personal consciousness by society and culture. Because the author can instantiate the alienated or marginal self into the pliable body of a protean text, the newly revised subject, emerging as the semifictive protagonist of an enabling counternarrative, is free to rebel against the values and practices of a dominant culture and to assume an empowered position of political agency in the world. (xv-xvi)

Engin Ertürk decides to write his next novel (following *Nur der Hauch vom Paradies*) about the life of a Turkish friend of his who was killed by the German police upon false suspicion. He says that Germany has different faces for different foreigners, thereby also referring to himself as a "foreigner." There is no doubt that his prospective biography of Enis Çakar will also call embody elements from a large pool of identities to call into question essentialist conceptions of identity, which often lead to oppression.

Nur der Hauch vom Paradies displays the ongoing process of re-inscription of identity in the interaction between infinitely layered communities in multicultural environments, all of which affect and transform each other in multiple ways. These hybrid identities, which are in a constant state of becoming, open vistas into pluralistic, multi-faceted, transitional and transnational conceptions of nation, race, ethnicity and subjectivity. Situating self-representation in relation to a range of critical and disciplinary discourses such as gender and nation, the novel represents "the increasingly transdisciplinary agenda of contemporary autobiographical studies" (Ashley, Gilmore, and Peters 3-4).

Works Cited

Ashley, Kathleen, Leigh Gilmore, and Gerald Peters, eds. *Autobiography and Postmodernism*, Amherst: University of Massachusetts Press, 1994.

Benstock, Shari. *The Private Self: Theory and Practice of Women's Autobiographical Writing*. Chapel Hill: University of North Carolina Press, 1988.

Bergland, Betty. "Postmodernism and the Autobiographical Subject: Reconstructing the 'Other.'" Ashley, Gilmore, and Peters 130-166.

Bourdieu, Pierre. "Structures, Habitus, Power: Basis for a Theory of Symbolic Power." *Culture/Power/History: A Reader in Contemporary Social Theory*. Eds. Nicholas B. Dirks, Geoff Eley, Sherry B. Ortner. Princeton, New Jersey: Princeton University Press, 1994. 155-199.

Gilmore, Leigh. "The Mark of Autobiography: Postmodernism, Autobiography, and Genre." Ashley, Gilmore, and Peters 3-18.

Gusdorf, Georges. "Conditions and Limits of Autobiography." Olney, ed., 28-48.

Henke, Suzette A. Henke. *Shattered Subjects: Trauma and Testimony in Women's Life-Writing.* New York: St. Martin's, 2000.

Hesse, Herman. *Der Steppenwolf.* Frankfurt am Main: Suhrkamp, 1972.

Hunsaker, Steven V. *Autobiography and National Identity in the Americas.* Charlottesville and London: University Press of Virginia, 1999.

Kristeva. *Nations without Nationalism.* Trans. Leon S. Roudiez. New York: Columbia University Press, 1993.

Olney, James, ed. *Autobiography: Essays Theoretical and Critical.* Princeton: Princeton University Press, 1980.

___. "Some Versions of Memory/Some Versions of Bios: The Ontology of Autobiography." *Autobiography: Essays Theoretical and Critical* 236-267.

Smith, Sidonie. *A Poetics of Woman's Autobiography: Marginality and the Fictions of Self-Representation.* Bloomington: Indiana University Press, 1987.

___. *Subjectivity, Identity, and the Body.* Bloomington: Indiana University Press, 1993.

Tekinay, Alev. *Nur der Hauch vom Paradies.* Frankfurt am Main: Brandes & Apsel, 1993.

Theorizing Life:
Argentinean History Recovered

Claire Emilie Martin
California State University, Long Beach

Abstract: Argentinean writers in the last two decades have set out to recuperate—in wildly disparate ways—the memory of the country's most complex and painful historical events. Some have drawn inspiration from the struggle for independence and from the colorful and bloody characters of national reconstruction during the nineteenth century, while others have dealt with the Peronist era, the "Dirty War," the coups, the juntas, the "disappeared," the Mothers of the Plaza de Mayo, the Malvinas war, the return to democracy, the economic and political debacle of the past few years. Many Argentinean writers have turned to the autobiography, the epistolary narrative, the memoir, and the recreation of the collective memory to attain the understanding denied to them otherwise. Through the act of writing a life and constructing the self and the other, Argentinean fiction is grappling with its tormented past. In this study, I propose to theorize life writing at the service of history in a country where historical writing has been unable to quench Argentineans' thirst for answers, for a collective memory recuperated and made whole. I have chosen the first two narratives by Sara Rosenberg, *Un hilo rojo* (1998; A Red Thread) and *Cuaderno de invierno* (1999; Winter Notebook), to illustrate this marked tendency in Argentinean letters.

Argentinean fiction in the last two decades has shown a remarkable ability to engage in a dialogue with its ghosts. Writers have set out to recuperate—in wildly disparate ways—the memory of the country's most complex and painful historical events.[1] Some have drawn inspi-

---

[1] Authors such as Liliana Bellone in *Fragmentos de siglo* (1999; Fragments of the Century), Carlos Gorostiza in *Vuelan las palomas* (1999; The Flight of the Doves) and *La buena gente* (2002; The Good Folks), Andrés Neuman in *Bariloche* (1999), Emilce Rotondo in *El 74* (1999; 1974), Paula Winkler in *Cartas escritas en silencio para el viento* (2001; Letters Written Silently for the Wind), among dozens of others, utilize the intimate and self-reflexive act of the recreation of the self to graft on to their stories the life of the nation.

ration from the struggle for independence and from the colorful and bloody characters of national reconstruction during the nineteenth century, while others have dealt with the Peronist era, the "Dirty War," the coups, the juntas, the "disappeared," the Mothers of the Plaza de Mayo, the Malvinas war, the return to democracy, and the economic and political debacle of the past few years. Writers and intellectuals of all stripes have been hard at work uncovering the truth of the recent past—a past shrouded in lies and deception. How can a nation so seeped in this violent malaise be true to itself and look forward to its future? Fiction attempts to give an answer to these and many more questions. Argentinean fiction of the nineties and the first years of the twentyfirst century has become the repository of the country's forbidden memories; it has emerged as the public conscience of a people too disheartened to seek the truth; it has taken the initiative to question the mad dash of recent governments and the private sector towards neoliberal chimeras that have depleted the vast natural resources of what used to be one of the richest lands on earth. In sum, it has dared to expose the resounding and persistent failure of this once promising nation. Fernando Reati, in *Collective Memory and Politics of Forgetting*, analyzes the transcendence of the lexicon of memory: "Amnesty, Amnesia, anesthesia [. . .] these words acquire a particular importance in Latin America [. . .] If the seventies are the years of terror, the eighties and nineties are those of the conflict between a will to remember and an effort to forget" (11).

The theme of revisiting the past is a common thread throughout Latin American fiction writing. However, in the last quarter-century, these perennial issues have taken a new turn as—in the case of Argentina—the political, economic, social and ideological realities have defied the wildest imagination and the direst predictions. The nation defaulted on its foreign debt; politicians are vilified (with good cause) in the media; corruption and theft have become a national sport practiced by all sectors; the "brain drain" started in the mid-sixties has intensified; the educational system, once patterned closely after Horace

Mann and Dewey's democratic ideals is in shambles. Social unrest paired with economic turbulence and predatory governments have extolled a heavy price on the population. Faced with the anger—masked in patriotism—of an embittered youth, Argentinean writers offer the modest comfort of their lucidity. To the unemployed seeking work, to the well-educated driving taxis, to the exiles sending dollars, Argentinean authors offer the gift of looking back without the screen of nationalistic discourse and uncritical patriotism. In a country in which non-fiction reads just like fiction and where its tales of horror and injustice have become the primary materials for comics and crooks, the narratives published in the last fifteen years provide readers a space in which to reflect about their nation and its future guided by its past. Sara Rosenberg offers a meditation on the evil face of Argentina during the "dirty war," examines it, dissects it, and tries to give birth to a new future from the broken bodies of the "disappeared."

Rosenberg was born in the province of Tucumán in 1954. In 1975 she went into exile to Canada and then to Mexico where she continued her studies in *beaux arts* and anthropology. She resides in Madrid since 1981. The simple premise of her first novel, *Un hilo rojo* (A Red Thread) is the kidnapping and disappearance of a young woman, Julia Berenstein, in 1976. The most apparent objective of the narrative is the recuperation of her life through the prism of those who knew her. Miguel, a long-time friend and still in love with Julia has secured funding to film a documentary on her life to ultimately find the place where she has been buried and record her life within his own personal narrative in a palimpsest of voices woven into the written account, the audio cassettes and the film. Ultimately, *Un hilo rojo* is as much a biography as it is Miguel's autobiography and the record of an era that persists in spite of the laws that tried to erase memory in the eighties and nineties. While weaving in fragments of Julia's journal, the tapes, the narrator's voice, Rosenberg offers a locus in which different sectors of the population from all sides of the ideological spectrum can meet and establish a dialog. Fernando Reati comments: "To allow for ambiguity and doubt, to elaborate paradigms of failure, to emphasize hesitation, to deny certitudes, is equivalent, in Argentinean letters, to questioning Manichean political and cultural discourse" (75). If exclusive truths have resulted in chaos and violence, then truth must be seen or arrived at through the filter of relativism and the instability of the sign. In Rosenberg's novels, language tries to give reality a plurality of meanings without falsifying or betraying it.

The novel is framed by the famous verses by the Spanish poet Miguel Hernández' "Elegy" from 1936 and Julia's own words in her notebook (now in Miguel's possession). Both the poem and Julia's words are uttered/written shortly before their deaths (during the Spanish civil war and the Argentinean "Dirty War" within forty years of one another). Framed by this balanced symmetrical structure, the novel groans under the weight of a cacophony of voices emerging from the interviews, the documents and the reflections of the narrator who follows the testimonial model in its most ample definition. This strategy allows for the inclusion of less mediated forms such as eyewitness accounts, a journal, several letters, the film documentary, and the confession (There are seven recordings divided into 17 parts scattered throughout the text in no particular chronological order).

Julia's voice emerges from her diary just a few months before being kidnapped and "disappeared": "To be blank, to be nobody, to erase again and again is to be filling with death each movement as if I had done away with myself. I must leave the cemetery, return to reconstruct the house, water the plants, open the book, continue breathing" (115). The erasure plagues the lives of those who knew her. Miguel and those who loved Julia search for her bones or even her shadow to unearth her from the limbo of the forgotten, a state that she was consigned to by her torturers. Echoing the verses by Hernández, grieving before the untimely death of his friend, the one who is left behind defies death:

> I want to dig up the earth with my teeth
> I want to take dry fiery bites
> Pulling it apart bit by bit.
>
> I want to tear up the earth until I find you,
> so I can kiss your noble skull
> unbandage your mouth, and bring you back to life. (99)

The literal and metaphorical decomposition of Julia/Argentina's body is filtered through a fragmentary language with a Cubist sensibility to emphasize the rupture between subject and object of desire. Nothing is whole or complete in this life; nor is it in the documentary or in the interviews. But Miguel has to continue to dig to know the truth:

> I reassemble the body. The song of the cicadas and the toads mixed with the smell of mist carries me to your hand, I see your fingers, I climb your arm to reach your smile. The eye is not whole, I move from the eyebrow to the pupil, and when you see me, you leave. You disappear. I insist. Underneath the tree, your mouth moves, but the words are only noises among the leaves. Only in my dreams I see you whole. (199)

The Manichean ideology that permeates the seventies in Argentina and in much of Latin America eases the reification and demonization of the other. Rosenberg explores in this novel the dehumanization of the "enemy," the victim and the torturer as a necessary process to attain the complete negation of the other. Miguel considers that this denial implies a partial knowledge of the self. The narrator has to follow all the traces that lead to some sort of knowledge through the voices that emerge in his narrative in order to confront the final truth about his unwilling participation in Julia's death. Julia is objectified by those who closed their eyes to the atrocities and uttered the lapidary phrase "there must be a reason" (por algo habrá sido) when confronted with the evidence of floating bodies in the River Plate or disappearances in the middle of the night. That Julia disintegrates in the tapes, becomes a ghost to add to the long list of "disappeared." However, when her friends remember and give their accounts of Julia's life, she becomes a body again, a presence, an individual capable of contradictions, obstinate and generous at the same time. When explaining his project to a friend, Miguel hesitates: "It's not a film about Julia. It's a way to think myself. If I were Lacanian, I would tell you that I'm placing the body of my ghosts.—I try to reflect on memory. Only those who remember can talk... Then it's a documentary.—No. I try to construct characters, I don't want people to sit in front of the camera and tell their story; it's as if the character appeared from the traces left behind, from the footprints, never in close up" (158).

In her second novel, *Cuaderno de invierno*, (Winter Notebook) the novel takes the shape of the protagonist's personal journal during the long winter of exile in which the narrator has not dared to live, still buried under the rocks to hide the fear that has become the self. At the same time, the novel constitutes the process of unfreezing of the self through memory to save itself from death in life: "Winter, time of hidden spaces, of lairs, when life obeys other laws and it hides under the stones, in the cold seeds, in silence. Time of profound exhaustion that covers all the every day little things as if it were a blind man's cloak" (87). Once her body comes back to life, Ana will be able to remember and unearth her loved ones and undertake her voyage to her future: "To go back to the land that his father had made his [. . .] And we start all over again."

The text is constructed on two fundamental and recurrent images: body and water. Ana's body (and by extension, the "disappeared"), and the water seen as salvation or baptismal water before a new life. But, also water points to torture, separation and exile through the image of the Río de la Plata and the Atlantic.

In the metaphorical physiology of the novel, the body contains essential fluids, rivers, waves, icebergs melting slowly, the Río de la

Plata with its bed of reddish mud, little stones, fragments of life and refuse. The aquatic imagery emerges through the text: "and she felt again the crisp noise in her skull, as if a liquid mass were displaced [. . .] The days feel like threads of water [. . .] threads of water and the rest anesthesia" (107). The voyage home initiated because of her father's eminent death is punctuated by a state of terror: "Ezeiza, the airport and the river, that immense naked nerve that carries silt, dark clay [. . .] and all of the figures of absence. To start. To reconstruct. She held onto the armchair, but as a fissured dam, she shuddered again. And water seeped through her eyes, announcing the flood" (18). The psychological dams painstakingly constructed in exile begin to show the fissures that compromise its structural safety and threaten to flood Ana's body and the world in which she temporarily resides.

In her solitary drunkenness, Ana realizes that she carries with her a white and frozen mass: "An enormous iceberg broke silently and slowly the surface of the water, and she saw it travel caressing the horizontal line of the sky that coincided with the tips of her boots on the snow. She felt cold, a strange sensation of coldness" (31). The iceberg crosses her field of vision once and again. The ice cube that clings to her drink also melts like the barrier that blocks her memory. Only towards the end of the novel, Ana will confront her ghosts and reveal that if she's alive is because her sister gave her life in order to save her. The only memory that persists is the white blotch of her sister's blouse while she runs from her pursuers trying to save her little sister. The white blouse, the white trace among the trees, the iceberg and the ice cube of guilt are a constant menace and reminder that Ana survived and Inés did not.

In *Un hilo rojo*, the body of Julia Berenstein lies in an unmarked common grave in an unknown place. The novel represents the search for the individual body, the container of a life lived and a memory that Miguel is trying to sustain. *Cuaderno de invierno* offers the possible salvation of the body. Ana is a survivor who has been practicing medicine in Madrid for fifteen years. She returns to Buenos Aires to see her dying father, a survivor of the Holocaust. In this second novel, Rosenberg looks for the universal element in the specificity of the national history binding together in Ana the Holocaust and the "Dirty War": two faces of evil perpetuating itself. Before it, only the integrity, the memory and the courage of the survivor remains.

After her father's death in Buenos Aires (she arrives too late), anesthetized by terror and alcohol, she writes a document about the literal destruction of the body, the obliteration of her mark as survivor in a long chain of survivors. Her body betrays her, turns against her, becomes foreign: "The leg tremors; old tremor of the knee caps [. . .] Fear installed again, as if the bony support of the body did not exist, and in the knee caps, instead of bones I had a turbulent water more appropriate for an ameba than for this gravitational animal that now walks with difficulty towards home" (16-17). While briefly in Buenos Aires, she loses her voice. Only when closing her eyes she can make herself heard. Eyes shut close. Voluntary blindness. She denies what is outside her interiority. Throughout the novel, the absence of hunger and her dependence on alcohol will be the choice vehicles of her carnal self-flagellation and expiatory repentance for her sin: that is, her will to forget. Ana acts as her own judge and her body becomes her prison. To escape it she must master its appetites and destroy it. The daily certitude of possessing a body denied to the "disappeared" and their families, pushes Ana to refuse its existence, to drown it in a sea of vodka and red wine until an overdose becomes a more effective means. The process of alienation from the body is affirmed in a dialog with it: "One day you get up and it looks at you askance saying: 'Where do you think you're going?' and you tell it 'I'm going to work, like every day,' but it tells you that it does not feel like going with you, that you may go alone, that you need to continue with your obligations. You dress it, you cover it, you transport it to the clinic without anyone noticing" (143).

While reconstructing her memory, Ana starts to piece together the past and to name her ghosts: "Antonio. It's not possible to understand what absence is just by naming it. There is something in that name, in that instant of seven articulated sounds capable of giving back the body [. . .] And when it's named, the body, arms, hands, the way of sitting, come from anywhere, without order like the changing waves [. . .] The name is a scar in the air" (100). Body and memory are recuperated at the same time. Once saved from herself she is able to look for and unearth the loved bodies: Hernán, Caty, Antonio and Inés.

In the stupor induced by an overdose of narcotics, Ana finally arrives at a cathartic state in a scene that echoes the last supper:

> They all rest finally at your own table. Don't keep hidden in your broken pockets those you want to hate, it's better if you give them a place, because otherwise they will jump over the fence and will sit anywhere [. . .] Set the table, so that in the depths of each plate there will be a part of your body, a landscape of your own geography. They will eat with spoons, or are you not pure liquid, water contained in unknown shores. Give them to drink, let them go, they have come after a long drought to put their tongues in your cavity and to gather you in their throat. [. . .] You let them be while you take a few more blue pills; they drink and you hear their satisfied breath, and you spill over, you spill over the broken crystal of the ice, splintered in the immensity of the ocean where now the fish jumps towards the sun [. . .] and wakes up all who were asleep and have been dreaming during a long winter with the warm surface of the earth. (238-239)

To wake up from death is to finally assume the past and to dare to hope for a future in spite of the fear of failing. Ana will go back to Argentina, will bury her dead, and will finally shake off the long and white winter cloak of exile and guilt to continue the life interrupted brutally by hatred and violence.

In conclusion, Sara Rosenberg has turned her craft into a weapon and a healing tool to write and record the lives and the silenced voices of the disappeared and the survivors. Biography and autobiography lend their discursive apparatuses to people the narratives with the intimate voices of the forgotten and of those who refuse to forget.

Works Cited

Aguinis, Marcos. *Las redes del odio: Recursos para desactivar la violencia.* Buenos Aires: Planeta, 2003.
Bellone, Liliana. *Fragmentos de siglo.* Salta: Robledal, 1999.
Bergero, Adriana, and Fernando Reati, eds. *Memoria colectiva y políticas del olvido.* Rosario: Beatriz Viterbo, 1997.
Feitlowitz, Marguerite. *A Lexicon of Terror: Argentina and the Legacies of Torture.* Oxford: Oxford University Press, 1998.
Hernández, Miguel. "Elegy." *The Selected Poems of Miguel Hernández.* Ed. and trans. Ted Genoways. Chicago: University of Chicago Press, 2001.
Gorostiza, Carlos. *Vuelan las palomas* Buenos Aires: Planeta, 1999.
___. *La buena gente.* Buenos Aires: Planeta, 2002.
Neuman, Andrés. *Bariloche.* Anagrama, 1999.
Partnoy, Alicia. *The Little School.* Virago, 1988.
Reati, Fernando. *Nombrar lo innombrable.* Buenos Aires: Legasa, 1992.
Rosenberg, Sara. *Un hilo rojo.* Madrid: Espasa, 1998.
___. *Cuaderno de invierno.* Madrid: Espasa, 1999.
Rotondo, Emilce. *El 74.* Buenos Aires: Dock, 1999.
___. Winkler, Paula. *Cartas escritas en silencio para el viento.* Buenos Aires: Corregidor, 2001.

Resisting Dis/closure:
Autobiography and Orhan Pamuk's *İstanbul*

Dilek Doltaş
Boğaziçi University

Abstract: Self-writings *disclose* the impossibility of depicting a comprehensive, consistent and *closed* self-portrayal. In autobiographical narratives, because the self that is written is shown to be in process and historically and socio-culturally contingent, the radical split between the self that writes and the self that is written is more apparent. What all forms of autobiography actually display is that narrational selves are more obviously constructed than real ones and disclosure of the self through writing is not possible.

Orhan Pamuk's autobiography, *İstanbul: Hatıralar ve Şehir* (*Istanbul: Memories and the City*) is an example of self-writing which both embodies these concerns and constitutes a site where they are foregrounded and discussed. Pamuk's text continually deconstructs itself denying the possibility of narrative closure although stylistically it has unity and a closed structure.

It is my contention, and I am not alone in this, that what all forms of autobiography display is that narrational selves are more obviously constructed than real ones, therefore disclosure of the self through writing is not possible. Furthermore, in autobiographical narratives, because the self that is written is shown to be in process and historically and socio-culturally contingent, the radical split between the self that writes and the self that is written becomes more apparent. Consequently, self-writings actually *disclose* the impossibility of *closure*. Orhan Pamuk's autobiography, *İstanbul: Hatıralar ve Şehir* (2003; *Istanbul: Memories and the City* [2005]), is an example of self-writing which both embodies these concerns and constitutes a site where they are foregrounded and discussed. Aesthetically Pamuk's autobiography has unity and a closed structure but at the thematic level the narrative continually deconstructs itself denying the possibility of closure.

Philip Lejeune in "The Autobiographical Pact" states that autobiography "is a retrospective prose narrative produced by a real person concerning his own existence, focusing on his individual life, in particular on the development of his personality" (qtd. in Marcus 191).

"The author," Lejeune claims, is "a personal name, the identical name accepting responsibility for a sequence of different published texts" (qtd. in Marcus 253). In other words, for Lejeune autobiography is a life-writing in which the author, the narrator of the story and the central character are the same. This identity is ensured by the "personal name" of the author and constitutes "the autobiographical pact" creating what Lejeune calls "the autobiographical space" (Marcus, 253-254). In attributing a central function to the author's name, Lejeune seems to uphold a Foucauldian stance. But while Foucault in "What is an Author?" refuses to associate the person of the author with his name, for Lejeune the "I" manifest in the narrative is identical with the "I" of external life.

In *Roland Barthes by Roland Barthes* Barthes denies the possibility of self-writing, and refuses to be a party to the "autobiographical pact". The signed authorial directive that appears in his handwriting, on the page between the title-page and the so-called body of the text reads: "It must all be considered as if spoken by a character in a novel." In other words, in Barthes' autobiography, as in his theoretical work, "to write" is presented as an intransitive verb divorced from its doer, the writer. Thus for Barthes, the focus of autobiography, as all other modes of writing, is the reader. In "The Death of the Author" he claims that "The reader is the space on which all the quotations that make up a writing are inscribed, [. . .] a text's unity lies not in its origin but in its destination" (171).

Paul de Man in "Autobiography as De-Facement" expresses weariness over theories of autobiography. He argues that the apparently "referential" status of autobiography reveals the fictionality of all referentiality. De Man claims that "empirically as well as theoretically, autobiography lends itself poorly to generic definition: each specific instance seems to be an exception to the norm" (qtd. in Marcus 240). The assumption that the life produces autobiography may indeed be reversed according to de Man and we may come to realize that autobiography produces and determines the life. Like Barthes he is skeptical about generic classifications based on the text or the author. For him "autobiography [. . .] is not a genre or a mode; but a figure of reading or of understanding that occurs, to some degree, in all texts" (qtd. in Marcus 241).

Rita Felski, in her article "On Confessions" gives both the history and the definition of the genre in the following words:

> Autobiography in the modern sense [. . .], first emerges as a distinctive form in the eighteenth century. Rousseau's *Confessions* is usually held up as the first example of autobiography, as a celebration of unique individualism, and thus fundamentally different from earlier texts, such as the Confessions of Augustine [. . .] in which self-analysis is valued not for its own sake but as a means of exposing the fallibility of humanity. (87)

According to Felski, "Protestantism's emphasis on the importance of the individual struggle for salvation prepared the way [. . .] necessary for autobiography proper" (87).

Unlike the poststructuralists Barthes, Foucault and de Man, Felski does not deny the author subjecthood. She treats autobiography as a specific genre, and she even concedes the identicalness of the author's name with the narrator's and the protagonist's selves. But in her essay Felski also underlines the constructed nature of all "subjectivities" and so-called "authentic selves". She writes: "[T]his attempted emancipation of the self can expose a self-defeating dialectic in which the history of confession [. . .] as subjection to external authority, returns in new form" (87). In other words, for Felski, the attempt to assert the self's privileged autonomy as "authentic" merely helps to disclose its profound dependence upon the cultural and ideological systems through which it is constituted.

In the 1760s Jean-Jacques Rousseau begins his *Confessions* with the following words.

> I have resolved on an enterprise which has no precedent, and which, once complete, will have no imitator. My purpose is to display to my kind a portrait in every way true to nature, and the man I shall portray will be myself.
> Simply myself. I know my own heart and understand my fellow man. But I am made unlike any one I have ever met; I will venture to say that I am like no one in the whole world.
>
> (17)

The quotation brings to the foreground both the ideology of the age and its assumptions relating to "self" and "identity." Seen as a personal account meant to be exemplary, Rousseau's confessions can be read as a secular version of the *Confessions* of St. Augustine. But seen as a text in which Rousseau displays himself and tries to justify his deeds to the public it is not a confession but an apologia. For Rousseau, as for the people of his age, self-knowledge was very important. It was both the means to know others and by comparison to others, yourself. In the *Confessions* Rousseau says: "I want [to expose my inner self] so that if we are to learn to appraise ourselves, we have at least one piece of comparative evidence: [. . .] everyone will know both himself, and one other and that other will be me" (qtd. in Marcus 23). In order to provide his readers with a proper example Rousseau promises his readers truth, sincerity and transparency.

Colin Campbell explains that the word 'self' in the hyphenated form as in 'self-confidence,' 'self-pity' etc. begins to appear in the English language in the sixteenth century but is widely used in the eighteenth. The term 'self-consciousness' is apparently first employed by Coleridge to point to the awareness which foregrounds the "objectness" of the world and the "subjectness" of man himself (Campbell 73; Marcus 50). This has clear implications for subject/object, inner/outer relationships in autobiography which is acclaimed to be an "objective" account of the "subjective" or an "external" depiction of the "internal." With the growing emphasis on self and self-awareness autobiographical writing begins to spread in the late eighteenth and throughout the nineteenth century. But during these years the tension between spiritual autobiography as self-scrutiny and secular self-writing meant for public consumption was central to the discussions on autobiography. On the one hand, writings about the self, as suggested by Rousseau and explained a few years later by Isaac d'Israeli, served the function of self-discovery and self-knowledge, on the other, their publication allowed for self-eulogizing, self-regard, self-absorption and turned into an apologia for the autobiographer's deeds. D'Israeli stresses the significance of self-analysis and self-knowledge to be attained through diary and memoir writing (D'Israeli; qtd. in Marcus 18-19). He goes so far as to say that people like Oliver Cromwell could not write a diary because they could not face themselves in "solitude and darkness." For D'Israeli "Diaries form that other Self, which [. . .] every thinking being possess; and which to converse with [. . .] accounts the highest wisdom" (D'Israeli 100; qtd. in Marcus 19). Laura Marcus aptly argues, however, that "once the analysis of self ceases to be solely for the self and/or for God, it must inevitably become a display of some kind" (13).

According to Marcus, the nineteenth century saw a gradual alignment of autobiography with the value accorded to authorship. Autobiography gradually came to be the site where genius, and in particular literary genius, could be established as "internally" valuable, without reference to other "outside" judgments. The literary geniuses were the "prophets of their times," their life stories were valuable in their own right and their signature inscribed the text with value. Linda Anderson points out that in the nineteenth century self-writing was expected to belong either to people of "lofty reputation" or to people who had something of "historical importance" to say (8). Similarly, autobiographical narrative came to be equated with developmental stories where both time and the personality of the narrator were controlled by a purpose and a goal. The primary concern of these narratives was the charting and analysis of the psychic and intellectual development of the self, and the deterministic or naturalistic accounts of individuality and society. Roy Pascal argues that because of this, the "great autobiographies" of the nineteenth century had a major influence on the novelistic writing of the period, in particular on the *Bildungsroman*, where the character is depicted as "becoming" (qtd. in Marcus 239). The *Künstlerroman*, the story of the development of the artist, also came to be popular in that century. The *Künstlerroman* was particularly important in confirming the essential "literariness" and the "constructedness" of both the autobiographical form and of the identity of the autobiographer (Marcus 239).

Felicity Nussbaum points out that for the eighteenth-century writers, the apparent incoherence, lack of integrity, scantiness and inconclusiveness of the narration of public and private events in journals, memoirs and diaries were more valuable, because they were more natural, life-like (Nussbaum 16; Anderson 9). In the nineteenth century there emerged a hierarchy of values in relation to self-representation, with memoirs occupying a lower order since they did not aim at fulfilling the higher function of autobiographies (Anderson 8; Marcus 237-239). But as Laura Marcus argues, it is the eighteenth-century novel, which displays similar formalistic narrative devices as eighteenth-century memoirs, and journals that inspire modern autobiographical writing (237).

For many critics today, the function of autobiographical writing is problematic, its boundaries as a genre are vague, the autobiographical self and the inner and outer worlds the narrative is supposed to depict are complex and amorphous. Domna Stanton in *The Female Autograph: Theory and Practice of Autobiography from the Tenth to the Twentieth Century* even claims that today autography is defined as an act of self-situating or signature and it is no longer burdened by the task of representing life (qtd. in Marcus 197). Contemporary critics believe that the hybrid nature of autobiographical writing, its being literary and historical at the same time, makes it a site where discussions on pressing oppositional topics such as subject/object, self and identity, private and public, fact and fiction, truth and falsehood are carried out at a variety of levels ranging from the epistemological, ontological and ethical to the cultural, the aesthetic and the political. Among the questions brought up during the discussions are the "truthfulness" and the "self-awareness" of the writer but also "the narrative (or narrational) unity of a life" which is governed partially by his/her life project (MacIntyre; qtd. in Ricœur158), the writers' gender, intention, the referentiality or non-referentiality of language and how such writing should be conceptualized in a more psychological or political register. In other words autobiography today appears as a microcosmic version of many of our present-day concerns, serving to articulate them. According to some critics, autobiography also provides at least partial solutions to such concerns, while for others, with whom I align myself, it may be viewed as an examplary instance of resistance to any solution to or closure of these problems.

Orhan Pamuk's autobiography is an example of self-writing which both embodies these concerns and constitutes a site where they are foregrounded and discussed.

In English, the original title reads "Istanbul: Memories and the City." The English translation, however, has been published under the title *Istanbul: Memories of a City*. Such a change of emphasis, I believe, neither does justice to the book's aesthetic and philosophical complexity nor does it reflect the text's predominantly autobiographical nature. There are similar unearned shifts of meaning in the main body and the chapter headings of the English translation so today I will take the Turkish text as my point of reference and use my own translations where and when necessary.

In *İstanbul: Hatıralar ve Şehir* Orhan Pamuk depicts himself as a Westernized, upper-class Istanbulite. However, his conception of himself is not unique and individualistic. It is fluid, communal, multiple, vague, as well as specific and historical. In the first chapter of the book we are told that the writer's identity is inscribed with the history and identity of his immediate family and with the history and the identity of the city into which he is born. Here Pamuk declares that just as the family he was born into, the body and the gender he happened to possess at the time of his birth, so does Istanbul, the place where he was born, determine his fate (15). But at the end of the same chapter Pamuk problematizes this causalistic, deterministic definition of the self. He claims that self is formed through memories and memories are inscribed by others' narrative accounts of what we do and experience. We read: "Once imprinted in our minds, other people's reports of what we have done end up mattering more than what we ourselves remember. And just as we learn about our lives from others, so too, do we let others shape our understanding of the city in which we live" (16).

Throughout the narrative on the one hand, material reality that is history and socio-cultural factors determine who Pamuk is, on the other, other people's accounts *and* his own fancy and aesthetic concerns are responsible in shaping his sense of self. In chapter 32, for example, talking about the violent fights he had with his older brother, Pamuk writes:

> Later, when reminded of those fights and violence my mother and my brother claimed no recollection of them, saying that, as usual, I'd invented them, just for the sake of something to write about [. . .] So anyone reading these pages should bear in mind that sometimes I am prone to exaggeration, sometimes, like a paranoiac I am obsessed with my own fears and anxieties. But what is important for a painter is not a thing's reality but its shape, and what is important for a novelist is not the course of events but their ordering, and what is important for a memoir writer is not the factual accuracy of the past but the symmetry of its account. (275)

For Pamuk "symmetry" does not imply aesthetic "balance and proportion" in the presentation of events and ideas but the "correspondence", the "fitting in" of these events and ideas to one another.

Seen from a Western perspective, Pamuk's sense of self and his relation to Istanbul have more affinities with the autobiographical selves of women and other marginal groups than with white, Protestant "individualist" Western men. In discussing the development of a woman's consciousness Stanford Friedman claims that when a woman or a minority looks into the mirror it does not reflect an individual identity, it displays a cultural representation into which the onlooker stares, to form an identity. Consequently, women and minorities develop a dual consciousness: the self as historically and culturally defined, and the self as different from this cultural prescription (Friedman 75-76).

Pamuk's writing clearly displays such a dual consciousness. That is why the title of his autobiography reads "Istanbul: Memories and the City." Orhan Pamuk's story is written through his memories of himself and the city. But his memories of the city are constructed through those of his parents, his grand-parents, and through those of five early twentieth-century Turkish men of letters who wrote on Istanbul (Reşat Ekrem Koçu, Yahya Kemal, Ahmet Hamdi Tanpınar, Abdülhak Şinasi Hisar, Ahmet Rasim), and finally through the memories of the eighteenth-century German painter Antoine-Ignace Melling, the nineteenth-century French writers Gérard de Nerval, Théophile Gautier, Gustave Flaubert and Pierre Loti. All these people have held a mirror to Istanbul and contributed to the formation of the Istanbulite culture and mood that Pamuk has made his own. The reflections of Istanbul in the mirrors of Westerners, we are told, were inscribed with their expectations of the city. Their drawings and descriptions were varied and sometimes contradictory but they never possessed an insider's depth and emotional complexity (224). In the majority of cases these Westerners either eulogized the city and its inhabitants for their exotic and "Eastern" particularities while pointing to the city's picaresque ruins like Pierre Loti, or like André Gide they detested the city and the Istanbulites for being other than Western (223), or they found everything about Istanbul to be "absurd," "amusing," "a tourist attraction" (224). The memoirs of these Westerners in different ways contributed to both the Istanbulites' construction of their image of themselves and their city and made them see their own difference from the Westerners. The result was a continual double consciousness, an "othering" of the self, that Istanbulites experience in describing themselves. Pamuk finds this state of mind both enriching and troubling:

> Istanbul's greatest virtue is its people's ability to see the city through both Western and Eastern eyes. [. . .] Even when I was a child, when the city was at its most run-down, Istanbul's own residents felt like outsiders half the time. Depending on how they were looking at it, they felt it was either too Eastern or too Western and the resulting uneasiness made them worry they didn't quite belong. (243-244)

These feelings of uneasiness and alieanation give rise to a deep feeling of *hüzün*, an emotion which Pamuk claims has no counterpart in the Western culture. For Pamuk *hüzün* is a collective feeling of "sorrow" that also connotes communal loss and lack. Through the course of the narrative, as the author-protagonist Pamuk situates and resituates himself with respect to the aforementioned Turkish and Western artists, and with respect to his contemporary Istanbulites from different socio-economic backgrounds we see him perform before us this "othering" process. The "othering" act of Pamuk, on the one hand gives the narrative depth, making it dialogical and open-ended, on the other it underlines the fluid, contingent and essentially constructed nature of the narrated self.

Structurally *İstanbul: Hatıralar ve Şehir* consists of 37 chapters which can be categorized thematically into three groups: chapters that narrate the episodes of Pamuk's life in a vaguely chronological manner—they are structured like a *Bildungsroman* and a *Künstlerroman* and they constitute the frame story; then chapters that focus mainly on different districts of Istanbul, its inhabitants, and the city's historical, economic and socio-political problems; finally chapters that portay Istanbul through the lenses of Turkish and Western artists. All these chapters are "symmetrical," that is they are linked to one another through Pamuk's presence, and through the unities of place, mood, image, metaphor, attitude, color and form of analysis. Furthermore, thematically the chapters discussing Pamuk's memories of the city, its inhabitants and other artists' views of Istanbul, are interlaced into the frame story

As stated earlier, the frame narrative in *İstanbul* is Pamuk's growing up into adulthood and his development into an artist. Interdependence, dual consciousness, historical and communal identities are presented as key elements thoughout Pamuk's account of his development as an artist and a self. The lives and memories of his family and of those who have contributed to the cultural memory of the city are presented as being so thoroughly entangled with his own that the center of Orhan Pamuk's story seems to be "everywhere and its circumference nowhere" (Friedman 74). What makes the narrative aesthetically symmetrical and unified, as suggested earlier, is the fact that it is structured around one person—Orhan; one theme—his coming of age and choosing to become a writer; one topography—Istanbul; one metaphor—the metaphor of mirrors and mirroring; one mood—*hüzün* ('sorrow' or 'mournfulness'); one image—ruin, loss, impoverishment; one color—black and white; one attitude—the attitude of an observant, the artist gazing; and one form of analysis which is historico-aesthetic.

The 37 chapters with seemingly disconnected headings and content are linked to one another by way of these unities.

The first chapter of the autobiography is an overture which sets the tone for the rest of the book. Called "Another Orhan," it is both a kind of a summary of the main issues dealt with throughout the text and an introduction to the main characters, topics, emotions and impressions of the city. The opening paragraphs read:

> From a very young age I believed that somewhere in the streets of Istanbul, in a house resembling ours, there lived another Orhan so much like me that he could pass for my twin, even my double. I can't remember where I got this idea or how it came to me. It most likely emerged from a web of rumours, misunderstandings, illusions and fears. [. . .]
>
> When I was five I was sent to live for a short time in another house. It was the end of one of their many stormy separations that my parents arranged to meet in Paris, and it was decided that my older brother and I should remain in Istanbul. [. . .] My brother remained in the heart of the family, with my grandmother in Pamuk Apartments, in Nişantaşı. But I was sent to stay with my aunt in Cihangir. Hanging on the wall in this house [. . .] was a picture of a small child. Every once in a while my aunt or uncle would point at him and smile, "Look! That's you."
>
> The sweet, doe-eyed boy inside the small white frame did look a bit like me, it's true. He was even wearing the cap I sometimes wore. But I knew I was not that boy in the picture (a kitsch representation of a 'cute child' that someone had brought fom Europe). Yet I kept asking myself—is this the Orhan who lives in that other house? (11-12)

Istanbul, Nişantaşı, Pamuk apartments and Cihangir are the places where Pamuk spends most of his life. His brother, his grandmother and his parents are the main actors in his life. The frequent quarrels and separations of his parents which he mentions above leave him in a state of anxiety and fear. At the root of his double consciousness, we are told, lies his fate of being born into this family and this city. He explains that as the self that is immediately present to him feels rejected, unhappy, and puzzled, he thinks of and assumes his other self which is far away, "always in another house," happy, welcomed and secure. We read:

> Whenever I was unhappy, I imagined going to the other house, the other life, the place where the other Orhan lived, and in spite of everything, I'd half convince myself that I was he and took pleasure in imagining how happy he was, such pleasure that, for a time, I felt no need to go to seek out the other house in that other imagined part of the city. (13)

Then Pamuk draws our attention to the philosophical questions relating to fate and identity, insisting that his own fate and sense of self are intricately woven with the fate of the city. He writes:

> Here we come to the heart of the matter: I've never left Istanbul—never left the houses, streets and neighbourhoods of my childhood. Although I've lived in other districts from time to time, fifty years on I find myself back in Pamuk Apartments... Such attachment to the city causes one's character to be moulded by its fate. [. . .] Often I realize that Istanbul [. . .] is my fate in the same way as my body [. . .] and my gender [. . .] This book is about this fate. (14-15)

Here Pamuk not only moulds his life-story with the history and the economic and socio-political state of Istanbul but he also implies that in talking about Istanbul he will be talking about himself and vice versa. In the same section he says,

> The city into which I was born was poorer, shabbier, more isolated than it had ever been in its two-thousand year history. For me it has always been a city of ruins, loss, poverty, and end-of-empire sorrow. I've spent my whole life either battling with this sorrow or like all Istanbulites finally making it my own. (15)

Although the first chapter of the book is also the beginning of Pamuk's *Bildungsroman*, his *Künstlerroman* does not begin until chapter 17. Here we learn that at the age of seven Orhan begins to paint. He says he painted because he found it blissful. We read: "The sweet praise I would enjoy when I drew a picture gave me to imagine that I'd been given a machine that compelled people to love, kiss, and adore me" (140). Later on in the same chapter, Pamuk cites more reasons as to why he liked to draw. He says he is looking back to his childhood and putting a distance between himself, the "fifty-year-old memoir-writer," and the child who painted (142). The reasons he gives, however, all point to the writer's approach to life, art, his sense of the self and others. Here Orhan Pamuk talks about the psychology and the ethical/aesthetic concerns relating to art and artists:

> As I watched the pencil race across the page, I would look on it in amazement, as if someone else had taken up residence in my body. [. . .] This division between my mind and my hand, the sense that my hand was acting of its own accord, had something in common with the sensation of escaping into my dream world [. . .] To draw was to find a second world whose existence was not cause for embarrassment. [. . .] The things I drew, no matter how imaginary the house, the tree, the cloud, had a basis in material reality [. . .] I felt I owned everything I drew [. . .] The world I created through drawing, like the second world I hid in my head, enriched my life; even better it gave me a legitimate escape from the dusty, shadowy world of everyday life, not only did my family accept this new habit of mine, they accepted my right to it. (142-143)

The following eight chapters all deal with his life as a painter. How he begins to paint by first imitating simple drawings in coloring books, then draws members of his family, sections from within his house, scenes from his neighborhood, from his walks within the city etc. The way he draws a thing might not be the way that thing appears to others but his drawing contains his truth and something from "material reality." Orhan's mother allows him to use her house in Cihangir as his studio and he goes there regularly to paint. At the age of 19 he falls in love with a girl who accepts to pose as his model. The girl's parents break up their friendship, finding his interest in painting unacceptable in a candidate for her hand. After their separation Orhan's interest in painting begins to recede and finally in his second year at the faculty of architecture he decides to quit school and become a writer. The final chapter of the autobiography is interesting because it is the only chapter where the narrative incorporates into the reported speech of the writer the direct speech of his mother. The mother's arguments against his dropping out of school to become a painter are interlaced into the mental debates and fantasies of the narrator. The chapter ends with the only direct statement Orhan makes throughout the narrative. He says "I'm not going to be a painter, I'm going to be a writer" (345). Thus the last chapter is the end of both the *Bildungsroman* and the *Künstlerroman*.

Going back to the first chapter we see that the last section of chapter 1 moves from Orhan's account of himself and his world to more philosophical and linguistic issues relating to life and art. Here most of the theoretical and aesthetic issues which have a bearing on the autobiographical genre are surfaced. Pamuk states that the Turkish language tries to distinguish what one sees and experiences directly from what one is told about by others. He believes that these two forms of acquiring knowledge so merge in forming one's memory of the past that the person begins to give priority to what he hears from others over his own feelings and experiences. We read:

> In Turkish we have a special tense, which I like very much, that allows us to distinguish hearsay from what we've seen with our own eyes; when we are relating dreams, fairytales, or past events we could not have witnessed, we use this tense. Our parents tell us our earliest life experiences, our cradles,

> our baby carriages, our first steps and we hear them being told as if we are hearing the stories of others. [. . .] This leads us into the habit of learning the significance of what we live through, even the pleasures we experience, from others. [. . .] And just as we learn about our lives from others, so too, do we let others shape our understanding of the city in which we live.

In the final paragraph Pamuk makes yet another claim about memory and reality formation. He explains that his memories are not only shaped by the stories of others but also by his own fantasies and dreams. We read:

> At times when I accept as my own the stories I've heard about my city and myself, I'm tempted to say "Once upon a time I used to paint. I hear I was born in Istanbul, and I understand that I was a curious child. Then, when I was twenty-two, I seem to have begun writing novels without knowing why." I'd have liked to write my entire story this way—as if my life were something that happened to someone else, as if it were a dream in which I felt my voice fading and my will succumbing to enchantment. Beautiful though it is, I find the language of epic unconvincing, for I cannot accept that the myths we tell about our first lives prepare us for the brighter, more authentic second lives that are meant to begin when we awake. Because—for people like me, at least—that second life is none other than the book in your hand. So pay close attention, dear reader. Let me be straight with you, and in return let me ask for your compassion. (16)

As the author/narrator addresses us directly in the last sentence we become aware of the paradoxes and dilemmas inherent in autography. We realize the contradictions intrinsic to the dynamics of identity formation, to writing and reading, to the problems of categorizing or defining autobiographical writing and turn to ourselves for reflection and interpretation. Pamuk tells us that "often the beauty of a place or a scene, the warmth and charm of the people is dependent on what the writer looks for in a city and what his/her readers expect to find there" (327). If Istanbul makes Pamuk what he is, and Pamuk sees in Istanbul what he expects to see, just as we readers see the writer the way we want to see him, then the significance of the story or the portait of the artist displayed in the narrative are in fact nothing other than the productions of our own mind. Therefore if anything is disclosed in the course of reading Pamuk's autobiography it is the state of our own mind. That is why Orhan Pamuk asks us to show him "compassion."

Works Cited

Anderson, Linda. *Autobiography*. New Critical Idiom. London and New York: Routledge, 2001.

Barthes, Roland. "The Death of the Author." *Modern Criticism and Theory: A Reader*. Ed. David Lodge. London and New York: Longman, 1988. 167-172.

___. *Roland Barthes by Roland Barthes*. Trans. Richard Howard. London: Macmillan, 1977.

Campbell, Colin. *The Romantic Ethic and the Spirit of Modern Consumerism*. Oxford: Blackwell, 1987.

de Man, Paul. "Autobigraphy as De-Facement." *The Rhetoric of Romanticism*. New York: Columbia University Press, 1984. 67-81.

D'Israeli. Isaac. "Literary Miscellanies" *Literary Character of Men of Genius*. By D'Israeli. London: Frederick Warne, 1822. 97-100.

Felski, Rita. "On Confession." Smith and Watson, eds., 83-95

Foucault "What is an Author?" *Modern Criticism and Theory: A Reader*. Ed. David Lodge. London and New York: Longman, 1988. 197-210.

Friedman, Susan Stanford. "Women's Autobiographical Selves: Theory and Practice." Smith and Watson, eds., 73-82.

Lejeune, Philippe. "The Autobiographical Pact." *On Autobiography.* Ed. Paul Eakin, trans. Katherine Leary. Minneapolis: University of Minnesota Press, 1989. 141-162

MacIntyre, Alasdair. *After Virtue: A Study in Moral Theory.* Notre Dame, Indiana: University of Notre Dame Press, 1981.

Marcus, Laura. *Auto/biographical Discourses: Theory. Criticism. Practice.* Manchester and New York: Manchester University Press, 1994.

Nussbaum, Felicity A. *The Autobiographical Subject: Gender and Ideology in Eighteenth-Century England.* Baltimore and London: Johns Hopkins University Press, 1989.

Pamuk, Orhan. *İstanbul: Hatıralar ve Şehir.* İstanbul: Yapı Kredi, 2003. English trans.: *Istanbul: Memories of a City.* Trans. Maureen Freely. London: Faber and Faber, 2005.

Pascal, Roy. *Design and Truth in Autobiography.* London: Routledge and Kegan Paul, 1960.

Ricœur, Paul. *Oneself as Another.* Trans. Kathleen Blamey. Chicago and London: University of Chicago Press, 1994.

Rousseau, Jean-Jacques. *The Confessions of Jean-Jacques Rousseau.* Trans. and introd. J. M. Cohen. London: Penguin, 1953.

Stanton, Domna C. *The Female Autograph: Theory and Practice of Autobiography from the Tenth to the Twentieth Century.* 2nd ed. Chicago and London: University of Chicago Press, 1987.

Smith, Sidonie, and Julia Watson, eds. "Women's Autobiographical Selves: Theory and Practice." *Women, Autobiography, Theory: A Reader.* Wisconsin: University of Wisconsin Press, 1988.

Traces of the History of Turkish Modernization in Orhan Pamuk's *Yeni Hayat* (*The New Life*): The Oscillation between Fascination with and Resistance to the "West"

Ayse F. Ece
Marmara University

Abstract: Orhan Pamuk's fifth novel, *Yeni Hayat* (*The New Life*), relates the adventures of a young university student who sets out on a bizarre journey to find the new life depicted within a book he has read at one sitting. The protagonist who meticulously describes the Anatolian towns he visits, the people he meets who have also read the book, his own strange feelings and thoughts, does not provide the slightest clue as to what the book which forced him to leave his former life contains. This study is based on an interpretative hypothesis which claims that the book stands for a particular text focusing on the guidelines of a Westernized life determined by the secular Turkish Republic established in 1923. Moving on with this assumption, the responses of the characters of *Yeni Hayat* who have read the book might be thought of as the counterparts of Turkish people's reactions to the destruction of their age-old traditional life and to the radical changes that occur in every domain of both their public and private lives under the rule of the new regime. When the entwined web of responses to the book is interpreted as the reflections of Turkish people's feelings towards the modern way of life, the oscillation between fascination with and resistance to the "West" comes to the foreground in the form of Turkey's age-old dilemma. The characters of *Yeni Hayat* are well aware of this dilemma and instead of trying to resolve it, they strive to learn to live with it through embracing the cultural hybridity which shapes their existence. The readers—both the characters of *Yeni Hayat* who have read a book and the "real" readers of *Yeni Hayat*—ultimately find happiness and peace of mind on the threshold, which is not a bridge to another life, but a third space where East and West coexist in a circular understanding of time.

"I read a book one day and my whole life was changed" (Pamuk 3). This intriguing sentence is uttered by Osman, the narrator of Orhan Pamuk's fifth novel, *Yeni Hayat* (1995; *The New Life*), set vaguely in the 1970s or 1980s (see Wright). Osman, a 22-year-old university student, sees the book first in the hands of a girl he has been admiring from afar and he immediately decides to buy a copy and read it as soon as possible to get an insight into the thoughts and dreams of this beautiful girl named Janan. Once Osman sits at his desk to read the book, he feels that his life will change entirely. Throughout the book Osman's intuitions prove to be true; he leaves his home, his mother and the city he has been living in since he was born and sets out on a bizarre journey to find the life described in the book. In fact, not only Osman's life, but also Janan and her boyfriend Mehmet's lives change thoroughly after reading the book. They, too, begin to take buses and travel to the remote parts of Anatolia in the search of the "new life" depicted within the book. However, apart from implying that the book suggests a "new life," the author does not give the readers the slightest clue as to what the book contains. Thus, the book's content is open to a variety of interpretations ranging from the advocation of a religious treatise to a political creed. Although the text is fluid, indeterminate, and open-ended, on one level it can be read as a manual containing the guidelines of a Westernized life determined by the secular Turkish Republic established in 1923. This reading enables us to interpret and evaluate the reactions of the characters who have read the book in a meaningful way. Moving on with this assumption, it can be hypothesized that the responses of the book's readers correspond to the Turkish people's reactions to the destruction of their age-old traditional life and to the radical changes that occur in every domain of both their public and private lives under the rule of the new regime. The characters undergo a radical transformation after reading the book just like the Turkish people who were forced to adopt a new way of life following the initiation of the modernization project. The hybridity of the social, cultural, and political lives of Turkish people which stems from being neither thoroughly Eastern nor Westernized was a considerable obstacle for the heated supporters of the modernization project. However, this in-betweenness is, in fact, not only a distinguishing feature of Turkish people but it also is a source of happiness and well-being for them. Similarly, the characters who have read the book find happiness and peace of mind on the threshold of two seemingly different worlds; i.e. in a third space where cultures, worlds, and lives meet without suppressing one another.

The author relates the psychological changes the narrator, Osman, goes through during and after the process of reading the book step by step without leaving out the smallest details. In this sense, *Yeni Hayat* can be read as the memoirs of the people who have read it, especially as a record of Osman's reactions to the book which has changed his whole life. Recognizing that the book invades both his soul and his identity, Osman says: "It was such a powerful influence that the light surging from the pages illuminated my face; its incandescence dazzled my intellect but also endowed it with brilliant lucidity" (3). The light, on the one hand, blinds the narrator's intellect, on the other hand it furnishes his intellect with an ability to predict the strange situations, events, thoughts, and feelings he will have to encounter in the near future. His intellect will be then so blind as to make him forget the past, but at the same time it will be brilliant enough to guide him in the new world shaped by the radical changes. Osman feels that he is entrapped in a place illuminated only by this strange light: "This was the kind of light within which I could recast my self; I could lose my way in this light; I already sensed in the light the shadows of an existence I had yet to know and embrace" (3). This new existence could be interpreted as a Westernized existence which would replace the Eastern one. The narrator will have to reformulate his identity by following this light, and in this process he eventually will come across a new existence which is quite foreign to him. The anticipation of all these inevitable personal transformations makes Osman feel all alone in his room: "[. . .] I was overtaken by a feeling of loneliness I had never before experienced—as if I had been stranded in a country where I knew neither the lay of the land nor the language and the customs" (3-4). Osman feels lonely as he has to slip out of his former identity and go through a turmoil in the search and formulation of a Westernized identity which in *Yeni Hayat* is referred to as a "land" whose language and customs are completely foreign. In order to find a way out of this depressing solitude, Osman decides to look for others who were previously caught in this trap: "Finding others who were in the same predicament as myself was of the utmost necessity to save myself from the feeling of unbearable loneliness that beset me in the new world into which I was projected" (16). He desperately seeks the ones who have experienced a similar kind of loneliness, the loneliness triggered by the feeling of in-betweenness, by the loosening of the links with the past, and by the emergence of a Westernized understanding of the world.

Osman and Janan set out on a journey to find Mehmet, who is the first among them to read the book. Mehmet is fascinated by the book just like Osman, but at the same time he has his reservations about it due to his conviction that it might be impossible to attain the "new life" described in the book. Janan's reactions to the book are similar to Mehmet's. In fact, her ideas concerning the book are shaped, to a wide extent, by Mehmet who is intimidated by the fading memories of the traditional culture and also thrilled by the modernization of daily life. When Osman decides to find Mehmet, leaving Janan in Mehmet's father, Doctor Fine's, mansion, he learns that a few people, who pretend to be ordinary citizens working and living in Anatolian towns, have also read the book. He meets all these people one by one to see to what extent their lives have changed after reading the book. He has learnt to recognize the readers from the expression on their faces: "The faces of those who have read the book and have faith in it are distinct; they all have the same melancholy [and] desire in their eyes [. . .]" (69). This melancholy stems from the blurring of memories and the desire is related to the urge of becoming a Westerner. Among these sad and impatient people, a doctor living in the city of Samsun attracts Osman's attention. To his surprise, this doctor has managed to cope with the book without going through a spiritual crisis. He goes on living in peace and happiness despite the book's impairing influences on him. Towards the end of *Yeni Hayat*, the author rewards the doctor for his successful reading experience by making him marry Janan, the narrator's beloved.

Doctor Fine, who tries to alleviate the book's effect on its readers by hiring spies to follow the people who have read it and by letting one of the spies kill its writer, asks the narrator a crucial question during one of their intimate conversations: "Tell me, is this possible in this day and age? Can a book change someone's whole life? [. . .] By what power can such a strong spell be cast in this day and age?" (120). Could it be the power of the Turkish Republic that Doctor Fine insistently questions? A reformulation of this question may read: Can the new way of life imposed by the Republic overthrow the age-old traditions and customs of Turkish life? Undoubtedly, the modernization process triggered a clash between the traditional existence and the new Westernized way of life. The people had to be taught the principles of this new life and they had to be persuaded to adopt them without questioning its underlying norms and paradigms. Consequently, the book containing the guidelines and principles of this new life should be read by as many people as possible. Mehmet who undertook this responsibility "tried distributing 'the work' in all sorts of possible places all over town [. . .]" (146). Here the book is referred to as "the work" in quotation marks. It is interesting to note that Kemal Atatürk, the founder of the Turkish Republic, also referred to the new, secular republic as "the work" while addressing the youth in his speeches (Nabi 105). The phrase "the work" which denotes both *Yeni Hayat* and the Turkish Republic reinforces the link between the reactions of its readers to the book and the reactions of the Turkish people to the new way of life initiated by the Turkish Republic.

During one of his trips to the small Anatolian towns, the narrator meets a group of firemen who have read the book. The firemen are so happy to meet someone who knows it that they begin immediately to recite the lines of the book they like most. The narrator is not surprised to witness such a scene; to him, it is not unusual to see people who either rewrite the book by copying each sentence, each word, and each punctuation mark to a notebook or quote from the book during their conversations with their friends at the tea gardens or restaurants. However, he is astounded when the firemen show him the place where they keep it: "As to the book, they showed me later that they kept it in the cab of their only fire truck as if it were the holy Koran" (193). In this context, the book is seen as a holy text containing all the secrets of life and death revealed within a logic that cannot be questioned. The modernization process is accompanied by the secularization of public life which tolerates the presence of the holy books only in religious activities carried out in the private realm. When *Yeni Hayat is* endowed with the characteristics of a holy book, it becomes a part of the private life of its readers. On the other hand, as it offers the guidelines of a new way of life to them, it is also integrated into their public lives. The impacts of the same book on both public and private domains signify the blurring of the boundaries between public and private lives.

Although the author avoids disclosing what the book contains, he feels the need to categorize the reactions of the people who have read it. He classifies them under three groups:

> Some went into solitude with the book, but at the threshold of a serious breakdown they were able to open up to a new world and shake off their affliction. There were also those who had crises or tantrums upon reading the book, accusing their friends or lovers of being oblivious to the world in the book, of not knowing or desiring the book, and thereby criticizing them mercilessly for not being anything like the persons in the book's universe. There was another set of organizer types who read the book in order to apply themselves to humanity rather than to the text. (154)

Consequently, there are three ways of responding to the book: One group consists of people who are frustrated and disappointed because their relatives, friends, and lovers do not approve of the new order as much as they do. Another group includes those who take the book too seriously and see it as encompassing the human life in all its aspects. According to the members of this group, it is not sufficient to persuade the people around them to lead a different way of life; in their view, all human beings must change their lives radically and adopt the new lifestyle. The last group to which the narrator, Mehmet and Janan belong suffer a nervous breakdown in their endeavors to adopt to the new order. These people feel painfully lonely and they want to reach the threshold which, they believe, would open the door to the new world for them.

"The threshold" is the place where the narrator, Mehmet, and Janan hope to find happiness, peace of mind, and tranquility. They do not know how to reach it, but they sense that during one of their bus rides they will set foot on this sacred place. At this magical moment, an angel will appear and in her unique presence they will enjoy the discovery of the meaning of life, death, and time.

"The threshold" by virtue of standing between the old life the characters used to lead before reading the book and the new life they want to discover and be a part of evokes an indecisive but happy existence in purgatory. The narrator says: "[. . .] I really wanted to be someplace else, in a time other than this, like that felicitous moment of being when one has not yet chosen between life and death [. . .]" (54). A moment marked with the inability to choose one path and the urge to stay at the converging point of two different paths is an ultimately happy moment for the narrator. Once he makes a decision to choose one path he feels that he will no more be happy. In a way, he enjoys contemplating his choices and multiple ways of existence open to him. The author addresses the narrator at one of his moments of sheer indecisiveness between his old and new lives: "You are pleasantly swaying in anticipation" (58-59). Anticipating a new existence and yet not embracing it thoroughly, and oscillating between the old way of life and the new one bring happiness to the narrator's restless soul. To overcome his frustration and bitter feelings, he always wants to be somewhere else: "Suddenly that same impatient desire rose once more from deeper depths and besieged my entire body, the desire to be both here and there" (59). Not only the narrator but Janan also looks forward to being at two different places at the same time. While talking about her childhood she says: "[. . .] I was afraid, and I liked my bed, but I wished I were out there too" (67). She was happy in bed, but she still wanted to be outside as well. The precious moment of not being here or there is highlighted by the narrator several times throughout the book. "Ah, to be neither here nor there! To become someone else and roam the peaceful garden that exists between the two worlds!" (54). Peace can only be found in a place which belongs to no definite worlds. The narrator clearly indicates where the "peaceful garden" exists while commenting on the felicitous moment of being neither here nor there: "[. . .] how precious was this unique moment which existed in between our victorious past and our gruesome and miserable future" (101). "The victorious past" obviously stands for the traditional Turkish way of life and the "gruesome and miserable future" signifies the Westernized way of life which requires a traumatic break-up with the past. The eventual result of dissociating from the past abruptly is expressed by the manufacturer of New Life Caramels the narrator meets on his last trip to Eastern Anatolia: "Today we were struggling to understand our own sensitivities through their [Western] rational methods, assuming this is what becoming civilized means" (281).

The passengers the narrator and Janan meet on their bus trips are also looking forward to meeting the Angel on the threshold. While describing a scene of crash the narrator analyzes the facial expression of an old woman who was on the point of dying "[. . .] the elderly woman is not in reality dying to reunite with her sisters and nieces but to reach the threshold of the nether world" (54). The narrator and Janan are fascinated by bus wrecks because these are the scenes that provide an encounter with a large number of people who are neither thoroughly alive nor literally dead. They meet a young girl among the wounded passengers on one of their trips on the dusty roads stretching away to the remote towns of Anatolia. Just before passing away the young girl describes her encounter with the Angel:

> I now see that it is your gaze, Angel, that is the unique moment that the book had promised, this moment of transition between the two realms; now that I'm neither here, nor there, I understand what is meant by departure; and how happy I am to comprehend the meaning of peace, death and time. (81)

Being in-between the two worlds helps the young girl to acquire an understanding of life, death, and peace.

Attempting to question culture as a fixed construct of modernist ideologies, the eminent postcolonial critic Homi Bhabha claims that the meaning of culture could only be negotiated within "a third space": "[. . .] it is the 'inter'- the cutting edge of translation and negotiation, the *in-between* space - that carries the burden of the meaning of culture" (38). "The third space" provides an appropriate time and place for the confrontation of two different cultures. Thus, in order to comprehend any cultural issue one has to stop by at this space and observe how two cultures coexist, albeit not in peace. Given this, it is not surprising to see that the characters who have read *Yeni Hayat* and consequently internalized a new understanding of life can find peace and solace only in between the old and new realms where they can negotiate and translate into one another the different ways of existence.

The characters who have finally gained an understanding of the meaning of life and death, and tranquility by oscillating between two different worlds gradually recognize their hybrid identities. Their former identities shaped by the social forces undergo a radical change on the threshold. These characters feel that they are no more the people they used to be. They begin to live in a flux of time which they cannot label simply as past, present or future. In fact, the slice of time that the threshold provides is just a moment, a moment which is characterized by the co-existence of the linear divisions of time, past, present and future. To put it another way, at the threshold the linear understanding of time is replaced by a circular one which can accommodate the past, the present, and the future together. During this period, one is neither forced to forget the past nor to contemplate only the future. Consequently, the tranquility and peace of mind which welcome the characters of *Yeni Hayat* as well as its readers outside the text on the threshold is triggered by the recognition of the liberating power of the crucial moment where the past, the present, and the future coexist.

When the entwined web of responses to the book is interpreted as the reflections of Turkish people's feelings towards the modern way of life, the oscillation between fascination with and resistance to the "West" comes to the foreground in the form of Turkey's age-old dilemma. The characters of *Yeni Hayat* are well aware of this dilemma and instead of trying to resolve it, they strive to learn to live with it through embracing the cultural hybridity which shapes their existence. The happiness and peace of mind they desperately need lies in the threshold, which is not a bridge to another life, but a third space where East and West coexist in a circular understanding of time. Orhan Pamuk refers to the hybrid identity of Turkish people on the threshold in one of his interviews as follows: "We will never be thoroughly Easternized or Westernized. Turkey's identity is actually its complexity. We have to learn to live easily with it" (qtd. in Lanham).

Works Cited

Bhabha, Homi K. *The Location of Culture*. London: Routledge, 1994.

Lanham, Frintz. "A Fine Turkish Blend: Orhan Pamuk Book Playful, Subversive." *HoustonChronicle.com* 16 Apr. 1998. 1 Dec. 2006 <www.chron.com/cgi-bin/auth/story/content/chronicle/ae/books/9798/04/19/pamuk.html>.

Nabi, Yaşar. *K. Atatürk Diyor Ki*. İstanbul: Varlık, 1970.

Pamuk, Orhan. *Yeni Hayat*. Istanbul: İletişim, 1995. English trans.: *The New Life*. Trans. Güneli Gün. New York: Vintage, 1998.

Wright, Ronald. "From a Breeze-Block Istanbul." *Times Literary Supplement* 10 Oct. 1997: 23.

Home Away from Home: Diaspora Experiences of Turks and Greeks in the 1920s

Banu Özel
Haliç University

Abstract: Once Greece had gained its independence from Ottoman rule (1832), it followed an irredentist policy hoping to reclaim Hellenic territory and revive the old dream of a new Byzantium. Known as the *Megali Idea* (Great Idea), this policy lasted until the defeat of the Greeks in the Greco-Turkish War (1920-1922). In the aftermath of the war, the Treaty of Lausanne (1923) paved the way for a compulsory population exchange between Greece and Turkey that rooted almost two million Greeks and Turks apart from their homes. The diaspora population living in Greece and Turkey today has carried the memory of this expulsion and relocation, and it is the force of these memories that plays the central role in the novels *Farewell Anatolia* by the Greek author Dido Sotiriou and *Kritimu: Girit'im Benim* (Kritimu: My Crete) by the Turkish author Sabâ Altınsay. The aim of this paper is three-fold: Firstly, to examine the texts as personal life narratives, which tell the lives of Turks and Greeks before and during the wars; secondly, to expound on how personal life stories may also represent and shape the collective history/memory of a community/nation (in this case, the collective history of modern Greece and Turkey); thirdly and lastly, to discuss the texts as works that go beyond national boundaries and seek to revive the collective memory of an entire region, be it the Aegean, the Mediterranean or the Balkans.

> And now
> Nostalgia is a narrow strait
> Me on one side
> The Mainland on the other side.
>
> —Yu-Kwang-chung, "Mainlander"

At the height of its power, the Ottoman Empire, which existed for more than 600 years, stretched from North Africa to the Balkans. In Ottoman times Greeks and Turks lived side-by-side for centuries. The rise of nationalist movements throughout the Balkans in the nineteenth century, however, led to many political and social upheavals, combats, and population expulsions. Once Greece had gained its independence from Ottoman rule (1832), it followed an irredentist policy hoping to reclaim Hellenic territory and revive the old dream of a new Byzantium. Known as the *Megali Idea* (Great Idea), this policy lasted until the defeat of the Greeks in the Greco-Turkish War (1920-1922). Greeks still refer to this event as the Asia Minor Catastrophe, signaling as it does the end of a centuries-long nationalist aspiration.

By contrast—not surprisingly—the Turkish people name this war 'The War of Independence' and the date when the war was won, 30 August 1922, is referred to as 'Victory Day,' marking the moment when the remains of a disintegrating empire began to be rebuilt into a new nation. To cite this event as either a catastrophe or a victory is of course simplistic; in any case, the consequences of this war were far more dreadful than the war itself. In its aftermath, the Treaty of Lausanne, signed in 1923, paved the way for a compulsory population exchange between Greece and Turkey that uprooted almost two million Greeks and Turks from their homes. Many people lost their lives on the way, and the survivors went through terrible ordeals, social and financial, in their respective new countries (Köker and Keskiner 198). Language was another problem for these refugees. Most of the Turks coming from Greece, especially from Crete, knew little or no Turkish; similarly, Greeks of Asia Minor were generally more proficient in Turkish (see the contributions in Hirschon). The diaspora population living in Greece and Turkey today has carried the memory of this expulsion and relocation, and it is the force of these memories that play the central role in the novels *Benden Selam Söyle Anadolu'ya* (*Farewell Anatolia*) by Dido Sotiriou[1] and *Kritimu: Giritim Benim* (Kritimu: My Crete) by Sabâ Altınsay.

---

[1] The works cited to this paper lists the Turkish translation of Sotiriou's work under the Turkish spelling 'Sotiriyu.'

Both of these novels, which narrate the lives of Turks and Greeks before and during the wars, are biographical and refer back to real-life experiences. Dido Sotiriou is herself an Asia Minor refugee expelled from Turkey in 1922. In Greece, she interviewed Manolis Axiotis, one of the survivors of the Greco-Turkish war and narrated his story in *Farewell Anatolia*. Sabâ Altınsay is the grandchild of a Turkish family uprooted from Crete in 1923, and *Kritimu* tells us the story of Altınsay's grandparents, İbrahim and Fatma Yarmakamakis. Being personal life narratives, the stories of Manolis and İbrahim also represent the stories of millions of Greeks and Turks forced to relocate. In this regard, it would not be wrong to claim that these novels also serve as narratives of the collective history of modern Greece and Turkey, and are instrumental in retaining or shaping the collective memory of each nation. Moreover, on an even broader level, Sotiriou's and Altınsay's works go beyond national boundaries and seek to revive the collective memory of an entire region.

In *Farewell Anatolia*, Sotiriou chronicles the story of Manolis Axiotis—an Asia Minor Greek born and raised in Aydın. Manolis' family deals with farming, mostly raising figs and olives. Unlike his father and big brothers, Manolis is not interested in farming; therefore, he is sent to Izmir—a multi-ethnic city inhabited by Turks, Greeks, Armenians, Jews, and Levantines—to learn business. Manolis stresses that the Asia Minor Greeks in his village led comfortable and peaceful lives before the outbreak of World War I:

> If paradise really exists, Kirkica, our village was a little corner of it. We lived close to God, high up on a hillside among forested mountains with the sea in the distance. As far as the eye could see, the fertile valley of Ephesus stretched out at our feet, thickly planted with fig and olive groves, and fields of tobacco, cotton, wheat, corn and sesame; and it was all ours. (15)

> Could it have been the natural warmth of Anatolia, or perhaps the fertile soil?... Whatever the reason, we were always singing. [. . .] We had never known anxiety about our daily bread—or the fear of death. Until 1914 there had never been a killing in our village [. . .]. (18-19)

World War I triggers a painful period of quarrels and battles for the Asia Minor Greeks and Turks. When the war breaks out, Manolis is called up to the Ottoman Army, yet like all the other distrusted Christians he has to work in the Ottoman Labor Battalions, which he describes as unbearable. He deserts from the Labor Battalions several times, but is caught every time by the Turkish forces who are constantly looking for absconders. Referring to the war years, Manolis says, "in our village, the singing died out. The houses emptied, the fields dried up, joy vanished. Everywhere there was terror and anguish" (90). With the end of the war, he and his brothers Kostas and Stamatis set off to revive their fields again. Nevertheless, another series of combats starts in Anatolia as the Greek Army prepares for the Asia Minor campaign to capture Istanbul. Most of the Asia Minor Greeks enlist in the Greek Army as volunteers. At first, Manolis is very reluctant to participate in another war, yet he cannot resist the pressure from his villagers and joins the Greek forces eventually. The Greek Army's defeat leads to thousands of Asia Minor Greeks' taking refuge in Greece. *Farewell Anatolia* concludes with the narration of Manolis' escape to a Greek island.

Moving from *Farewell Anatolia* to *Kritimu*, we see another story of Turkish-Greek relations, war, and displacement. *Kritimu* narrates the story of İbrahim Yarmakamakis, a Greek-speaking Turkish Cretan. İbrahim and his father Mustafa are talented goldsmiths in Crete respected by both Turkish and Greek. İbrahim has two beloveds: Cemile, his fiancée, and the Crete Island. He marries Cemile, yet she dies while giving birth to their daughter Azize. It is not easy for İbrahim to get over Cemile's death; to make the matters worse, his much-loved

Crete is on the brink of disintegration. The Ottoman Empire is about to pull back its soldiers and officers from the island, and the tension between Muslim Turks and Christian Greeks is very dense due to two opposing views on Crete's future: Greek Cretans look forward to the union with independent Greece whereas Turkish Cretans expect the Ottoman government to use its influence concerning the rule on the island. As years pass, destabilization and the bitter conflicts between Turks and Greeks increase considerably. Occasional fights between the two groups turn into insurrections, now and then causing casualties. İbrahim loses his best friend Piçiriko in one of the Greek uprisings. After the Balkan Wars, the Ottoman Empire declares that it will give up Crete, and soon afterwards Crete unites with Greece. This makes the situation of the Turkish Cretans much more complicated and desperate due to the fact that they lose the financial and social security they used to enjoy for centuries. Although it is very painful for them, many Turkish Cretans leave the island and head towards Turkey.

When the Greco-Turkish War in Anatolia is won by the Turks in 1922, the new Turkish parliament in Ankara desires to have all Muslim Turks in the same territory and hence wants the compulsory relocation of those of them who live outside Turkey. İbrahim, at the time married to Fatma, has to take his wife and five children to Küçükkuyu, Turkey, leaving their home and land in Crete to the Asia Minor Greeks expelled from Turkey—leaving his parents, his beloved Cemile and Piçiriko in their graveyards. They, together with the other Turkish Cretans, embark on the ship that will take them to their "new homes." Tired of war and violence, hurt by his losses, full of questions and disappointment, İbrahim cries: "Girit mi bizim gurbetimiz, Türkiye mi? Bilmem, ah bilemem" (286) ("Is Crete our exile or Turkey? I don't know, o I don't know"). As the ship leaves the port, thousands of people on board all together sing the famous Crete folk song "Kritimu! Omorfi nisi!" (287) ("My Crete! My beautiful island!").

While conveying tragic stories of ordinary people, these life narratives also dwell upon some consequential historical events of the late nineteenth and early twentieth century. As they narrate the stories of two men, they also portray the end of Greek communities in Anatolia and the end of the Turkish presence in Crete; or, in more general terms, they demonstrate how nationalism and war can give rise to ethnic conflicts and ruin communities. Therefore, it can be claimed that personal testimonies can lend a voice to groups or larger communities when historical events and personal experiences mingle. In *Farewell Anatolia*, Asia Minor Greeks collectively live at ease before the social and political upheavals in Anatolia and go through catastrophic days during and after the wars; most of them experience the fear and violence in the İzmir Quay when the city is burned to ashes, and except those captured as war prisoners they are all forced to migrate. Likewise, in *Kritimu*, social and financial ordeals and enforced relocation concern not only İbrahim, but all Turkish Cretans. This point reveals the connection between personal and collective history. Before they leave Crete, İbrahim questions this connection and tries to make sense of their collective tragedy:

> Böyleydi; yazıları böyleydi. Bu toprakta doğup büyüyen bunca insanın, hepsinin mi yazgıları ortaktı peki? İbrahim sanırdı ki her kula başka bir kader düşer. Bunlarınkinde nasıl oluyordu da aynı yazı, herkese birden düşüyordu? (253)

> It was their destiny. Yet, did all these people, born and raised on this land, have a destiny in common? İbrahim had thought that each person has a destiny of his own. If so how come people here in Crete could share the same destiny?[2]

Just like İbrahim, Manolis is also troubled with the bitter reality of their shared history. When he reaches Greece, he verbalizes the Asia Minor Greek refugees' dreadful collective experience as follows:

---

[2] Translations from *Kritimu* are mine.

There, across the water, we abandoned our homes, our bolted storerooms, our wedding wreaths laid atop the iconostase, our ancestors in their graveyards. We abandoned our children and parents and brothers, left our dead unburied, the living without a roof over their heads. Haunted dreams. There. Over there, until just yesterday, it had been our home.

(Farewell 297)

On the other hand, in *Kritimu*, Hüseyin Aziz, a prominent Turkish journalist, seems to be more successful in acknowledging collective history as a fact. He says: "Tıpkı insanlar gibi toplumların da kaderleri vardır. Bu kader, bazen çok acı yazılır" (286) ("Just like people, communities have their destinies, too, and sometimes this destiny is very painful"). Both in *Farewell Anatolia* and in *Kritimu*, personal tragedies, especially of the main characters, and painful destinies of the communities go parallel with each other. Thus, these texts go way beyond being only the life narratives of Manolis and İbrahim; they rather represent the stories of millions of Turks and Greeks who endured the very same struggles and conflicts.

A further point concerns with collective histories are remembered by communities or nations. What are the trajectories in which personal recollections transform into collective memories? And why does collective memory matter, really? Collective memory—a term coined by French sociologist Maurice Halbwachs in 1925—relates to a group's continual remembering of what has been experienced in common. According to Halbwachs, collective memory is socially constructed (Couser 22). When personal memories of a traumatic past are put into writing as life narratives, they evolve as collective memories, which means they are not only recollected by a single individual but also by members of the group having experienced the events, and even by those who did not. Hence, collective memory has the power to shape societies and their understandings of the past, present and future. When it comes to diasporas, the issue of collective memory gains a further significance. In *Farewell Anatolia* and *Kritimu*, the relationship between personal and collective memory can be discussed in two respects. On a textual level, Manolis and İbrahim—two representatives of the early twentieth-century Turkish and Greek diasporas—are preoccupied with the issue of memory. In order to reinforce and sustain their memories of Crete, a few days before they leave the island, İbrahim takes his family to the Crete Castle where they can have a panoramic view of the island. İbrahim and Fatma tell the children to look at the view carefully for the last time so that they will never ever forget it (*Kritimu* 264). "Her biri kendi Girit'ini seyrediyor, onu hatıra diye yanlarına alabilmek için gözlerini, zihinlerini, akıllarını sonuna kadar açıyor, bir mücevheri kutusuna kilitler gibi gönüllerine kilitliyorlardı" (264) (Each was watching his or her own Crete; to take it with them as a memory, they were opening their eyes and minds wide; they were locking her into their hearts as if locking jewelry into its box). Before Manolis flees to Greece, he passes through his own village, and he realizes that "every house, every lane, every tree and shrub" and every stone of that earth is a living part of his heart and his memories (*Farewell* 290).

On an extratextual level, the emergence of these texts in contemporary literature demonstrates that the two authors, as members of diaspora populations, sustain "a collective historical and cultural memory of the dispersion" and a "will to transmit heritage" (Chaliand and Rageaux iv-xvii). Hélène Cixous considers writing "a way of leaving no space for death, [. . .] of never letting oneself be surprised by the abyss" (3). Having written *Farewell Anatolia* and *Kritimu* so as to contribute to the collective memory of Greek and Turkish people, Sotiriou and Altınsay give a credit to Hélène Cixous' truthful remarks. Sotiriou states in his forword:

> Anadolu Rumları, atalarının toprağından kopup ayrılalı kırk yıldan fazla zaman geçti. Bu fırtınayı yaşamış olanlar birbiri ardından göçüp gitmekte ve yaşantılar kaybolmakta. [.

. .] Anadolu Rumları'nın bir atasözü vardır: "Ölü gözünden yaş akmaz". İşte bu nedenle hayatta olanların anılarına kulak verdim ve sevgiyle dayadım kulağımı yüreklerine. [. . .] Bir daha geri gelmemek üzere çökmüş bir alemi gözlerinizin önünde canlandırmak amacıyla yaptım bu işi. Yaşlılar unutmasın, gençler bütün olup biteni çırılçıplak görsün, öğrensin diye... (*Benden* 7)

It has been more than 40 years since the Asia Minor Greeks were uprooted from their ancestors' land. Those who experienced these tempestuous days are now passing away one after the other and the memories of these lives are vanishing. [. . .] The Asia Minor Greeks have a proverb: "The eyes of the dead don't shed tears." It is for this reason that I have lent an ear to the memories of those who are still alive and affectionately leaned my ear on their hearts. [. . .] I have done this to bring alive again before your eyes a lost world that will never come back. For the aged not to forget, for the young to clearly see and learn what happened...[3]

Sotiriou draws attention to the importance of averting forgetfulness and unconsciousness, because retaining a memory is essential to maintaining an identity. Through narratives of collective memory, diasporas can form and reinforce memories of their homelands and establish points of identification with the rest of their communities. Thus, they can even create a national identity based on a shared history.

At this point, the rigorous role of "discourse" in the creation of a national identity is worth some discussion. Retaining and conveying a national history and memory is generally realized through mass public education and cultural assimilation, which are, according to Michel Foucault, "political means of maintaining or of modifying the appro-

---

[3] The translation of this quotation from the author's foreword to *Benden Selam Söyle Anadolu'ya* is mine.

priation of discourse, with the knowledge and the powers it carries with it" (227). Modern nation-states carefully select history—purposefully discounting certain events and/or periods and overemphasizing others—and in this way they construct their own sense of the past. Then this selected history is collectively represented through various media such as national narratives, national holidays, commemorations, anthems and songs by using certain discourses. For Foucault, "the production of discourse is at once controlled, selected, organized and redistributed according to a certain number of procedures [. . .]" (216). For decades, the controlled and selected political and nationalist discourses in Greece and Turkey have formulated Greek and Turkish subjects, respectively, as "others," as "opponents"—or even "enemies," though this may seem a politically incorrect claim.

Examples of these types of discourse can be found in the texts under discussion here. For instance, in *Kritimu*, Meletyos, a Greek coppersmith, says to his wife Hrisula, who is a good friend of Turkish Cemile: "Girit'te Hıristiyan mutluysa Müslüman mutsuzdur" (63) ("In Crete, if the Christian is happy, then the Muslim is unhappy"). *Farewell Anatolia* reveals similar attitudes, especially when narrating the Asia Minor Campaign. Asia Minor Greeks, including Manolis, speak out the discourse of Greek irredentism: "This land is the breadbasket and the glory of our race and it's ours, all ours, from way back! [. . .] Greece should be the winner; Turkey is lying there in ruins" (207).

Nevertheless, Foucault also states that "a single work of literature can give rise, simultaneously, to several distinct types of discourse" (221). A close analysis of the texts reveals that they not only reflect the national and political discourses of Greece and Turkey, but also provocatively and remarkably challenge them by presenting competing and contrasting views and by making use of moralistic and humanistic discourses. What I mean by moralistic and humanistic discourses is the rhetoric of interrogation, interpretation and evaluation which question the dynamics and moral of wars without bias and mourn for the times of peace.

For example, in *Kritimu*, between the lines, the violent acts of Turks and Greeks are regarded as murder, although Greeks claim that the blood they shed is for free Crete, while Turks regard the events as a rebellion. Moreover, Dr. Ragıp Begakis, who leaves Crete and goes to Turkey in order to join the Turkish Army in the Greco-Turkish War, states: "Biz şimdi, kendi istiklalimiz için harp etmekte haklıysak, istiklali için Osmanlı ile harp eden Giritli Hıristiyanlar haksız mıydı?" (237) ("If we are right to fight for our independence now, were the Christian Cretans who fought for their freedom against the Ottomans wrong?"). His remarks do not blindly try to justify the Turks' struggle for independence, but equally consider the Greek efforts for liberty. Manolis, not being able to come to terms with their situation after the wars, cries: "Sevket! Don't you recognize me, my friend? For years we reaped laughter and tears together. *Ne yapior*, Sevket? Ah Sevket! We have turned into monsters. We have plunged knives into our hearts, destroyed them; and for what?" (*Farewell* 298). Like Manolis, İbrahim's mother Azize Hanım cannot comprehend the reason for the battles between Turks and Greeks: "Neyi paylaşamazlardı ki? Giritlilerin hepsi aynı sayılırdı üstelik. İşleri, adetleri bile benzerdi. [. . .] Neydi bu başlarına gelen, daha da gelecek miydi?" (*Kritimu* 39). ("What was it that they could not share? Besides, all Cretans were much the same. Even their jobs and customs were similar. [. . .] What was this misfortune that befell them? Would there be even more?") Both Manolis' and Azize Hanım's remarks stress that in the recent past Greeks and Turks were friends sharing joy and sorrow and imply that the hostility between the two is not really something self-originated, but something generated through external factors. Needless to say, wars, expulsions of populations and the casualties they cause trigger nostalgia for what is lost: Nostalgia literally is pain for a return home (*nostos* 'return home' and *algia* 'pain'; cf. *Merriam-Webster's*). In Greece, Manolis expresses his nostalgia in both of its meanings:

longing for the good-old days and longing for a return to the homeland:

> So much suffering, so much tragedy. Now my mind wanted to return to the past. If it could only all be a lie, if we could only go back to our land, to our gardens, to our forests with their songbirds, sparrows and tiny owls, to our orchards with their tangerine trees and flowering cherries, to our beautiful festivals... (*Farewell* 298)

Although the modern nation-states have favored the extrication and even alienation of the Greek and Turkish people in order to achieve ethnic homogeneity in their territories, and although the nationalist and political discourses in Greece and Turkey have represented the respective other side as the "Other" for the sake of sustaining national unity and identity, examples from contemporary literature have managed to provide an abundant ground where this otherness and alienation have transformed into interaction and mutual understanding. Bringing *Farewell Anatolia* and *Kritimu* together gives one much more than two simple life stories. Their powerful reflections on the issues of war, forced migration, collective history and memory demonstrate that they can also function as narratives of the collective history of Greek and Turkish diasporas or, broadly speaking, narratives of the national history of modern Greece and Turkey. Furthermore, their defiance and deconstruction of entrenched nationalist viewpoints through the eloquent use of different discourses as well as their highlighting of various contradictory views in both countries strike one as diligent and innovative attempts to move beyond abiding nationalist representations. These texts reveal that the two nations are not essentially "others" as which they are usually pictured; on the contrary, they are very much alike in the psychological and physical traumas and the social and financial ordeals they have suffered as well as in their ways of living, their manners, songs and cuisines. From this perspective, it can also be claimed that *Farewell Anatolia* and *Kritimu* represent the collective history of an entire region, be it the Aegean or the Mediterranean or the Balkans.

Works Cited

Altınsay, Sabâ. *Kritimu: Girit'im Benim*. Can: İstanbul, 2004.
Chaliand, Gerard, and Jean-Pierre Rageau. *The Penguin Atlas of Diasporas*. Trans. A. M. Berrett. New York: Viking, 1995.
Cixous, Hélène. *"Coming to Writing" and Other Essays*. Ed. Deborah Jensson. Cambridge, Massachusetts: Harvard University Press, 1991.
Coser, Lewis A. Introduction. *On Collective Memory*. By Maurice Halbwachs. Ed., trans, and introd. Lewis A. Coser. University of Chicago Press: Chicago, USA, 1992.
Foucault, Michel. *Archaeology of Knowledge*. Trans. A. M. Sheridan Smith. New York: Pantheon, 1972.
Hirschon, Renée, ed. *Crossing the Aegean: An Appraisal of the 1923 Compulsory Population Exchange between Greece and Turkey*. New York: Berghahn, 2003.
Köker, Tolga, and Leylâ Keskiner. "The Experience of Forced Migrants in Turkey." Hirschon 193-208.
Merriam-Webster's Collegiate Dictionary. 11th ed. Springfield, Massachusetts: Merriam-Webster, 2003.
Sotiriou, Dido. *Farewell Anatolia*. Trans. Fred. A. Reed. Athens: Kedros, 1991.
Sotiriyu, Dido. *Benden Selâm Söyle Anadolu'ya*. Trans. Atillâ Tokatlı. Can: İstanbul, 2004.

The Dancer and the Dance: A Study of Mrinalini Sarabhai's Autobiography

Leena Chandorkar
Abasaheb Garware College, University of Pune

Abstract: *The Voice of the Heart* (2004), the autobiography of Mrinalini Sarabhai, one of the most respected classical dancers of India, was unable to live up to the expectation it aroused. Had Mrinalini subtitled the book "The Autobiography of a Dancer," she would have been free to make the theme of her public role of dancer the central focus. In the present form it lacks a "wholeness" that was there in her best dance performances.

The dualities of East-West, public-private, spiritual-secular, science-art, commerce-culture, tradition-modernity are constantly evoked in *The Voice of the Heart* only to sink under their own contradictions. The projected Self in the autobiography is strong enough—the innumerable quotations praising Mrinalini are the thread that holds the pastiche of memory together—yet the endless self-glorification hints at a lurking feeling of inadequacy. The voice of the heart rings hollow.

My paper analyses the contradictions within this autobiography. It is not merely the failure to follow the confessional ideal of a conventional autobiography or the total lack of perspective but the absence of an inner voice that makes this autobiography a truth half-told.

> O body swayed to music, O brightening glance,
> How can we know the dancer from the dance?
>
> —W. B. Yeats, "Among School Children"

The Voice of the Heart is the autobiography of an exceptional woman. Mrinalini Sarabhai is one of the most respected and well-known names in Indian classical dance. The blurb on the jacket of her stylishly produced autobiography published by Harper Collins holds her "single handedly responsible for taking classical Indian dance beyond the shores of India and making Bharatnatyam a dance form that is revered throughout the world."

If Mrinalini Sarabhai is exceptional, her autobiography is even more so. This is because, unlike women of her generation, Mrinalini Sarabhai in her autobiography makes no attempt to dilute or tone down the fame that her art fetched her. She takes no recourse to literary devices that would throw a veil of modesty over her achievements. She has no fear of being charged with egoistic self-exaltation. On the contrary, her autobiography seems to revel in self-praise and self-congratulation. The reason could partly be her very public profession—a dancer needs to feed off the adulation of her audience; and partly her emotionally deprived childhood: "My mother always emphasised the fact that I was not worth much. I don't think I have got over that. Only my art gave me the courage to live, and through the years, my marvellous friends and my audiences have helped me build up my self esteem [. . .] every little instance of kindness mattered to me" (35). The impact that childhood memories can have on a person! With a bull-dog like tenacity Mrinalini Sarabhai sets out to prove her mother wrong by becoming somebody worthwhile. The autobiography is a systematic chronicling of all the praise Mrinalini Sarabhai ever received in her life, starting with the pat on the back for her first stage performance at age eight to the last paragraph of the autobiography where she quotes somebody who calls her a "Goddess of Dance."

In this unabashed glorification of her own achievements *The Voice of the Heart* is atypical. Autobiographies written by Indian women tend to be modest about successes. Women's autobiographies relate the price they had to pay for their fame rather than the happiness that their achievement brought them. There seems to be an unspoken injunction amongst women autobiography writers about speaking out in public. But here the title itself articulates the autobiography as a mode of breaking the silence, of giving voice to an untold story.

The way this story unfolds, or rather the way this writer chooses to articulate her life, is significant. *The Voice of the Heart* is a study in dualities: classes vs masses, East vs West, tradition vs modernity, public vs private, science vs art, spiritual vs secular. This begins in the very first chapter.

Mrinalini Sarabhai was born in Chennai in pre-independence India (before 1920, the exact date of birth is not given), the youngest of the children of a well-known lawyer and academician, Subbaram Swaminathan. The first chapter "Father" delineates the steady rise in fame of a boy born in a small village in Sekharipuram in the Palghat district of Kerala. With his brilliant mind and studious nature, "especially his knowledge of English" (1), Swaminathan shifted from the village school to the district school. From there to Kozhikode, a bigger town in Kerala, and then to college in the famous Madras Christian College where he won the Gilchrist scholarship for further studies abroad. The next stop was London University College and Gray's Inn, from where he took his BSc degree. Writes Mrinalini Sarabhai: "Having conquered London and Edinburgh, he now set his vision on the Harvard Law School" (2). This vocabulary of "conquering" and "defeating" the world at its own game continues like a thread through the book, even when Mrinalini Sarabhai is describing the reaction to her own concerts abroad.

This was the beginning of the twentieth century, when colonial India was just waking up to the call of nationalism. It was in this atmosphere that Swaminathan, with the help of his British mentors, started his law practice in Chennai. His successful career was soon to make him an important and influential person in Chennai.

It was in this Anglicised household that Mrinalini Sarabhai grew up. She completed her schooling at a finishing school in Switzerland. Ironically, after her father's death, her mother became an active member of the Indian National Congress and later became one of the first woman Cabinet Ministers of free India. Mrinalini Sarabhai's sister, Capt. Lakshmi Sehgal, became a communist and joined Subhash Chandra Bose's Indian National Army. All this fervent nationalist activity was funded by the money left by her lawyer father!

It was undoubtedly a privileged childhood. Born into wealth, Mrinalini Sarabhai married into wealth. There was a yawning chasm between the "haves" and the "have-nots" in colonial India. Mrinalini Sarabhai's family was definitely amongst the élite. The oppression that the colonised suffered in the India of her time was class-based. If you were fortunate enough to be on the right side of the fence, you could live in complete ignorance of your country's slavery. It was the good fortune of Mrinalini Sarabhai to marry into "old-money." The Sarabhais were the most important industrial group in Ahmedabad. Vikram Sarabhai, her husband, was the most brilliant and the most versatile of the four Sarabhai sons. Theirs was a family that followed Gandhian principles. Gandhi's influence put a moral obligation on the well heeled to do something constructive for the downtrodden. The classes were expected to come out of their ivory towers and help the masses. In spite of all this social awareness in her childhood as well as marital houses, Mrinalini Sarabhai remained the quintessential aristocrat. She quotes:

> Umashankar Joshi, the great poet, was already a dear friend of Vikram's and mine. At one of our Arangetram (inaugural) ceremonies he said, 'Princes of Gujarat always married princesses from other states. Minaldevi came from the South and created huge tanks and reservoirs for the people. This prince (Vikram) has married Mrinalinidevi who has brought us the classical arts of the country.' A lovely compliment from a great poet. (180)

Mrinalini Sarabhai's second chapter entitled "Mother" is more about herself than about her mother. This is strange because her mother was a remarkable woman. Writes Mrinalini Sarabhai:

> My mother was strangely rigid in some ways. She became involved in politics even before my father died and was very much a leader in the social life of Chennai. She was a mem-

ber of the ladies' club, she took part in the dramatics, usually as the heroine. She also played tennis and was one of the first women to drive a car. She was a very talented person, a gracious and charming hostess, but she had no time for her children. (32)

After these damning words, her mother's accomplishments are mentioned no more and the rest of the chapter is dedicated to the description and praise of Mrinalini Sarabhai.

The figure of the mother is revered highly in Indian culture and the mother who is also a serious career woman is an embattled figure even in modern India. In this regard, Mrinalini Sarabhai was fortunate to have an enlightened and liberal man like Vikram Sarabhai for a husband. This brilliant man, "the father of Atomic Science in India" understood Mrinalini Sarabhai's commitment to dance and undertook his parenting responsibilities without grumbling. Mrinalini Sarabhai quotes from an article written by her daughter Mallika: "Papa was with us frequently and for lengthy periods of time, adjusting his work schedules to suit Amma's dance ones" (158). She ends thus: "For me Amma has been the embodiment of everything positive—strength, love, kindness, humour. As a mother, if I can be the same kind of mother to my children, then that would be enough" (158). This certificate from her grown-up child validating her role as mother is important if her achievement in the outside world is to have any meaning at all. For, in the eyes of the world, success in the public field is cancelled out if you fail as a mother.

Mrinalini Sarabhai was young and idealistic at a most important time in the history of modern India. The nationalist movement spearheaded by Gandhi was sweeping India. Gandhi, also known as Bapu, the Father of the Nation, was responsible for giving an equal status to women in the Freedom Struggle. Having strong women like her mother and her sister in her family, Mrinalini Sarabhai did not lack a role model as far as a social role for a woman was concerned. Therefore it is no surprise that she was determined to fashion a strong identity for herself that would be apart from her identity as a daughter/sister/wife/mother. This identity she found in dance. Says Mrinalini Sarabhai:

> I got proposals of marriage almost every week and I was getting tired of them. Whenever anyone proposed, my stock reply was: 'I am sorry. I want to be a career girl.' That notion itself used to upset people. Vikram was so different. He understood my commitment to dance. It was some deep yearning within me that found a perfect answer in him. He loved the arts and knew instinctively what was right. We had so many things in common: our love for beauty, for honesty, for tradition, and, at the same time, our excitement about new developments in civilization. (79)

In that sense, both Vikram and Mrinalini Sarabhai are children of Nehru's "modern," socialist India—seeking to make a place for themselves on the world stage while holding on to their Indian roots. He in the sphere of science and she in the sphere of art and culture (and both close to the powers that be!). The first Prime Minister of India, Jawaharlal Nehru, also referred to as Chacha Nehru, Uncle Nehru, is portrayed as a charming and loving father figure:

> Nehru was a family friend and treated Vikram like a son. I hero worshipped him and thought that he was one of the finest persons I had met [. . .] The first time Vikram and I went to a party at his home, he made me sit beside him, put his arm around me and asked me what I did. 'Dancing,' I said. (125-126)

Nehru, whose daughter Indira Gandhi went on to become one of the most powerful Prime Ministers of India, was committed to bringing talented and intelligent women out of the four walls of their homes and into the mainstream of society. That he should ask the young Mrinalini Sarabhai what she did, apart from being a glamorous wife to a brilliant scientist, is significant. An identity apart from that of the familial roles thrust upon a woman was an important contribution of the nationalist struggle.

According to Dipesh Chakraborty "[c]olonial Indian history is replete with instances where Indians arrogated subjecthood to themselves precisely by mobilizing, within the context of 'modern' institutions and sometimes on behalf of the modernizing project of nationalism, devices of collective memory that were both antihistorical and antimodern" (239). It is true that Indian culture provides a space for a truly talented woman to reach a position of power because of this strong identification of the Country with Mother—the concept of Bharat Mata, Mother India.

Ambalal, Mrinalini Sarabhai's father-in-law, invited his sister Anasuyaben to work with him in the family business. A strong woman, she often travelled alone to their sugar mills in Bihar. This was in 1918. She founded and ran the Ahmedabad Textile Labour Association at a time when her brother, Ambalal, headed the Mill Owner's Association. Writes Mrinalini Sarabhai: "Often my evenings were spent with her, watching with amusement the way she treated labour union leaders as lovable young boys, amongst them Khandubhai Desai, Gulzarilal Nanda (later our Prime Minister), Arvind Buch and others, who came to see her frequently—chiding them all as only a loving mother could" (95).

Later Mrinalini Sarabhai herself would become the grand matriarch. Referred to as *Amma* (Mother) not only by her own children, but by all her students and those who came in contact with her. According to Chandra T. Mohanty, "That women mother in a variety of societies is not as significant as the value attached to mothering in these societies. The distinction between the act of mothering and the status attached to it is a very important one—one that needs to be stated and analyzed contextually" (179).

Mrinalini Sarabhai contrasts the attitude of the West towards the image of the mother with that of India. On her first tour of Paris, she had her husband and one-year-old son with her. Says she:

> One of the reporters of the *Daily Mail* said, 'The thought struck me that few European ballerinas would find it convenient to bear a child and take him on tour.' I was considered out of the ordinary for not only having a child, but also being proud to show the world that I was a mother. 'We in India take such things in our stride,' I said when the reporters questioned me about it. A husband and baby on tour would be unthinkable for a ballerina in the West. (131)

Mrinalini Sarabhai sees herself as not merely a dancer, but as a cultural ambassador: "When I came to Paris, I was rather worried about how classical South Indian dancing would be received by the audiences. Yet inside me was the great desire to show to the West what to me was a most perfect technique" (131). This idealism, this need to showcase the best of India to the world, particularly to Europe and the US, was also a part of the Nehruvian dream: "One of the remarks by our ambassador in Paris, which has been repeated many times since, was, 'I have never seen such a highly disciplined and well dressed group, not to speak of the marvellous dancing. You make us proud of being Indian" (213).

Nehru worked in close association with the pioneers of Indian Science and Culture after independence. One of these pioneers and one of Nehru's favourites was undoubtedly the handsome, well-bred Vikram Sarabhai. Cambridge-educated, polished in manners, a visionary, modern in thought and traditional in upbringing, he was the epitome of the modern Indian man that Nehru thought suitable for representing India. Yet his scientific development was to go hand-in-hand with social upliftment. "When Vikram started India's space programme, he always spoke of using Space for national development" (189). This commitment to social upliftment is shared by Mrinalini Sarabhai. In the chapter entitled "Communicating Social Issues Through Dance" she talks about *Memory*, a dance drama she created on dowry deaths:

> It was the first time that Bharatnatyam spoke of a social problem. I did not change the technique but used it very differently. [. . .] Editorials were written by leading newspapers on how for the first time dance spoke of contemporary problems. My creative urge had at last begun to find fulfilment and direction. From then on there was no looking back. (227, 228)

Her husband's scientific work was complementary to her dance. She writes:

> Vikram often talked of the marvellous universe beyond the Milky Way, and both of us, lying on our cots on the veranda of our bedroom, gazed at the stars differently, yet united in a shared experience of wonder. [. . .] Art and Science both explore our invisible world. Once Vikram wrote, 'The important aspect is to be able to make abstractions in art, in dancing, in astronomy or in Physics and Mathematics. We observe a little but from there onwards we take wings in a way and project ourselves onto a new plane—it satisfies a need to soar. (233)

She projects her marriage with Vikram as a coming together of Yin and Yang. A two-in-one kind of package at the disposal of social and national causes. She says:

> Science is so similar to Art, both disciplines are a search for unknown galaxies in the universe, both spiritually aware of the indivisible wholeness of the cosmos. A scientist looks for new horizons in knowledge, a dancer for inner horizons of understanding. A scientist speaks about the spaces beyond our planet and its mysteries. A dancer searches spaces within

for meaning. Vikram as a scientist, and I as a dancer, shared a togetherness that was hard to define. (80)

However, even this seemingly perfect marriage had fissures. Vikram's well-known and long-standing relationship with Kamla Kapur caused Mrinalini Sarabhai much heartache. She dismisses this liaison in one paragraph and quotes from a letter that Vikram wrote her assuring her of his undying love. Mrinalini Sarabhai is careful about keeping the "perfect marriage mask" intact. Sometimes though, the mask slips.

In one of the rare instances of self-awareness in the book, Mrinalini Sarabhai writes:

> Married into such an overpowering family, I felt very alone. Vikram was immediately immersed in the business and his laboratory and did not have much time to be with me. The whole family was extremely self-contained, and seemingly so confident that I felt inadequate. To live up to the high ideals of the family—never put into words but made very obvious to me from my mother-in-law's behaviour—gave me a sense of isolation that has lasted all my life. (98)

Is this the reason why the autobiography of Mrinalini Sarabhai is filled with self-praise and self-congratulation to the point that it can be labelled as a tome of vainful boasting? Is it to cover her feeling of inadequacy? Is she even aware how me-centred the autobiography has become? Actually, the autobiography as a genre is problematic. It is basically, the writing of a life—where the writer and the main protagonist of the story are one. To lift the autobiography from being an endless ego trip, the writer has to achieve a balance between the subjective and the objective. It is this objectivity that *The Voice of the Heart* lacks.

Even the language is mundane and hardly lyrical. For a woman who claims to be a writer, this is surprising. The tone adopted veers between obscure preachiness and a dull detailing of events. The innumerable quotations, praising Mrinalini Sarabhai, are the thread that hold the narrative together. Humour is lacking and so is an easy felicity with the English language. There is neither the aura of erudition in the narration as in Pearl S. Buck's autobiography, nor the disarming simplicity that one finds in Laxmibai Tilak's autobiography.

Repeatedly, Mrinalini Sarabhai calls her dance a spiritual experience. True spirituality seeks a oneness with God and a dilution of the Ego into the limitlessness of His powers. Where is the need then to quote after every few paragraphs some admirer or other? Why has Mrinalini Sarabhai not been able to set aside her me-centred focus when talking of any topic or person? The Self that is projected here is at a variance with the Ego-less entity a truly spiritual seeker would present. If dance is the medium to reach the Creator, why should there be a separation between the dancer and the dance?

In the words of Swami Ishwarchandji, the spiritual guru of Mrinalini Sarabhai, "Give up all (in the real sense, in the core of yourself) for Him. Don't you see that life is trying to bring about this giving up on your part without your being aware of it?" (250). Mrinalini Sarabhai quotes her guru and then says, "In dance, the presence is constantly there and I am one with the universe, never aware of my audience or surroundings" (250).

Unlike scientific research, which is a lonely and reclusive activity, dance is a very interactive art. Dance in seclusion is not possible. The public performances that Mrinalini Sarabhai gave, ostensibly to showcase Indian culture to the world, are at odds with the spirituality she ascribes to it. If dance is devotion and she is Mira, the saint poet who worshipped Lord Krishna, she would not bother about public acclaim. This contradiction within herself regarding where to place her Self is transmitted to the fashioning of her autobiography. Mira was totally immersed in her devotion towards Lord Krishna. She was not bothered about the outside world. The secular world and all its attractions and plaudits held no importance for her.

What Mrinalini Sarabhai describes is ultimately show-business, the very antithesis of spirituality. Her performances (when they are not state-sponsored) have all the attendant compulsions of showbiz—albeit an elitist kind of showbiz: the impresario, the sale of tickets, the critics' reviews, TV/print interviews. It would be presumptuous to call all this spiritual. In fact the nickname that Vikram gave her is more appropriate: Urvashi, the celestial dancer who danced in the court of the Gods!

In the final analysis, *The Voice of the Heart*, its rather grand title notwithstanding, leaves us strangely indifferent to the main protagonist. There is no feeling of empathy for her. The voice from the heart is inadequate to describe the ups and downs of a rather privileged life. It reads like the diary entries of a dancer with a fairly packed schedule. Where are the self-doubt, the questions, the inner workings of an evolved mind? Readers had hoped for a more introspective and learned autobiography. Especially because it is the only autobiography in English published in recent years by a well-known Indian dancer, it fails to live up to its promise. *The Voice of the Heart* lacks depth. For, as Mrinalini Sarabhai observes about dance: "Putting some known vocabulary together is not creativity. There must be something vibrant that is a tangible quality of one's own truth" (113). Pity her autobiography does not follow this!

Echoing the sentiments of Yeats, Mrinalini Sarabhai ends her autobiography thus: "There is no separateness in dance and my entire being" (305). As the grand matriarch of Indian Classical Dance, perhaps we cannot grudge Mrinalini Sarabhai this grandiose claim. Yet, the "wholeness" that was there in her best performances is absent in her autobiography. It lacks the focus and the centredness that one would have expected from a dancer of Mrinalini Sarabhai's calibre. The interiorised Self who looks within and places herself/himself in the larger context of society is not found here. The lack of cohesiveness in *The Voice of the Heart* is at odds with the centrality that Mrinalini Sarabhai arrogates for her dance.

The basic contradiction lies between what Mrinalini Sarabhai professes and what the autobiography presents. The language of the autobiography claims to highlight the underlying unity in human experiences. However, as my paper has shown, a close reading of the text exposes the dualities that are constantly invoked—the Public and the Private, the Spiritual and the Secular, the East and the West, the Traditional and the Modern. To bring the dualities on a level plane, Mrinalini Sarabhai overcompensates on one side or the other. Ultimately, the dancer and the dance do not come together, the author and the reader cannot meet halfway. *The Voice of the Heart* is unable to present a cohesive picture of Mrinalini Sarabhai's journey through life.

Works Cited

Chakraborty, Dipesh. "Postcoloniality and the Artifice of History: Who Speaks for Indian Pasts?" Mongia 167-181.

Mohanty, Chandra T. "Under Western Eyes: Feminist Scholarship and Colonial Discourses." Mongia 232-241.

Mongia, Padmini, ed. *Contemporary Postcolonial Theory: A Reader*. London: Arnold, 1996.

Mrinalini Sarabhai. *The Voice of the Heart*. Delhi: Harper Collins, 2004.

Wire Writing as Life Writing: The Portraits of Alexander Calder

Barbara B. Zabel
Connecticut College

Abstract: The visual manifestation of life writing is, of course, portraiture. My essay focuses on the modernist portrait sculpture created by Alexander Calder (1898-1976) while living in Paris in the 1920s. Produced prior to Calder's well-known mobiles, these portraits are made of wire, an unorthodox sculptural medium. Calder's method of drawing in space with a flexible material resulted in provocative auto/biographical portraits of a wide range of personalities, including his future wife Louisa Cushing James, well-known entertainer Josephine Baker, and singer-model Kiki of Montparnasse.

This essay considers Calder's sculpture in terms of the radical transformations of the genre of portraiture in the modern era, and also in terms of relationality, a concept central to scholarship on life writing. Calder's portraits engage a complex nexus of the relationships: between artist and subject, viewer and subject, and viewer and artist. I discuss the implications of such relationality for self-portraiture, as well, how self examination becomes a form of self-understanding, for artist as well as viewer. Through discussion of several portraits by Calder, I have attempted to read portraits as cultural documents which imply narratives having to do with dynamic relational identities.

Life writing can take visual as well as written form. The obvious visual expression of life writing is, of course, portraiture, a genre with a long tradition in western art. Though well established by the Renaissance, portraiture has been viewed as a rather lowly art historical genre. In this sense, it shares with life writing a status as somewhat marginalized in the critical hierarchy of genres. In recent years, however, scholars in both fields have reassessed the genres of portraiture and life writing, resulting in a great boom in scholarship. While scholars of literature have pushed the limits of life writing to include underrepresented subjects, art historians have expanded the discourse of portraiture to include modernist and postmodern theory.[1] The received wisdom in art history has been that, with the advent of modernism and the rejection of traditional notions of representation, the genre of portraiture was doomed to disappear altogether as a genre. However, just the reverse seems to have occurred. Far from disappearing, portraiture has undergone radical transformations in the modern era, transformations that have broadened the scope of portraiture. Artists have turned to portraiture as a major vehicle for addressing larger social issues, including those having to do with identity and gender, race and class, the advent of the machine and information ages, and myriad other issues. Indeed, portraiture has assumed a central role in the discourse of modernism and postmodernism.

This revitalization of portraiture is amply demonstrated in portraits by American sculptor Alexander Calder (1898-1976). Created while Calder was living in Paris in the late 1920s—and prior to the artist's more celebrated mobiles—Calder's portraits are made of wire, an unorthodox sculptural medium. Instead of working with mass by shaping a lump of clay, casting in bronze, or carving a chunk of wood—the traditional practice in sculpture—Calder chose to work with a flexible linear material. This choice would seem particularly limiting, because wire has no color and only one dimension. However, the artist managed to shape thin rods into three-dimensional portraits of considerable character and nuance. Calder typically suspended the portraits from the ceiling or wall, so that they would be free to move and shift position. And the fact of their mobility is particularly significant in regard to their genre. Because of this mobility, Calder's portraits seem, like their subjects, to have a life of their own.

Calder applied this technique of drawing in space to a wide range of personalities—entertainers he encountered in Paris and New York: Kiki of Montparnasse, Josephine Baker, and Jimmy Durante; art-world colleagues: painters Fernand Léger and Amedée Ozenfant and

---

[1] Recent publications include Anthony Bond and Joanna Woodall, Gen Doy, Shearer West.

composer Edgar Varèse; sports stars and icons of American culture: baseball hero Babe Ruth, tennis champion Helen Wills, and aviator Charles Lindbergh (Calder actually witnessed Lindbergh's historic landing on an airfield outside Paris in 1927); and portraits of his friends and family members, including his wife, Louisa.

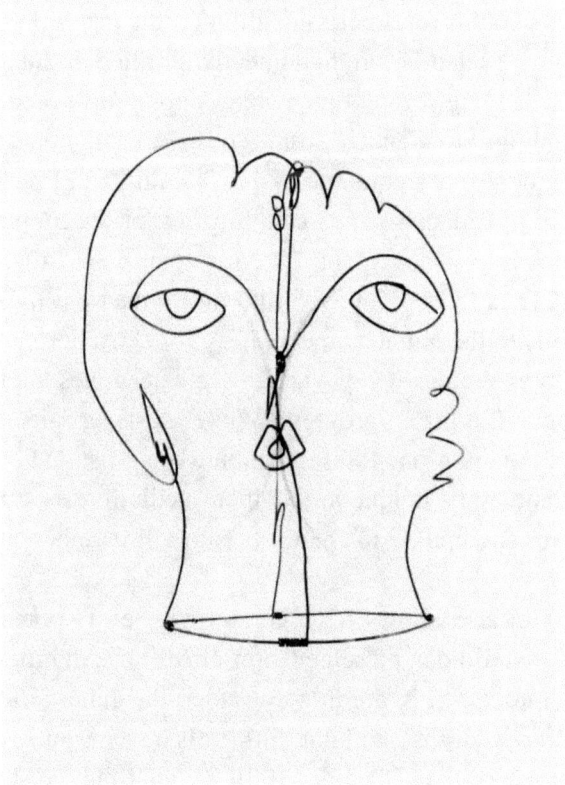

Illustration 1[2]
Alexander Calder: *Kiki of Montparnasse*

---

[2] Alexander Calder, *Kiki of Montparnasse*, 1929. Wire, 12 ¾ in. Musée National d'Art Moderne, Centre Georges Pompidou, Paris, France. Copyright © CNAC/MNAM/Dist. Réunion des Musée Nationaux/Art Resource, NY. Copyright © 2006 Estate of Alexander Calder/Artists Rights Society (ARS), New York.

Calder's creative process is key to the making of and interpreting these works. We have a visual record of that process in still photographs from a film made in 1929 by Pathé Films, which documented the making of one such portrait, Kiki of Montparnasse (ill. 1). Born Alice Prin in 1901, Kiki was an aspiring artist and writer, who by 1920 had made a name for herself as a singer in bars in Montparnasse, and who also earned money as an artist's model. Calder invited Kiki to come to his studio for a portrait sitting on the occasion of the making of the film. Seated before his model with pliers in hand, the artist shaped wire, bending it to define a chin, looping it to render eyes and nose, or spiraling it to simulate strands of hair. From his twistings of a single wire emerges a unique face full of vitality and life. Kiki seems to come alive in Calder's hands as a function of the looping rhythms of wire, which imply movement. As critic John Baur wrote, it is "as if a tremor of life ran through them" (qtd. in Lipman 237). The finished work responds to the slightest touch: her eyes shift, her mouth moves, her hair vibrates. Calder's free wheeling line generates the feeling of a work in progress, a life in progress. While most portraits come about as a result of a one-on-one transaction between artist and subject, Calder's portraits may be unique in that their medium resists being fixed; wire is forever susceptible to change because of its inherent flexibility and mobility.

The medium also allows for a certain degree of spontaneity. One story has it that Calder presented himself at an exhibition venue at Harvard with no work. According to Calder, the gallery director "protested that I arrived with nothing but a roll of wire on my shoulders and pliers in my pockets" (Calder 108). By the time the show opened a few days later, Calder had created all the works for the show on the spot, while interacting with gallery personnel, patrons, and friends. This was often Calder's modus operandi; indeed, he typically carried his tools with him and appropriated materials close at hand, creating works wherever he happened to be. As he commented in 1929, "I was always a junkman of bits of wire and all the prettiest things in the garbage can" (qtd. in Rimanelli 123). His process, indeed, his life, was quite improvisatory, and the works themselves retain a sense of immediacy, a feeling of living in the moment, of a life or lives unfolding.

This process of portrait-making is, of course, dependent on the relationship between artist and subject—the close scrutiny of the artist, the response of the subject, and the interaction between two individual personalities in close proximity to one another. Such interaction is, of course, dictated by social conventions; for instance, how close one can scrutinize another human being without creating discomfort in both scrutinizer and scrutinized; how close one can look without seeming to stare. The act of portrayal thus involves a give-and-take, what Marcia Pointon has called a "perpetual oscillation" between artist and subject, between observer and observed (193). Artist and sitter both have an invested interest; both come to the portrait session with expectations; both are affected by the resulting transaction. The dual involvement and investment of artist and subject is, of course, implicit in the naming of portraits. When we refer to a portrait, we typically name two individuals, rather than one (Pointon 193): Gilbert Stuart's George Washington, Copley's Paul Revere, Picasso's Gertrude Stein, or Calder's Kiki of Montparnasse. Furthermore, any human interaction takes place over time, so the idea of time is necessarily embedded in the work itself. The artist is not trying to capture a single moment; rather he interacts with his subject over time, to create a sense of shifting identity, thus reflecting a human truth: that the self consists not of a single, stable entity but of multiple identities.

The inscription of time in these works also suggests narrative, which, as John Eakin has written, "is a—if not the—principal mode in which relational identity is transacted" (*True Relations* 63). Although portraits do not impart an obvious sense of narrative, I would argue that as a result of an ongoing human interaction, they may imply a kind of narrative. And this is reflected and extended in the process by which the viewer interacts with the portraits. Once the works are suspended, it is the viewer's turn to enter into the relationship, to inspect the work from all sides, taking in shifting views of individual faces. In doing so, we are implicated in the process, in the life of sculpture and the life of the portrait subject, as our identities are interwoven with those of both the artist and the sitter. Calder's mode of drawing in space thus encapsulates not one static view or moment but an unfolding of identity or identities, an unfolding of a life or lives.

Although modernist portraiture departs from the conventions of earlier portraiture, the premodernist history of the genre can illuminate its narrative impulse. Often considered America's first art form, portraiture is of relatively recent origins. Emerging as a major genre in late eighteenth-century America, portraiture recorded the colonists' attempts not only to make a fresh start in a new land, but, more important, to invent fresh identities to personify the new experiment in democracy. The key motivating principle in politics was egalitarianism, and this is embedded in many early portraits. A prime example is John Singleton Copley's *Paul Revere*, of 1768, which has become an icon of American identity. Copley gives us a down-to-earth portrayal of Paul Revere (1735-1818), who was soon to become a hero of the American War of Independence. The portrait is based on meticulous mimesis. With great precision, the artist has represented Revere dressed in simple work clothes and engaged in the labor of a skilled craftsman, a silversmith. As if momentarily interrupted from his task of engraving a teapot, Revere is shown contemplating the viewer. The exquisite reflections on the table and on the teapot that he is engraving are clearly designed to signify his own reflectiveness. Copley gives us a thoughtful, dignified individual involved in honest labor, a new kind of hero for the new country. We can read such a portrait, like many portraits, as a kind of narrative and as a cultural document.

Traditional sculptural portraiture likewise suggests narrative, containing as it does clues to status, profession, and position in society. Even though three-dimensional portraits dispense with setting and other narrative devices of painted portraits, they can establish narrative through facial expression, clothing, and bearing of the figure.

Nineteenth-century sculptor Hiram Powers, for example, draped his bust of *General Andrew Jackson* (c. 1835) in classical garb, so as to link the American president to venerated generals of the Roman past. This classical allusion contrasts markedly with Jackson's unidealized, craggy features, which suggest a person of strength and determination, someone well equipped to tackle the monumental task of nation building. Powers gives us a figure with bulk and mass—a physical reality. We experience a specific individual as a "bounded whole," a "center of awareness" (Brilliant 170-171).

Calder's portraits are cultural documents equally as rich as Copley's and Power's, but they speak to us in a different language, the language of modernism. While Calder perpetuates something of Copley's straightforward and unembellished approach to portraiture and of Power's attention to detail and respect for material, his portraits represent a radical departure from the tradition of eighteenth- and nineteenth-century portraiture. No longer can we intuit rank or status, nor are we shown period clothing or hair style. In his *Self Portrait*, for instance (ill. 2), Calder gives us the outlines of his head and his features, but that is all. No longer do we have the traditional context of the self in the world; indeed, he affects a total erasure of the self in the traditional understanding of the term. This is not the vision of a unified self seen in John Singleton Copley's oil portrait; nor does it have the massive presence in the world of the nineteenth-century sculpture of Hiram Powers. There is no context to provide unity, no obvious narrative, no timeless unified moment. What Calder achieves instead is a greater sense of changing perspectives and ever-shifting relationships. The viewer experiences the sense of a self changing over time, as intimated in an early review in the *New Yorker*: "He makes a mockery of the old-fashioned frozen-stone school of sculpture and comes nearer to life in his creations than do nine-tenths of the serious stone-cutters" (Pemberton).

328 *Barbara B. Zabel*

Illustration 2[3]
Alexander Calder: *Self Portrait*

---

[3] Alexander Calder, *Self Portrait*, 1930. Wire, Copyright © 2006 Art Resource, NY/Estate of Alexander Calder/Artists Rights society (ARS), New York.

In decontextualizing the individual in this way, Calder follows up on the innovations of other modernists. For example, in the Cubist portraits by Pablo Picasso, such as *Portrait of Ambrose Vollard*, of 1910, the artist has described his subject as a series of shifting planes which seem to ascend the canvas. Picasso has given us the suggestion of a face and a name, but not much of a likeness. He has pushed portraiture's traditional obligation to "likeness" and "resemblance" to its limits (Pointon 189). A decade later Russian modernist Antoine Pevsner built on followed up on the implications of Picasso's novel portraiture, that is, the notion that art could be a construction rather than an illusionistic representation. Rather than simulating construction in oil paint, he used thin sheets of celluloid and copper to assemble his *Portrait of Marcel Duchamp*, 1926. The Russian thereby translates Picasso's suggestion of oscillating planes into three dimensions. Although Pevsner's planes do not in fact oscillate, they suggest an interchange of mass and space. As in Picasso's *Portrait of Ambrose Vollard*, Pevsner's *Portrait of Marcel Duchamp* provides the viewer with a human face; however, one without hard and fast boundaries or mimetic details to make it a likeness or to give it context.

Likewise, in Dadaist Francis Picabia's self-portrait entitled *Le Saint des Saints*, the artist has entirely extinguished likeness, creating a portrait devoid of every trace of resemblance. Still, we can decode it as a richly allusive cultural document. Picabia has superimposed an automobile horn on a cross-section of a combustion chamber, in a way that is erotically suggestive, playing on his own reputation as a womanizer. Picabia's portrait represents its subject through implicit correspondences between machines and individual personality, through metonymy as opposed to direct mimesis. This impulse to create analogies between individuals and machines announces the radical transformation of identity-construction in the machine age, whereby principles of mechanical construction have superseded mimesis.

Calder, too, allies his art and his conception of self with the dominant realm of the machine by his use of wire: a material produced for industrial rather than artistic purposes. However, while he lends a technological note through his unorthodox material, he is not as willing as the other modernists I've shown to forfeit conventional notions of what constitutes a portrait. Calder's innovations remain within traditional expectations of portraiture in several respects. In his *Self Portrait*, Calder retains, first of all, a reliance on drawing; and, secondly, he shows us a likeness.[1] And, because it is a likeness of the artist himself, Calder's *Self Portrait*, like all self portraits, is a mirror image. The viewer thus sees what the artist sees in the mirror. And, indeed, this self-portrait resembles photographic records of Calder as a young artist.

Moreover, Calder's *Self Portrait* may also conform to another convention of portraiture: that what the artist sees in the mirror goes beyond strict adherence to appearance. Comparing his early sculpture to a later image of the artist as an old man suggests a sense of foresight, a sense that Calder is projecting into the future to an older, more serious, self than was the case in 1930. The viewer encounters what Eakin has called "a present consciousness which is moving into the future" (roundtable discussion). Such a portrait conforms to the traditional notion that a portrait imparts not just likeness, but a sense of scrutiny, a process of inquiry, "an attempt to break through the surface to some truth within" (Clark 116). Self-examination becomes a form of self-understanding. Calder gives us not just a likeness of himself, but a representation of the activity of self-scrutiny, of coming to terms with one's self, one's past, present, and future.

The viewer, too, has a role in the act of viewing a portrait; in fact, all viewing of art involves the viewer. In the case of Calder, when all we are given, literally, is a kind of outline, then the viewer's role becomes magnified. Calder's portraits make explicit the incorporation of the viewer's gaze into the subject matter of portraiture. As viewers, we are invited to project ourselves into the image in front of us, to

---

[1] Calder shares this tendency to innovate within tradition with Matisse, as discussed by Klein.

scrutinize ourselves. The truths Calder gives us are meshed with our own truths, and here again portraiture becomes a record of multiple and relational identities.

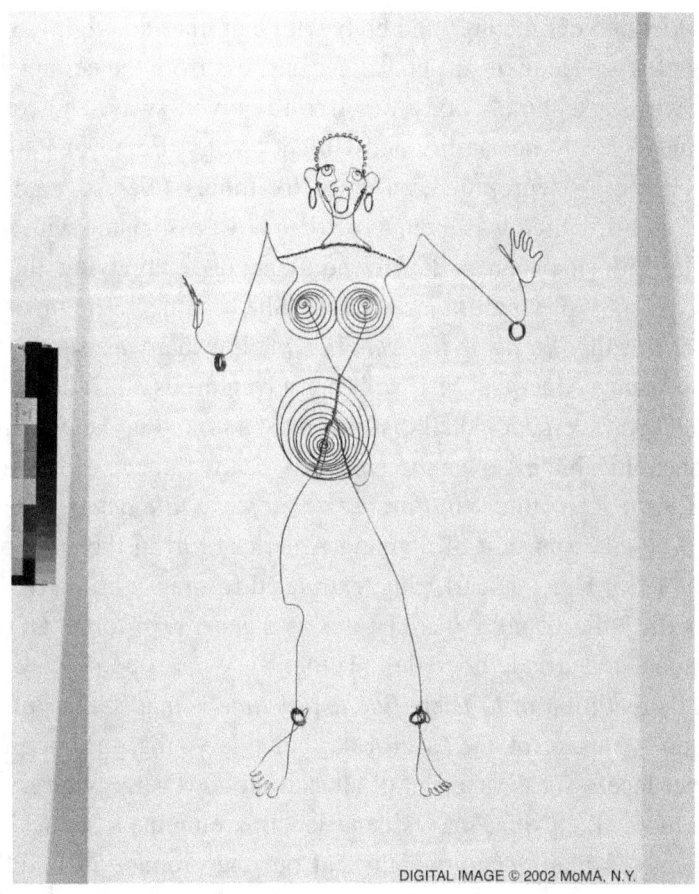

Illustration 3[2]
Alexander Calder: *Josephine Baker*

---

[2] Alexander Calder, *Josephine Baker*, 1927-1929. Iron-wire construction, 39 x 22 3/8 x 9 ¾". Gift of the artist. Digital Image © The Museum of Modern Art/Licensed by SCALA/Art Resource, NY. Copyright © 2006 Estate of Alexander Calder/Artists Rights Society (ARS), New York.

This relationality is most powerfully exposed in Calder's portraits of American entertainer, Josephine Baker (ill. 3). In 1925, Baker arrived in Paris, where she became the star of the Folies Bergère. In order to capture the pulsating energy of La Baker, as she was called, Calder defined her features and body with taut lines and tightly wound spirals of wire. He then suspended her likeness from the ceiling with a single wire. Josephine's body was free to quiver, sway, and rotate at will, underscoring her agility and vibrant energy. Post-war Paris was experiencing a "negrophilia," a craze for things "Negro," and especially for jazz, which was then, more than now, associated with America. The French avant-garde viewed Baker as embodying this new American spirit of youthful jazz culture. She became a version of what the French called *la jeune fille américaine*. For many artists and writers, the young American girl, with her adventurous spirit and unconventional ways, embodied all that was most admired in America itself.

Francis Picabia gives us the most provocative image of this archetype of American culture in *Portrait d'une jeune fille américaine dans l'état de nudité* (portrait of a young American girl in the state of nudity) of 1915. Here, a spark plug, extricated from its automotive function, defines the young American girl as a generative force, an image of personal and artistic liberation (Turner 8). What is perplexing about Picabia's rendition of *la jeune fille américaine* is that she has no face. What do we make of the facelessness of this young girl? We might view her facelessness as a sign of alienation; however, a viewer of the 1920s more likely may have identified this emptiness as a kind of tabula rasa, a blank slate, which held out the promise of building a new identity for a new era (Lavin 46). For Calder it was Josephine Baker who finally gave *la jeune fille américaine* a distinct identity, as she constructed a new persona in Paris. In recognition of this feat, Calder seized on Baker as the embodiment of *la jeune fille américaine*, giving her a face and a specific identity.

The fact that Calder gives the young girl a black identity racializes this concept, and in doing so he gives tacit acknowledgment of the rich aesthetic collaboration between black and white cultural forms that produced modernism (Lemke 4). Paradoxically, this sense of creative collaboration is both challenged and enhanced by the fact that Calder's sculptures have no color. Blackness is implicit, of course, because we know this is Josephine Baker, but it is up to the viewer to fill in the contours. The literal openness of the sculpture elicits our participation, not only in supplying the color of her skin, but also in perpetuating or countering stereotypes. In this context, Zora Neale Hurston's essay, "What White Publishers Won't Print," is illuminating. Hurston disparaged "the Anglo-Saxon's lack of curiosity about the internal lives and emotions of the Negroes" (169):

> The question naturally arises as to the why of this indifference, not to say scepticism, to the internal life of educated minorities. The answer lies in [. . .] an intangible built on folk belief. It is assumed that all non-Anglo-Saxons are uncomplicated stereotypes. Everybody knows all about them. They are lay figures mounted in the museum where all may take them at a glance. They are made of bent wires without insides at all. (169)

Hurston's passage seems a perfect description of Calder's portrait of Josephine Baker. She consists of "bent wires without insides." It is up to the viewer to fill in the details, to flesh out a narrative to go along with the image. By eliciting the viewer's participation in "completing" the work, Calder piques our curiosity about the subject and challenges us to bring our own associations, our own assumptions into a dialogue with the portrait. As we do so, we begin to appreciate Calder's own dialogue with his subject. The artist foregrounds the playfulness and wit of Baker's performances, how Baker performs stereotypes of "primitivism," while at the same time mocking those stereotypes.

In her most notorious role as Fatou at the Folies Bergère in Paris, Baker entered the stage, designed as a dense jungle, wearing a skirt of bananas and little else (ill. 4). To the accompaniment of drums, Baker

Illustration 4[3]
Josephine Baker

danced, moving her hips so that the bananas bounced and swung while she simply laughed. As critic André Rouverge observed, "This girl has the genius to let the body make fun of itself," and to playfully mock the colonialist dreams of the French explorer sleeping nearby (*Mercure de France* 1 Sept. 1926; qtd. in Hammond and O'Connor 42).

---

[3] Josephine Baker, Photograph from program for the Folies Bergère, 1926-27. Courtesy of Maureen McCabe, Quaker Hill, CT.

Baker thereby exposes the absurdity of "primitivist" stereotypes, while also suggesting her own sense of creative autonomy. Calder's images, too, engage humor to undermine stereotypical perceptions of Josephine Baker as "primitivist" erotic dancer. Yet another early critic described Calder's wire as "deliberately tantalizing. [. . .] Of its own volition, [it] jokes and teases" (Harris). In this way, Calder honors Baker's genius and wit as well as her agency in acting out and challenging stereotypes.

Just as we implicitly read Calder's wire figure of Baker as black, we understand its musical counterpart as jazz; the wire sculpture is, after all, not a passive static construction but made to be active. The lines of the sculpture define a body in movement; but here, too, it is the spectator who fills in the gaps, intuiting the syncopated beat to which Baker moves. This meshing of black and white in Calder's work mirrors the wider collaboration of the two—in the world of entertainment and of modernism; indeed, it comprises a recognition of the challenges confronted by blacks in modern culture as well as the contributions of black culture to postwar modernism. Moreover, such engagement between viewer and sculpture demonstrates a kind of relationality, the sense that we create our own identities through coming to terms with the other.[4]

I'd like to conclude with one of Calder's most intriguing portraits: that of Louisa Cushing James, soon to be the artist's wife (ill. 5). This work inspires similar readings, now having more to do with gender than race. Calder entitled this portrait *Medusa*, thereby establishing a mythic resonance. In the original myth, Perseus cuts off the head of Medusa so as to appropriate the formidable power of her gaze, which could turn men to stone. The process of creation itself assumes the artist's exertion of control over his subject; the power of Medusa's gaze becomes his own, signifying a collapsing of other into self. Such a

---

[4] For an extended discussion of Calder's portraits of Baker, see my chapter, "Expatriate Portraiture: Alexander Calder and Josephine Baker in Paris" (*Assembling Art* 109-132).

conflation is particularly potent because of the charged relationship between the artist and model.

Illustration 5[5]
Alexander Calder: *Medusa*

---

[5] Alexander Calder, *Medusa*, c. 1930. Wire, 31.1 x 43.8 x 24.1 cm. Private Collection. Art Resource, NY. Copyright © 2006 Estate of Alexander Calder/Artists Rights Society (ARS), New York.

The grandniece of novelist Henry James and of psychologist/philosopher William James, Louisa James was from a distinguished New England family. She was well educated, had lived in France as a child and had traveled throughout Europe with her family. Her liberal-minded father, Edward Holton James, fostered a sense of independence in his daughter. Calder met father and daughter the summer of 1929 aboard an ocean liner bound for New York. A shipboard romance ensued, and the couple was married 18 months later. Perhaps we should not make too much of the nickname Calder gave to Louisa; after all, the name Medusa was inspired by her windblown hair when he first met her on the deck of a ship. However, it's difficult to view such a name as purely descriptive, loaded as it is with gendered meanings. Indeed, Medusa had extraordinary tropic value for the culture of the 1920s. Classical myths have always been reinterpreted to comment on changing times, and the treatment of Medusa by artists has paralleled the evolution of women's cultural influence (Matilsky 40). For the newly empowered woman of the 1920s, Medusa seems to have taken on particular relevance as the embodiment of a whole constellation of archetypal meanings: she could stand for the ancient symbol of female power and wisdom; for "female mysteries"; for the forces of the primordial Great Goddess; and she signified universal creativity as well as destruction. She is archetype of the other, the "evil eye," and symbol of confrontation and even castration (Mack 571). Key to Perseus's success was the fact that Medusa's gaze remained active after her decapitation; at stake was not so much the need to kill the monster Medusa, as the need to take possession of her power (Mack 588). According to the myth, Perseus confronted the lethal gaze of Medusa and, by cutting off her head, assumed her power and ultimately the throne as King of Argos. The image of the disembodied Medusa thus represents the power of Medusa's gaze after it was taken from her and transferred to Perseus; that is, after Medusa was controlled and tamed.

Consider how Calder may have conceptualized the myth of Medusa for himself. He was clearly fascinated with this new woman in his life, but by naming her Medusa he also signaled a sense of intimidation. Representing her as Medusa may then have been his way of coping with his own vulnerability in the face of this new force in his life. In capturing her visage in wire and tethering her to the gallery wall, he symbolically domesticated and controlled her. However, because the original myth implicitly suggests a reciprocity between Perseus and Medusa, Calder also acknowledged that his power depended on hers. In assuming the power of Medusa's gaze as his own, Calder thus suggested a relational identity transacted through a complex narrative.

Calder's portrait of Louisa—as well as those of Kiki of Montparnasse and Josephine Baker—seem to reveal the male artist working through a crisis in his own identity and forging new identities through his transactions with the other. While on the one hand the portraits resolve the crisis by denying, or at least diminishing, differences between male and female, self and other, they also acknowledge and exploit difference. And it is the unresolved tensions and the open-endedness of the resulting narratives—the fact that so much is left out—that make these portraits so compelling.

Works Cited

Bond, Antony, and Joanna Woodall, eds. *Self Portrait: Renaissance to Contemporary*. London: National Portrait Gallery, 2005.

Brilliant, Richard. *Portraiture*. Cambridge, Massachusetts: Harvard University Press, 1991.

Calder, Alexander. *Calder: An Autobiography with Pictures*. New York: Pantheon, 1966.

Clark, T. J. "The Look of Self-Portraiture." *Yale Journal of Criticism* 5.2 (1992): 109-118.

Doy, Gen. *Picturing the Self: Changing Views of the Subject in Visual Culture*. London/New York: I. B. Tauris, 2005.

Eakin, John, "Relational Selves, Relational Lives: The Story of the Story." *True Relations: Essays on Autobiography and the Postmodern.* Ed. G. Thomas Couser and Joseph Fichtelberg. Westport, CT and London: Greenwood, 1998. 63-81.

___. Roundtable discussion. Symposium on the Theory and Practice of Life Writing: Auto/biography, Memoir and Travel Writing in Post/modern Literature. Haliç University, Istanbul. 20 Apr. 2006.

Emery, Lynne Fauley. *Black Dance from 1619 to Today.* 2nd ed. Princeton, NJ: Princeton, 1988.

Hammond, Bryan, and Patrick O'Connor. *Josephine Baker.* London: Jonathan Cape, 1988.

Harris, Ruth Green. "Paintings and Sculpture Show." *New York Times* Feb. 1929. Clipping in Alexander Calder Papers, Microfilmed Scrapbook 1927-1932. Washington, D.C.: Archives of American Art, Smithsonian Institution.

Hurston, Zora Neale. "What White Publishers Won't Print." 1950. *I Love Myself When I Am Laughing ...: A Zora Neal Hurston Reader.* Ed. Alice Walder. Old Westbury, N.Y.: Feminist Press, 1979. 169-173.

Klein, John. *Matisse Portraits.* New Haven and London: Yale University Press, 2001.

Lavin, Maud. *Cut with Kitchen Knife: The Weimar Photomontages of Hannah Höch.* New Haven: Yale University Press, 1993.

Lemke, Sieglinde. *Primitivist Modernism: Black Culture and the Origins of Transatlantic Modernism.* New York and Oxford: Oxford University Press, 1998.

Lipman, Jean. *Calder's Universe.* New York: Viking, 1976.

Mack, Rainer. "Facing down Medusa (An Aetiology of the Gaze)." *Art History* 25.5 (November 2002): 571-604.

Matilsky, Barbara C. *Classical Myth and Imagery in Contemporary Art.* Exhibition catalogue 15 Apr.-12 June, 1988. New York: The Queens Museum, n.d.

Pemberton, Murdock. "The Art Galleries." *New Yorker* 7 Feb. 1929.

Pointon, Marcia, "Kahnweiler's Picasso: Picasso's Kahnweiler." *Portraiture: Facing the Subject*. Ed. Joanna Woodall. Manchester and New York: Manchester University Press, 1997. 189-202.

Rimanelli, David. Exhibition review. *Artforum* 36.10 (Summer 1998): 123.

Turner, Elizabeth Hutton. "*La jeune fille américaine* and the Dadaist Impulse." *Women in Dada*. Ed. Naomi Sawelson-Gorse. Cambridge, MA, London, England: MIT Press, 1998. 4-21.

West, Shearer. *Portraiture*. Oxford History of Art. Oxford and New York: Oxford University Press, 2004.

Zabel, Barbara. *Assembling Art: The Machine and the American Avant-Garde*. Jackson, MI: University Presses of Mississippi, 2004.

ibidem-Verlag
Melchiorstr. 15
D-70439 Stuttgart

info@ibidem-verlag.de

www.ibidem-verlag.de
www.edition-noema.de
www.autorenbetreuung.de

www.ingramcontent.com/pod-product-compliance
Lightning Source LLC
Chambersburg PA
CBHW051627230426
43669CB00013B/2204